Designing ISP Architectures

John V. Nguyen

Sun Microsystems Press
A Prentice Hall Title

The publisher offers discounts on this book when ordered in bulk quantities. For more information, contact: Corporate Sales Department, Phone: 800-382-3419; Fax: 201-236-7141; E-mail: corpsales@prenhall.com; or write: Prentice Hall PTR, Corp. Sales Dept., One Lake Street, Upper Saddle River, NJ 07458.

Editorial/production superviser: *Nicholas Radhuber*
Cover design director: *Jerry Votta*
Cover designer: *Kavish & Kavish Digital Publishing & Design*
Manufacturing manager: *Alexis R. Heydt*
Marketing manager: *Debby vanDijk*
Acquisitions editor: *Gregory G. Doench*

Sun Microsystems Press
Publisher: *Michael Llwyd Alread*

10 9 8 7 6 5 4 3 2 1

ISBN 0-13-045496-6

Sun Microsystems Press
A Prentice Hall Title

Acknowledgements

As with any major publication, the result is an aggregation of effort and collaboration from many contributors, both directly and indirectly. In particular, this book is the result of a major effort from the Advanced Internet Practice (Sun Professional Services) and the Sun BluePrints™ (Enterprise Engineering) groups within Sun Microsystems. The outcome is a collective knowledge of design principles and preferred practices based upon professional experiences, gained from designing very large-scale solutions for service providers.

Special thanks to my manager Dan Berg (Director, Advanced Internet Practice) and Bill Sprouse (Manager, Enterprise Engineering) for the opportunity with this initiative. Additionally, special thanks to Barbara Jugo (Publications Manager, Sun BluePrints), Jeff Wheelock (Manager, Sun BluePrints), and Charles Alexander (Director, Enterprise Engineering) for their support in keeping things in perspective.

Thanks to Meredith Rose (Systems Engineer, Foundry) for technical assistance with network design using Foundry products, Nikki Kester (Regional Sales Manager, Foundry) for support and resources, and Robert Cosme (Systems Engineer, Cisco Systems) for technical assistance with network design using Cisco products.

Thanks to all reviewers for their insights and comments: Tom Bialaski (Enterprise Engineering), Kirk Brown (Advanced Internet Practice), Jason Carolan (Advanced Internet Practice), Ron Cotten (Advanced Internet Practice), David Deeths (Enterprise Engineering), Alex Noordergraaf (Enterprise Engineering), and Kemer Thomson (Enterprise Engineering).

Finally, last but not least, a very special thanks to Rex Casey (Senior Technical Writer, Sun BluePrints) for spending countless hours in translating my complex thoughts and technical jargon to something that is readable and understandable. Special thanks to Terry Williams (Technical Writer, Sun BluePrints) and Dany Galgani (Graphic Designer, IPG Publications) for transforming napkin sketches into beautiful artwork; Tim Marsh (Enterprise Engineering) for his hard work in setting up the prototype in the lab; and Minerva Ontiveros (Enterprise Engineering) for handling all the administrative logistics. Without all of you and your support, I could not have done it with such an aggressive schedule.

Contents

Figures

Tables

Preface

This book is one of an on-going series of books collectively known as the Sun BluePrints™ program. This BluePrint is a resource for designing an Internet Service Provider (ISP) architecture.

About This Book

In this BluePrint, you'll find practical advice and information helpful in making key decisions for designing platform-independent ISP architectures. Based upon industry standards, expert knowledge, and hands-on experience, this book:

- Details the design process
- Introduces fundamental design principles
- References sources for advanced design principles
- Shares tips, insights, and preferred practices for considering requirements, technology, and trade-offs
- Describes how to avoid common pitfalls
- Offers a low-cost approach for entering the ISP market and provides sources for obtaining market data
- Suggests criteria for selecting components, based on varying design scenarios
- Provides general guidelines for capacity planning
- Applies the material to a sample customer scenario, where applicable
- Includes appendices containing a prototype for small to medium-sized environments that we successfully implemented in the lab at Sun Microsystems in San Diego

Sun BluePrints Program

The mission of the Sun BluePrints program is to empower Sun's customers with the technical knowledge required to implement reliable, extensible, and secure information systems within the datacenter using Sun products. This program provides a framework to identify, develop, and distribute best practices information that applies across Sun product lines. Experts in technical subjects in various areas contribute to the program and focus on the scope and usefulness of the information.

The Sun BluePrints program includes books, guides, and online articles. Through these vehicles, Sun can provide guidance, installation and implementation experiences, real-life scenarios, and late-breaking technical information.

The monthly electronic magazine, *Sun BluePrints OnLine*, is located on the Web at *http://www.sun.com/blueprints*. To be notified about updates to the Sun BluePrints program, please register at this site.

Who Should Read This Book

This book is expressly for IT architects and consultants who design ISP architectures.

Portions of this book are beneficial to systems engineers, system administrators, security administrators, application designers, and network administrators who implement solutions. For this secondary audience, this book provides design fundamentals, configuration considerations and examples, and tips and resources for implementing a design.

Note – Operation and management issues are beyond the scope of this book.

Before You Read This Book

To provide the best focus for the subject of this book, we assume readers have experience in systems engineering, system administration, and network administration, and that now they are focused on designing solutions for ISP customers. This audience understands ISP services, components, infrastructure, networking, and related technologies.

Introducing FijiNet

Throughout this book, we use a fictitious company called FijiNet to demonstrate how to design an ISP architecture. Our goal is to apply the concepts and information to a realistic scenario while making the content enjoyable to read. Any resemblance to a past, present, or future company named FijiNet is purely coincidental.

Note – Use this book to design an ISP architecture for any size ISP. In our design and examples for FijiNet, we purposely limit the scope to an initial 10,000 subscribers, so that we can effectively cover subjects.

How This Book Is Organized

Chapter 1 "Introduction," introduces the ISP subject matter and briefly describes the market, value, challenges, and approach to solutions.

Chapter 2 "Formulating Design Requirements," introduces a systematic approach to obtaining and evaluating business and functional requirements for a new ISP architecture. Before you start designing an architecture, use this chapter to organize and derive the information you need to develop a design that meets requirements, takes into account unknowns (assumptions), and bases decisions on realistic data.

Chapter 3 "Establishing an Architectural Model," provides an architectural model and principles to use in designing an ISP architecture. Building upon the approach in Chapter 2 ", this chapter shows you how to apply an architectural model and principles to design requirements.

Chapter 4 "Creating a Logical Design," recommends engineering a logical design based on high-level topology of the architecture. It describes elements necessary for creating a logical design, and it presents these elements in a high-level structure, showing how to design an architecture from the top-level down.

Chapter 5 "Creating a Physical Design," builds on the previous chapter by using the logical design to construct a high-level network design and perform capacity planning. This chapter provides information to assist you in formulating estimates for how much capacity your design needs. Use it as a general sizing guideline for estimating storage and memory for services.

Chapter 6 "Selecting Components," provides general guidelines for selecting software, server, and network components for an architecture design. As part of this chapter, we provide tables listing commonly used commercial and Open Source products appropriate for ISP infrastructures. Think of this chapter as a shopping list for physical components needed to implement the design arrived at in earlier chapters.

Chapter 7 "Implementing a Solution," offers general practices and recommendations for implementing a design. Includes recommendations for developing a prototype prior to implementing a solution. Also in this chapter are considerations for adapting to change after an ISP has implemented a solution.

Note – Most of the following appendixes contain details of an implementation for FijiNet, the prototype that was built and tested in the Sun lab in San Diego. Although numerous details would obviously change with another implementation, based both on design decisions and changes in versions of base software, these appendices serve as a useful reference for the reader who wants to see an implementation.

Appendix A, "Questions for Obtaining Design Requirements," provides interview questions to use when you are obtaining and refining requirements for an architecture.

Appendix B, "Sample Network Configurations," contains sample configurations for routers, switches, network access servers, and domain name servers.

Appendix C, "Sample DNS Configurations," provides sample configurations for your domain name service (DNS) servers.

Appendix D, "DHCP Server Configuration," contains a sample configuration for the dynamic host configuration protocol (DHCP) server.

Appendix E, "NTP Server Configuration," provides a sample configuration for the network time protocol (NTP) server

Appendix F, "LDAP Configuration," contains a sample configuration for the lightweight directory access protocol (LDAP).

Appendix F, "DNS Benchmark Data for Sun Enterprise Servers," contains benchmark results from the *Sun DNS/BIND Benchmarking and Sizing Guide*, dated March 2, 2001. We use this data for making assumptions about performance.

Appendix G, "Network Capacity," contains specifications for network capacity.

Appendix H, "HTTP Throughput," provides a table for HTTP throughput for network capacity.

Chapter I, "Port and Protocol List," provides a *partial* list of protocols and ports helpful in identifying services and associated protocols/ports for firewall rules.

Ordering Sun Documentation

The SunDocs℠ program provides more than 250 manuals from Sun Microsystems, Inc. If you live in the United States, Canada, Europe, or Japan, you can purchase documentation sets or individual manuals through this program.

Fatbrain.com, an Internet professional bookstore, stocks select product documentation from Sun Microsystems, Inc.

For a list of documents and how to order them, visit the Sun Documentation Center on Fatbrain.com at:

```
http://www1.fatbrain.com/documentation/sun
```

Accessing Sun Documentation Online

The docs.sun.com℠ web site enables you to access Sun technical documentation on the Web. You can browse the docs.sun.com archive or search for a specific book title or subject at:

```
http://docs.sun.com
```

```
http://www.sun.com/blueprints
```

Recommended Publications

In addition to other sources we cite in this book, we recommend the following publications:

- *Dot-Com & Beyond - Breakthrough Internet-Based Architectures and Methodologies*
- *Sun Performance Tuning*, 2nd Edition
- *Capacity Planning for Internet Services*
- *Solaris and LDAP Naming Services*

Using UNIX Commands

This document does not contain information on basic UNIX® commands and procedures such as shutting down a system, booting a system, and configuring devices.

See one or more of the following for this information:

- AnswerBook2™ online documentation for the Solaris™ Operating Environment
- Other software documentation that you received with your system

Typographic Conventions

Typeface	Meaning	Examples
`AaBbCc123`	The names of commands, files, and directories; on-screen computer output	Edit your `.login` file. Use `ls -a` to list all files. `% You have mail.`
AaBbCc123	What you type, when contrasted with on-screen computer output	`%` **su** `Password:`
AaBbCc123	Book titles, new words or terms, words to be emphasized	Read Chapter 6 in the *User's Guide*. These are called *class* options. You *must* be superuser to do this.
	Command-line variable; replace with a real name or value	To delete a file, type `rm` *filename*.

Shell Prompts in Command Examples

Shell	Prompt
C shell	*machine_name*%
C shell superuser	*machine_name*#
Bourne shell and Korn shell	$
Bourne shell and Korn shell superuser	#

Sun Welcomes Your Comments

We are interested in improving our documentation and welcome your comments and suggestions. You can email your comments to us at:

> `docfeedback@sun.com` or `blueprints@sun.com`

Please include the part number (806-0917-10) or title of this document in the subject line of your email.

Introduction

This chapter provides an introduction to Internet service providers (ISPs), briefly describes market trends, provides market data resources, offers considerations for entering the market, and describes challenges.

This chapter contains the following topics:

- "Defining an ISP and Its Architecture" on page 2
- "Identifying Market Trends" on page 2
- "Obtaining Market Data" on page 6
- "Challenges in Becoming an ISP" on page 6

For information about the purpose, scope, and audience of this book, refer to the Preface. Also, for an introduction to our sample customer FijiNet, used throughout this book, refer to the Preface.

Defining an ISP and Its Architecture

An ISP provides Internet services to business and residential subscribers, also referred to as users. ISPs provide basic services such as email, web hosting, and news. Also, ISPs offer value-added services such as calendars, address books, search engines, chat rooms, instant messages, etc.

An ISP architect defines the overall structure, called the architecture, that sets forth structuring principles and patterns for an ISP's infrastructure, services, network, customer care system, and so on.

The architecture sets system-wide constraints that must be adhered to by each portion of the subsequent design. Within the architecture, the architect identifies major components and their interrelationships. An ISP architect defines how:

- Overall processing should be decomposed into components
- Major components should be organized and well integrated

Developing an ISP architecture is important because it becomes the fundamental organization of a system embodied in its components, their relationships to each other and to the environment, and the principles guiding an architecture's design and evolution.

Identifying Market Trends

In a relatively short time, the Internet has become a major marketplace. Service providers of every size and composition are active in the market, and both new and established companies are looking for ways to increase subscribers, services, and, ultimately, revenues.

Value Proposition

Even though the ISP market in the United States (U.S.) has matured, significant opportunities still exist, especially for international ISPs, to capitalize on niche and underdeveloped marketplaces and to add new residential and business subscribers.

As bandwidth becomes available at an increasingly affordable cost, ISPs look for new value-added services and ways to attract new subscribers. The ISPs with established infrastructures are uniquely positioned to leverage their expertise and scale. In addition, ISPs are seeking new channels for their services and opportunities to reach new subscribers.

Market Positioning

As the Internet market evolved, service providers were classified into three classes: network service provider (NSP), application service provider (ASP), and Internet service provider (ISP).

- NSPs are companies that offer high-speed backbone Internet access. These companies are usually large telecommunication providers and network equipment providers. These companies own and operate networked, wireless, and wireline telephones, cable, and satellite. For example, some NSPs in the market today are AT&T^{SM}, BBN®, Bell South®, Level3, Qwest®, and UUNet®.

- ASPs are companies that offer online application hosting to businesses. ASPs provide businesses such as ISPs with applications and infrastructure for running applications over the Internet. These applications are usually provided via a wide area network (WAN) from a centralized data center. Businesses operating over the Internet most often outsource Information Technology (IT) functions to ASPs, to save time and money. For example, some ASPs in the market today are PeopleSoft®, TIBCO™, VerticalNet™, ATG®, and Oracle®.

- ISPs provide Internet access and services to business and residential subscribers. For example, some ISPs in the market today are America Online^{SM} (AOL^{SM}), AT&T Broadband Internet^{SM}, Mindspring™, and Earthlink™.

The emergence of the Internet challenged the dominance of traditional telecommunication companies. In response to decreasing market share and new opportunities, most of them shifted business strategies and became NSPs, then integrated ASP and ISP characteristics. By having all classes under one roof, these companies provide a one-stop portal for both business and residential subscribers.

There are approximately 9,700 ISPs, and this number is steadily growing. Yet, six large ISPs dominate the market today. The largest ISP, AOL, has approximately 32.5 million subscribers world-wide. The battle for the top spots is fierce; however, the market for regional ISPs is open.

Consider the following market trend:

> *J.D. Power and Associates[™] reports that smaller ISPs are threatening the dominance of the six largest national providers, accounting for 52% of new household subscriptions in the past year [2000]. This indicates that the regional ISP market is still growing strong.*[1]

In the national market (U.S.) as of November 2001, the top ISPs by subscriber are as follows:[2]

1. AOL (26.3 million subscribers)

2. MSN® (7 million subscribers)

3. United Online (6.1 million subscribers)

4. Earthlink (4.9 million subscribers)

5. @Home (3.7 million subscribers)

6. Prodigy (3.5 million subscribers)

Note – In September 2001, United Online acquired both Juno Online® and NetZero®.

Smaller ISPs that offer high-speed Internet access via digital subscriber lines (DSL) or cable modems are more likely to grow in this competitive market. Growth patterns and customer satisfaction surveys indicate both national and regional ISPs that want to attract new customers have to offer high-speed service. In response to customer demand, local cable and regional telephone providers are gearing up to roll out more DSL and cable modem services.

1. Michael Pastore, "Smaller ISPs Netting More Subscribers," [http://www.isp-planet.com/research/small_growth.html] ISP-Planet, September 12, 2000.

2. Patricia Fusco, "Top U.S. ISPs by Subscriber: Q3 2001," [http://www.isp-planet.com/research/rankings/usa.html] ISP Planet, November 2, 2001.

Present and Future Trends

Change is constant on the Internet. The following provides a glimpse of present and future trends.

High-speed access appears to be the trend for the next four years. Predictions are that broadband will grow quickly, and that DSL and fixed wireless access will gain on cable.

The year 2000 showed residential high-speed Internet access in the United States (U.S.) growing more than 230 percent, according to research by The Strategis Group, outpacing dial-up access. Increasing consumer demand and technical innovations with self-provisioning are cited as the major cause for this growth. TABLE 1-1 shows residential high-speed growth and trends for the U.S.[3]

TABLE 1-1   U.S. Residential High-Speed Access Growth and Trends (by Millions)

Access Method	1999	2000	2001	2002	2003	2004	2005
Cable	1.25	4.11	7.12	9.57	11.88	14.19	16.13
DSL	0.58	1.93	4.22	6.88	9.38	11.87	14.22
Wireless	0.01	0.06	0.19	0.95	1.96	3.04	4.71

Fixed wireless and two-way satellite technologies are being deployed as alternatives to DSL and cable modem. These technologies substitute where cable modem and DSL services are unavailable. And in some cases these technologies directly compete with DSL and cable modem. In general, cable subscribers are more satisfied with their broadband service than DSL subscribers. DSL access remains popular among small businesses.

Experts predict that with high-speed access driving the market, residential subscribers will more than triple over the next five years, growing from 8.6 million subscribers in 2001 to more than 36 million subscribers in 2005, according to a report by Parks Associates. They estimate the cumulative value of the residential market will approach $3 billion by 2005.

---

3. Michael Pastore, "High Speed Access to Pass Dial-Up in 2005,"[http://www.isp-planet.com/research/bband_vs_dialup.html] ISP Planet, January 23, 2001.

Obtaining Market Data

For an ISP to conduct an objective, competitive analysis, the ISP needs objective data. To gain a wider perspective, ISPs can obtain market data from in-depth, impartial studies. The cost for market data is worthwhile compared to costly errors from making incorrect assumptions or adopting strategies that do not align with market trends.

The following are some market data resources available through ISP industry research analysts:

- *AllNetResearch*™ – The Superstore for Internet Research
- *The Burton Group* – Emerging network-computing technologies
- *Cahners® In-State Group* – Real-time research
- *CyberAtlas*™ – Statistics and research for web marketers
- *Forrester*™ – Technology changes
- *Gartner Group*SM – IT research and analysis
- *International Data Corporation*SM – Comprehensive resource for worldwide IT markets
- *META Group®* – IT research and unlimited analyst consulting
- *Patricia Seybold Group* – Strategic technology and business solutions
- *StatMarket®* – Real-time statistics and subscriber trends
- *The Yankee Group*SM – Strategic planning, technology forecasting, and market research

Challenges in Becoming an ISP

A new breed of businesses are looking to enter or expand their business in the ISP market. Entering the ISP market presents daunting infrastructure challenges. The entrance to the ISP market typically involves a significant commitment and a substantial cost associated with services. Infrastructure challenges include managing a large number of subscribers, subscriber and service provisioning, and operation and management.

Key Challenges

For the vast majority of companies, what it takes to be an ISP is far removed from their core business. A key factor for success in this market is delivering reliable and consistent services in a fast-moving market.

As small to medium-sized businesses approach this market, they lack the infrastructure and technical expertise to deliver services in an economical way. Most solutions require a large amount of time and effort, as well as a significant initial investment and on-going support costs. These costs include—and are not limited to—recruiting and retaining qualified technical and management staff. These businesses face a market where there is a severe shortage of skilled IT professionals, making it increasingly difficult to be self-sufficient in managing a variety of applications and platforms in-house.

Significant hardware, software, and integration costs are required, often amounting to hundreds of thousands of dollars. On an annual basis, operations and management costs can be as much as the initial entry costs. For many of these businesses, this investment can be a considerable financial strain.

Planning for applications in-house can be very difficult, if not impossible, without an army of qualified professionals.

The need to anticipate growth rates and forecasts in volatile markets can lead to inaccurate estimates and costly mistakes.

Consider the following advice to ISPs for defying difficult times:

> *The greatest challenge facing ISPs is profitability, and the perception of many ISPs is that adding subscribers is essential for enhancing their bottom-line profit. Keeping operating costs low and customer satisfaction high are equally challenging issues.*
>
> *ISPs seeking to increase revenues understand that they must extend their service offerings beyond providing Internet access and basic services alone. Responding to a survey, 84% of the ISPs stated that they generate additional revenue from services other than Internet access.[4]*

Many ISPs are marketing add-on services to current subscribers rather than spending large investments to attract new subscribers, because it is much more cost-effective. Value-added services can produce higher profit margins for services sold to current subscribers.

Most revenues earned by ISPs from residential subscribers are still a product of dial-up Internet access. However, market indicators show that ISPs may find it difficult to increase revenue from dial-up residential subscribers unless these subscribers either adopt high-speed technologies or sign up for value-added services.

---

4. Patricia Fusco, "How ISPs Plan to Defy Difficult Times," [http://www.isp-planet.com/research/2001/2001_market_survey.html] ISP-Planet, April 11, 2001.

In a market that includes multi-national conglomerates, it would be wise for independent ISPs to rely on the same business strategies that have helped other small businesses succeed when facing larger rivals—personal service, quick responses to customer service inquiries, and the idea that the customer always comes first. Local and regional ISPs should also utilize their geographic service area to their advantages by offering content or services specifically designed to appeal to local audiences.[5]

Considerations

The first, and foremost, consideration for any company entering the ISP market is whether it is necessary to build a new ISP from the ground up to serve its subscribers.

There are a variety of ways to provide ISP services without committing large capital expenses and ongoing operating resources necessary for a new ISP. In particular, some applications have become a commodity, and now it is easy to outsource to ASPs. Each of these relationships inherently has its own advantages and disadvantages. However, all of them off-load the expertise and much of the capital expense needed to build and operate an ISP. If an ISP does not have in place the qualified staff and expertise, then off-loading to ASPs is generally the best option, because these companies have core competency in the service provider market.

For mission-critical applications that drive a business, ISPs increasingly rely on a service provider's applications, such as accounting and provisioning, for essential and critical business processes.

The outsourcing model offers service level agreement (SLA) and around-the-clock dedicated operation and management staff. The outsourcing solution provides a level of operation and management excellence far beyond that economically viable for small businesses, at a very attractive rate.

Specific applications, such as a billing system, auto-registration, and customer self-care, can be outsourced, while others might be retained in-house. Small to medium-sized businesses can leverage professional expertise from outsourcing, instead of facing the high-risk and high-cost approach of the past. In fact, with variable costing models, minimal commitment terms, and often minimal integration work, tactical decisions on short-term outsourcing can be used in an economical way, allowing businesses to focus on their core business and leave provisioning, operation, and management to qualified professionals.

The trends driving outsourcing are clear: leveraged expertise, channel strategies, and financial challenges faced by small and medium-sized businesses. The variety of outsourced solutions is almost unlimited, available today from most ASPs, and will

5. Fusco, "How ISPs Plan to Defy Difficult Times."

likely grow rapidly, depending upon the pace of broadband access in the residential market. Those that do not adapt to this model may find the cost pressure to compete under the old model unbearable.

- For small and regional ISPs, performing everything in-house usually draws IT resources from critical marketing and sales initiatives. Without a focus on their core business, these small and medium-sized businesses quickly fall out of step with their market, relying increasingly on unprofitable and limited service offerings.

- The purchase of commercial off-the-shelf (COTS) products for these small ISPs proves to be a difficult business case to make.

- Low-end applications provide some required features, but lack the robust end-to-end functionality, the flexibility to add new value-added services, and the scalability to keep pace with the exponential growth in subscribers and new services.

- The full-feature, carrier-grade billing systems, necessary hardware, technical support, and deployment expertise required are impractical for small and regional ISPs. The high-cost of meeting these requirements cannot be justified within the business case. This fact leaves them settling for short-term tactical home-grown or low-end solutions, which obviously do not solve the problem of flexibility, reliability, and scalability.

Requirements

The following are some key requirements that small and regional ISPs should look for in an outsourced solution:

- *Resource leverage* - The decision to outsource provisioning is due to the fact that small ISPs can get a better solution than that available via purchasing.

- *Variable costs* – Small ISPs are looking for low up-front investment.

- *Flexible terms* - The solution must be low risk, without excessively long-term agreements.

- *Service level agreements* - Much of the value that a large service provider offers relates to the reliability and availability of a carrier-grade solution, including but not limited to, provisioning, online billing and payment, subscriber self-care, autoregistration, guaranteed availability, and disaster recovery.

- *Integration* – Small ISPs are looking for a seamless offer. Everything from online billing and auto-registration interfaces to subscriber self-care applications must be integrated with directory services.

These requirements create some significant infrastructure demands. While it is relatively easy to implement home-grown systems, this approach is proving to be unprofitable and difficult to differentiate. The support systems that facilitate these basic offerings are typically unable to scale to manage the phenomenal growth of the Internet, and they lack capabilities to generate revenue from value-added service.

Alternative Approach

An alternative for companies entering the ISP market is to enter a co-location or managed operation agreement with an existing ISP or hosting service provider. With this approach, a company commits capital resources necessary to build its own computing environment. This investment includes, and is not limited to, hardware, software, data center footprint, and Internet connectivity from a NSP or a telecommunication service provider.

The advantage of this alternative is that it gives a company as much control over the services as it wants, while still limiting the capital and operation expenses of building a new ISP from the ground up. In particular, this approach eliminates the need for a company to maintain its own in-house technical, operation, and management staffing. Also, it eliminates the need to build and maintain an expensive data center environment. At the same time, it allows a company to determine exactly what services to offer and what software to use to support services. Perhaps, most importantly, this approach allows a company almost complete flexibility to customize its product offerings and pricing, while reducing the up-front capital investment to start an ISP.

Although this approach is a far less expensive option for entering the ISP market than building and operating an ISP infrastructure from the ground up, there is still significant capital investment needed. Some hardware and software investment is necessary to support this model.

## CHAPTER 2

Formulating Design Requirements

This chapter provides guidelines for obtaining and evaluating requirements for an ISP architecture design. This chapter contains the following topics:

Formulating Requirements for a Design

Ideally, every design should be predicated on detailed requirements. Formulating requirements is a process that can vary greatly depending upon how well your ISP customers know their business challenges (present and future) and on how readily available their requirements are.

We recommend the following process when you are formulating requirements for designing an ISP architecture:

1. "Obtain Requirements" on page 12

2. "Evaluate Requirements" on page 16

3. "Establish Assumptions" on page 17

4. "Determine Design Trade-Offs" on page 19

5. "Address Architectural Limitations" on page 25

The following topics address each of these tasks within the process of formulating and evaluating design requirements.

Obtain Requirements

Obtaining requirements is the first and foremost step in the design process. These requirements should set forth business and functional requirements. A series of information interviews and meetings is usually necessary to gather requirements and to ensure that you interpret them accurately within the context of an ISP architecture. For a list of helpful questions to ask customers when designing ISP architectures, refer to Appendix A. As you gather requirements, record all information that may be helpful in designing an architecture.

Business Requirements

Business requirements are commonly found in a business plan, which defines a business's purpose, vision, mission, and road map. To be useful in formulating design requirements, the business plan must provide detailed goals and objectives.

Whether a business requirement is tactical or strategic, a business plan is critical in facilitating an architecture design that is best of breed while aligning with business strategies, both short-term and long-term.

A well-defined business plan helps you design an architecture that enables your customer to achieve corporate goals and objectives. Business plans often change over time, but the mission and vision are usually stable. No matter what the business might be, the essential elements stay the same.

Note – It is important to talk to business and technical representatives at several levels of a customer's organization to make sure that architecture requirements fit in with business requirements.

If your customer does not have a business plan, recommend that one be developed. Formulating a business plan can be a monumental task; however, the time and effort required to create a detailed business plan pays off in the long run.

In the absence of a business plan, interview the customer to determine business requirements, then review the requirements with the customer and ask questions to validate your interpretation and assumptions.

For a comprehensive list of considerations and questions to ask customers, refer to Appendix A.

The following are some factors used to establish business requirements:

- Services
- Service availability
- Time to market
- Future growth
- New technologies
- Capital investment

Functional Requirements

Functional requirements set forth design characteristics and desired results. They clearly define all functions required of an architecture and provide guidelines for how each component works and integrates to form an entire system. Also referred to as functional specifications, functional requirements are necessary in formulating the best design approaches and applying appropriate technologies to achieve a desirable architectural solution. A customer should provide detailed forecasts and requirements.

A typical functional requirements specification addresses the following:

- *Functionality* – What is the system supposed to do?
- *Interaction* – How does each component interact?
- *Performance* – What are the speed, availability, response time, and recovery time of components?
- *Attributes* – What are the portability, correctness, maintainability, security, and other related considerations?
- *Constraints* – Are there any required standards, security policies, internationalization, etc?

Design an architecture to meet functional requirements and align the design with business strategies. To be effective and practical, a design should meet business objectives.

Sources

Functional requirements are typically provided in the following ways:

- As part of a detailed customer business plan
- Prepared by a customer, specifically for the project
- Prepared by you and other engineers, after interviewing a customer for requirements and business strategies

Rarely do customers know all their requirements. Perhaps their core businesses are less technology-oriented, or their familiarity of the subject matter is less in-depth. They rely on architects and implementors to guide them through the process and deliver high-quality architectures that meet their business needs. In most cases where there is lack of requirements, you can use market analysis, industry standards, and design assumptions. Using this baseline, interview the customer to define and validate requirements. We highly recommend that you document the requirements and present them to the customer as a functional specification.

Factors

The following are examples of factors used to establish functional requirements:

- Service uptime level expectations
- Concurrent active session projections
- Future growth predictions
- Customer has multiple sites and requires a modular and replicable solution
- Customer wants to integrate new systems with legacy systems and existing technologies
- Customer wants to offer new services on demand
- Customer requires automated service and user provisioning
- Customer requires online billing and customer care capabilities
- Architecture must be expandable to support multiple points of presence (POPs)
- Customer requests a centralized authentication and authorization mechanism

Evaluate Requirements

After you obtain both business and functional requirements, carefully evaluate them. Determine how realistic each requirement is. What would be the best design approach to satisfy each requirement and related requirements? Consider all constraints such as cost, time to market, etc., and decide if any of the requirements should be modified, then recommend changes and solutions to the customer. In the absence of requirements, make assumptions for now and validate them later with the customer.

The following are common questions to ask yourself as you evaluate requirements:

- Can an architecture be designed to meet all requirements?
- Are any of the requirements unrealistic or unattainable within the constraints imposed by the customer or technology?
- Is the solution achievable with existing technologies?
- Will the design be cost effective?
- Does the solution rely on extremely complex technology that may be difficult to implement or manage?
- If technology is not readily available, would it be viable to develop a custom solution?
- Does the design integrate with customer's operating environment?
- Is the design scalable to handle additional services and subscribers?
- Is the design modular and replicable with minimum changes?
- Does the design depend on any proprietary technology?
- Will the design be adaptive to business and technological changes?
- How long is the hardware and software investment expected to last?

Analyzing each requirement and deciding how to meet it is critical. Several solutions may be considered for a single requirement, and sometimes alternative solutions are needed in case a component cannot be used.

As you analyze requirements, it's common that you will start forming ideas about making trade-offs and addressing limitations. (The next two sections address these topics.)

For example, if commercial off-the-shelf (COTS) or open source products cannot achieve the desired solution, resources such as time and skilled labor might be required to develop a custom solution, whether it is to be done in-house or outsourced. This constraint might have an affect on a business requirement (for example, time to market) and appropriate changes might need to be made to ensure that a solution aligns with the business plan. Ultimately, the choice is the customer's:

either change the constraint or the requirement. In situations such as these, it's best to have several options to present, thereby providing the customer some flexibility and insight into trade offs. Maintain an open dialogue with the customer.

If the customer has not prioritized requirements or some of the requirements conflict, involve the customer in reviewing and prioritizing requirements.

Establish Assumptions

During the design process, it's necessary to establish and make assumptions. The key to establishing good assumptions is to base them on as much reliable data and expertise as is available. Assumptions originate from the customer, you, and other engineers.

Some common reasons for making assumptions:

- Requirements are incomplete or lack sufficient detail
- Requirements do not accurately reflect industry data
- Missing data such as background information
- Inexperience with available technology
- Need a base line for capacity planning
- Need to anticipate future growth and usage patterns

Even when excellent requirements are available, some general design assumptions need to be made by you and the customer. For example, you need to establish a base line for capacity planning.

Tip – A common scenario is that a customer cannot estimate the percentage of concurrent active sessions. Because this assumption is important in estimating many other design variables, such as average bandwidth consumption and number of high-speed trunks required for access servers, you need to assume a percentage of concurrent active sessions. For information about how to calculate percentage of concurrent active sessions, refer to Chapter 5.

Other assumptions can be based on market data, customer forecasts, and industry averages so that you can create the best possible design that is optimal and realistic.

The following are some common factors used in establishing assumptions:

- Total number of subscribers
- Market forecast
- Concurrency percentage (total number of active sessions)
- Subscriber type (residential or business)
- User expertise (beginning, intermediate, advanced, or mixed)
- Expected growth and usage patterns
- Web content (static, dynamic, or combination of both)
- Storage for news (affects total storage requirement)
- Backup retention policy (affects how long data can be archived on backup media)
- Scale to next magnitude of subscribers (for example, 10K to 100K)
- Service availability (critical or not critical)
- Maximum quota (for example, email = 5 Mbyte, web = 5 Mbyte)
- Email access protocol (POP3, IMAP4, or both)
- Internal or outsourced provider for news, provisioning, management, etc.
- Daily peak times (for example, 8 a.m. to 10 a.m., 2 p.m. to 4 p.m., and so on)

Carefully examine and evaluate all assumptions, whether offered by the customer or established by you and other engineers. Make assumptions within a reasonable range so that actual results match or are close to intended results. To validate your assumptions, you may need to develop a design prototype (refer to Chapter 7). The goal is to achieve minimal distortion or bias resulting from inaccurate assumptions.

Tip – While capacity planning should cover the growth expected, it is critical that ISPs monitor subscriber growth and system usage. They should compare actual data with forecasts and assumptions to ensure that the capacity is capable of handling projected growth.

Determine Design Trade-Offs

Design trade-offs are benefits gained or lost from a substitution process that derives a "best-fit" solution, based on imposed design requirements and constraints. Choose design trade-offs where a benefit gained outweighs any benefit lost or reduced.

Realistically, there might never be the best or most ideal solution available to meet a challenge. However, design considerations and trade offs help you arrive at the best-fitting solution. Assess and mitigate all risks for every design trade off. Determine how a trade off affects the overall design, as well as short-term and long-term business strategies. Document all design trade-offs, including the rationale for each decision, reasons, and possible outcomes. You or the customer may need this critical information later.

Understanding design trade-offs is critical in taking the appropriate design approach toward achieving an optimal solution. Obviously, there is usually more than one way to arrive at a solution.

Tip – An optimal approach is one that achieves a desirable result, is simplistic in design, is straightforward to implement, and is easy to manage. For many reasons, it's best to avoid approaches that rely on overly complex designs, complicated implementations, and proprietary technology.

The following sections present common design considerations and provide comments about trade offs. For ease of reference, the design considerations are organized by what they apply to, for example, scalability, availability, and security.

Scalability

Should the design use low-end network equipment?

Many small-scale ISPs elect to use the smallest possible network equipment (routers and switches) to handle their current or projected number of subscribers. While this approach satisfies a short-term goal of reducing up-front capital investment, it may not be a good approach if the architecture is expected to scale multiple times to support many more subscribers in the near future.

In such a scenario, the network equipment cannot be scaled vertically to support a higher port density because the chassis is too small. Unfortunately, to achieve a higher level of scalability, the network equipment must be completely replaced. The costs in this scenario are obvious: new equipment purchases, old equipment's rapid depreciation, labor, and service down time for installing and upgrading equipment.

Tip – In most architecture designs, it's best for an ISP to start with a larger network equipment chassis with a minimal configuration. Although it costs more, it saves money and provides a more scalable architecture in the long-term. (Cost is dependent on the vendor and equipment the customer selects.) To minimize up-front costs with a larger chassis, have the network equipment configured with only the minimum configuration needed to handle the current subscriber level. As the ISP's subscriber base grows, they can add new capacity to scale.

Scalability applies to various components at different layers within an architecture. In general, scalability applies to network, systems, applications, and data. For each component, scalability can be applied in one or two ways: vertical and/or horizontal. The level of scalability is dependent upon the component and the layer of the infrastructure.

Scalability is usually done in stages and should be realistic. It is not realistic to design a 10,000-subscriber architecture that is scalable to 10 million subscribers. Allowing such exponential scaling would require significant up-front capital investment or redesigning an architecture from the beginning. A *factor of 10* is the recommended approach in planning for scalability.

From our experience, the factor of 10 approach is good for the following reasons:

- The level of scalability is realistic and achievable.
- It requires the lowest cost in upgrading various components within an infrastructure.
- It provides a life cycle that is viable to the business with the best return on investment.

No architecture has unlimited scalability. Each one has different levels of scalability. How much scalability an architecture has is dependent upon design requirements. It's possible to design an architecture with a very high level of scalability, but it might not be feasible for several reasons. First, the architecture might not ever need to scale that high; thus, it is unrealistic to have it. Second, the cost to have that level of scalability is high and may not be justifiable to the business case. Third, an architecture with too low a level of scalability can be costly because it has too short a life cycle, requiring it to be redesigned and redeployed.

Availability and Reliability

Should the architecture include redundancy?

High availability is expensive, and reliability depends on what is implemented for availability. ISPs that deem availability and reliability to be critical to their business success and service offering find ways to invest capital for purchasing redundant equipment.

Many small ISPs cannot afford to purchase redundant equipment, so they choose to reduce up-front capital costs by excluding redundancy throughout the infrastructure.

Redundancy can be implemented in the following layers: network, system, and data.

- At the network layer, redundant Internet connections, switches, routers, load balancers, and firewalls enhance availability and reliability.

- At the system layer, redundant power supplies, fans, system boards, and servers behind load balancers enhance availability and reliability. Also, clustering technology enhances availability and reliability.

- At the data layer, redundant data paths and storage arrays enhance availability and reliability.

Without redundancy, each component within a layer can cause a single point-of-failure, resulting in a partial or complete failure of the infrastructure. Without a doubt, adding redundancy is expensive, but so are the consequences of relying on architecture that is not reliable. It is up to each ISP to determine whether redundancy fits within the business model.

Tip – At the system layer, N+1 (extra server) minimizes overall cost while achieving higher availability. A complete failure is avoided, with the major trade off being a potential service degradation, depending on how much load the extra server handles. Another trade off is that N+1 can be complex to implement and manage.

Security

Should the design include a firewall?

Many ISPs choose not to implement firewalls, due to the bottlenecks they tend to cause. Some security experts debate whether a firewall is useful for ISPs, based on the cost and collateral impact, among other considerations.

Sometimes architects and their customers make a strategic decision to omit a firewall. The most common reasons for not implementing a firewall are as follows:

- It introduces single point-of-failure to the infrastructure.
- It adds to performance and scalability issues.
- It does not provide substantial security compared to cost for an ISP environment.

Should the design include a router access control list (ACL) and packet filters?

Many ISPs choose to omit firewalls and implement router ACL and packet filters instead. Some key considerations are the following:

- Routers are stateless and do not examine payload.
- Firewalls are necessary for stateful applications.

For small ISPs that have static content, a router ACL and packet filters may be sufficient. However, for dynamic content and state preservation, a firewall is necessary. Routers only examine packet headers; they don't examine payload. Stateful firewalls do. Many ISPs don't need stateful firewalls unless they have stateful applications to be managed, such as portals.

Caution – Implementing a router ACL and packet filters offers some protection; however, serious security breaches can occur. If an extreme assault against its infrastructure occurs, an ISP may experience downtime or system failure, resulting in lost revenue and subscribers. Firewalls can be important because they provide an additional layer of security beyond router ACLs and simple packet filters.

Should the design include an intrusion detection system (IDS)?

Hardware and software to implement an IDS is costly. However, without an IDS, an ISP cannot respond to attacks in a timely manner. Depending upon the security attack and an ISP's business, the cost can be substantial. Security breaches cost organizations billions of dollars every year.

Small-scale ISPs often want to exclude implementing an IDS for the infrastructure. This strategic business decision is based on the following:

- IDS is not mission-critical to the business.

- IDS does not fit within budget constraints.

Caution – Although excluding an IDS reduces capital cost, it exposes an ISP to potential loss and liability. Implementing an IDS allows an ISP to monitor who accesses data and services. If an extreme assault against its infrastructure occurs, for example, a distributed denial of services (DDoS) attack, an ISP may experience down time or system failure, resulting in lost revenue and subscribers. In addition to these costs, there may be litigation costs, for example, if subscribers take legal action.

Manageability

What are the best design techniques for accommodating manageability?

The best techniques are to design a modular architecture and to keep it simple. Using these techniques, you can design an architecture that is manageable and easily scaled.

Use the guiding principle that one should not make more assumptions than the minimum needed. This principle underlies all scientific modelling and theory building. It advises us to choose from a set of otherwise equivalent models of a given phenomenon the simplest one.

> *Pluralitas non est ponenda sine neccesitate.* —Occam's[1] Razor

Translation: plurality should not be assumed without necessity.

In any given model, Occam's razor (scientific precept) helps us to "shave off" those concepts, variables, or constructs that are not really needed to explain a phenomenon. By doing that, developing the model becomes much easier, and there is less chance of introducing inconsistencies, ambiguities, and redundancies.

---

1. William of Ockham (1285-1349), a 14th century logician and Franciscan friar.

A modular design allows an architecture to scale on demand and be easily replicated with minimal changes. Changes can be confined within a module so that they do not affect the operation of other components. Modularity makes it easier to control and manage the infrastructure. For example, a modular design allows additional front-end web servers to be replaced or replicated effortlessly without affecting operations or modifying the architecture. In contrast, with a nonmodular approach, a simple change might require modifying many components, and the change might affect many other components.

When an architecture design is based on a common operating environment and/or operating platform, it is easier to manage. The skills and knowledge required to maintain the system are far less than that required when a system is comprised of components from many vendors.

In most cases, there are multiple approaches for deriving a solution. However, some approaches and techniques are less complex than others, yet provide similar outcomes and satisfy an ISP's requirements. Keep your architecture design as simple as possible. A simple design costs less and is easier to implement. Also, it is easier to manage and troubleshoot.

Open System

Why should I design an architecture to meet standards for open systems?

In an ISP architecture design, many components must be tightly integrated to create a seamless infrastructure. If you design an architecture where all components, both hardware and software, are designed and produced based on industry open standards, the customer may achieve benefits such as the following:

- Seamless integration with current technology
- No dependence upon a single vendor
- Flexibility in adopting new technologies

If components in your design are based on proprietary technology (produced or supported only by a single vendor, or operated only within a proprietary operating platform or environment), try to minimize the amount of proprietary technology and the impact it has on the entire system. Carefully document where proprietary components are used, and suggest a back-up plan in case the customer needs to replace those components with another vendor's components.

Tip – After implementation, correcting or changing an infrastructure that was designed with non-standard technology is usually difficult and expensive because the architecture must be redesigned.

Outsourcing

When an ISP has significant cost constraints, is there an alternative way to meet some requirements?

Outsourcing is an excellent way to reduce up-front capital investment, to reduce ongoing operational and management cost, and to maintain a reliable service level agreement (SLA) with business subscribers.

This alternative provides ISPs, especially small- to mid-sized companies, an opportunity to enter the market without investing capital in resources and management staff. This alternative works best when applied to meeting requirements such as subscriber care, billing, and registration. Establishing and maintaining an internal solution would be cost prohibitive, and the ISP may not have qualified staff with the expertise and experience necessary for implementing, operating, and maintaining the system. For this example, a cost-saving approach would be to outsource to an application service provider (ASP).

Open Source Applications

Are open source applications a viable alternative?

Purchasing commercial off-the-shelf applications for Internet business can be very expensive, especially for small- to mid-sized ISPs entering the market. Developing applications in-house is very expensive too. Sometimes, open source applications are a good design trade off. The advantage is that applications and their source code are available at no cost and are freely distributed over the Internet. The disadvantages are lack of technical support, features, performance, security, scalability, and reliability.

Address Architectural Limitations

In general, architectural limitations result from constraints imposed on an architectural design. Specifically, these limitations reflect what can and cannot be achieved. You may encounter limitations initially when evaluating requirements or later, for example, due to changes requested by a customer.

An example of an architectural limitation is the inability to scale to support a larger number of subscribers. Another example is the inability to safely handle a higher level of transaction processes.

As the final task in formulating design requirements and evaluating them, it's important to address architectural limitations. In many cases, this task is simply documenting limitations and communicating them to your customer. In other cases, you may want to clarify requirements and strategy with the customer, present concerns, address risks, and recommend solutions, then agree on a resolution. It's far more advantageous to the customer and you to make any changes now, before progressing with further design work. If changes result from these meetings, go back to the affected areas and re-evaluate them.

Every architecture design has limitations, whether they result from requirements, tactical business decisions, inaccurate assumptions, or other causes. Evaluate all architectural limitations, so that risks can be assessed and mitigated. Also, when possible, take into consideration future limitations of an architecture.

Sometimes customers are unfamiliar with the technology included in their requirements. They may request features that are not possible with current technologies. Address all limitations early in the design phase, so that changes can be made with minimal impact. Advise the customer of limitations and recommend alternatives.

The following are common challenges during the requirements evaluation:

- Budget constraints
- Requirement cannot be satisfied with technology available or applicable to a customer's operating environment
- Technology exists; however, tools, applications, or solutions are proprietary, and, therefore, are not available or recommended for an open system environment
- Unrealistic requirement that cannot be met

If you encounter a major limitation in meeting a business requirement, and it cannot be addressed with alternatives, ask the customer to reassess the requirement and/or business plan.

The following are common challenges encountered after a design is completed and/or implemented:

- Customer expects architecture to do things beyond its original purpose and design
- Forecast contained inaccurate data, resulting in a non-optimal design
- Changes occur in business or functional requirements after a design is completed, for example, the customer changes the requirements for scaling; now wants to go from 100,000 subscribers to 1,000,000.
- More services added or running on infrastructure than planned (changes level of resource utilization, which puts the design at risk)
- Lack of qualified personnel and detailed procedures to manage infrastructure

- Tactical business decisions affect long-term strategies, for example, deploying a short-term solution to minimize cost, then later needing to scale to a larger solution (in these cases, the customer might have to replace the original solution rather than scaling it)

- Company representative strongly favors a vendor even though the vendor's technology would not provide an optimal design

Although initially your focus is on evaluating limitations based on requirements presented in a business plan and a functional specification, be aware that other limitations may surface later. If you think a customer may change expectations later, for example, some of the company's representatives are suggesting they expect the subscriber population to grow more dramatically than stated in the requirements, it's a good idea to query the customer now and present scenarios showing options and associated costs.

Formulating Requirements for FijiNet

A local telecommunication company on the Fiji Islands would like to offer Internet services to residential subscribers. The company, FijiNet, partners with Sun to develop a detailed architectural design for entering the ISP market.

With FijiNet as a fictitious sample customer, this section applies process and information presented earlier in this chapter to obtain and evaluate all requirements on which to base an architectural design within a realistic scenario.

In the next chapter, we show how to apply an architectural model and principles to FijiNet's requirements.

Note – Throughout this book, we use a fictitious company called FijiNet to demonstrate how to design an ISP architecture. Our goal is to apply the concepts and information to a realistic scenario while making the content enjoyable to read. Any resemblance to a past, present, or future company named FijiNet is purely coincidental.

Obtain Requirements for FijiNet

Using information from FijiNet's business plan, we become familiar with the company's background, market, and their initial requirements for an ISP architecture.

Through the business plan, we learn that FijiNet was established five years ago as a local telecommunication service provider, and FijiNet is the only local telecommunication service provider serving the Fiji islands. Islanders are very loyal to local businesses, and have for the most part resisted marketing efforts by larger telecommunication service companies. FijiNet's current market is 100,000 subscribers. In addition to providing telecommunication service, they also provide local cable service.

FijiNet's latest market research shows that approximately 10 percent (10,000) of their subscribers are interested in Internet access and services.

Business Requirements

TABLE 2-1 shows FijiNet's business requirements for the market they want to serve initially. In the column next to each business requirement, we noted what the requirement applies to in architecture design terms, for ease of reference later during the evaluation.

TABLE 2-1 FijiNet Business Requirements

Requirement	Applies to
Quick time to market: FijiNet wants to implement an ISP architecture and offer basic services within six months.	Business strategy
Initial offering must provide basic services: email, web hosting, and Internet news to residential subscribers.	Basic services
In the near future, FijiNet may offer the same basic services to business subscribers.	Basic services
FijiNet may offer some value-added services such as address book, calendar, web mail, chat, and search engine with subsequent product and service releases.	Value-added services
Service offering must accommodate 10,000 residential subscribers for the initial phase.	Base line assumption
Must be scalable to support 100,000 residential subscribers in 5 years.	Scalability
Should be highly available, providing 24x7 service availability.	Availability
Should be highly reliable, providing 99.99% uptime (four nines).	Reliability
Must integrate with existing environment.	Adaptability
Provide solution that has minimal up-front capital investment.	Business strategy
Can support broadband and wireless services in the future.	Value-added services
Expand ISP services to national level in 5 years.	Scalability
Provide service responsiveness with the best possible level of performance within given cost constraints.	Performance

Functional Requirements

TABLE 2-2 provides FijiNet's functional requirements for an ISP architecture. In the column next to each functional requirement, we noted what the requirement applies to in architecture design terms, for ease of reference later during the analysis.

TABLE 2-2   FijiNet Functional Requirements

Requirements	Applies to
System should be highly reliable, providing 99.99% uptime (four nines).	Reliability
System should be highly available, providing 24x7 service.	Availability
Support at least 5000 concurrent active sessions (50% concurrency).	Base line assumption
Scalable to support 100,000 residential subscribers in 5 years.	Scalability
System should be modular and replicable to multiple sites.	Manageability, Scalability
Integrate new architecture with existing operating environment and future technology.	Adaptability, Open system
Automate subscriber care, billing, and registration.	Manageability
Scalable to multisite configurations supporting multiple POPs.	Scalability
Central authentication and authorization.	Manageability, Security
Provide initial service offering of email, web hosting, and Internet news.	Basic services
Scalable to handle addition of new value-added services such as address book, calendar, web mail, chat, and search engine in subsequent product and service releases.	Scalability
User data and service access must be highly secure through firewalls, authentication, and authorization features.	Security

Evaluate Requirements for FijiNet

By conducting informational interviews and meetings with representatives from FijiNet, we interpret and clarify business and functional requirements. The primary constraint for the entire architectural design for FijiNet is cost, because FijiNet wants to enter the ISP market with the lowest possible cost.

The design goal for FijiNet is an absolute minimal configuration that can be used for basic Internet services. The solution needs to be modular, reliable, replicable, and highly scalable with minimal changes to the overall architecture to accommodate growth.

In our evaluation, we see cost as the overriding design constraint that affects the overall design and places other constraints upon the architecture. For example, it immediately removes high availability from the architecture. Other requirements can be outsourced to third-party vendors.

TABLE 2-3 shows an analysis of FijiNet's business requirements, and TABLE 2-4 shows an evaluation of functional requirements. For requirements that cannot be met within constraints, we provide recommendations or alternative solutions.

Evaluating Business Requirements

TABLE 2-3 provides our evaluation of the business requirements for FijiNet.

TABLE 2-3   FijiNet Business Requirements Evaluation

Requirement	Analysis
Quick time to market: within six months, FijiNet wants to implement an ISP architecture and offer basic services.	Depending on the size and whether the deployment is new or based on existing infrastructure, the average time to market varies from 6 to 18 months, depending upon the size of the ISP and other factors. Many factors are involved, for example, services offered, complexity, and scale of the design. For FijiNet, 6 months is achievable if a data center is in place with power and space available.
Initial offering must provide basic services: email (POP/IMAP), web hosting, and Internet news to residential subscribers.	Traditional ISPs don't usually offer Internet mail access protocol (IMAP) to residential subscribers. They only offer post office protocol (POP). This is due to the simplicity of the protocol and the low overhead. While this model is common and dominant in the market today, its days are numbered. The trend is moving toward feature-rich IMAP email service, especially for business subscribers.
In the near future, offer same basic services to business subscribers.	Business subscribers expect a service level agreement (SLA). The success of their Internet business may depend upon FijiNet's ability to provide reliable services. Service interruption might not be tolerable or acceptable to business subscribers. Therefore, for FijiNet to expand the service offering to business subscribers, a higher quality of service (QoS) level must be offered.
Some value-added services such as address book, calendar, web mail, chat, and search engine are planned for subsequent product and service releases.	It is essential that the deployment is planned in multiple phases. Value-added services are typically not deployed until all basic services are operating and have been trouble-free. To ensure manageability and quality control, we advise FijiNet to only deploy one service at a time. It is important to plan ahead for any service that will be offered in the near future. This planning is critical in ensuring that the infrastructure is scalable to handle new services and integrates with existing services.
Service offering must accommodate 10,000 residential subscribers.	We use this number to establish a base line assumption for the percentage of concurrency, as well as capacity planning for storage.

TABLE 2-3   FijiNet Business Requirements Evaluation *(Continued)*

Requirement	Analysis
Must be scalable to support 100,000 residential subscribers in 5 years.	Scalability is typically designed for the next 12 to 18 months for large ISPs and 2 to 3 years for small and mid-sized ISPs. Any plans 5 years out are too far to accurately predict usage patterns, changes in new technologies, and market trends. For FijiNet, we recommend revising this requirement to state that scaling to 100,000 subscribers will occur in 12 to 18 months.
Should be highly available, providing 24x7 service availability.	For small ISPs such as FijiNet, cost is the most important design constraint. Such a high level of availability is frequently requested, but ultimately not necessary or critical to the business because subscribers are residential subscribers. It is important for an ISP to provide a reliable level of service. However, in this case, it is not viable to FijiNet's business because too much capital would be invested to attain the highest level of availability, when it is not required. When FijiNet has a larger number of subscribers (≥100,000) and expands its business to a national level, then it will be necessary to implement high availability to the infrastructure to ensure service reliability.
Should be highly reliable, providing 99.99% uptime (four nines).	The 99.99% uptime is not realistic, especially for a small ISP such as FijiNet. The request for 99.99% uptime is equivalent to having down time of 4.30 minutes per month. This requirement is neither practical nor achievable without full redundancy and fault tolerance implemented throughout the infrastructure to remove all single points of failure. For most small- to mid-sized ISPs, 99.5% uptime (3.6 hours down time per month) is much more realistic. For FijiNet, we recommend 99.5%. For telecommunication service providers and online financial institutions, achieving the highest level of uptime, such as 99.99% or higher, is mission critical to the business and justifies the cost for redundancy.
Must integrate with existing environment.	Because FijiNet is a local telecommunication company, it probably has a billing system in place to handle user provisioning and a mechanism for authentication. If these components exist and can be leveraged, FijiNet can take advantage of them and minimize costs. It is not economical to manage two separate billing systems and directory services in a single operating environment. If these components do not exist or cannot be leveraged, this responsibility should be outsourced to an ASP, so that cost constraints and time-to-market can be met.

TABLE 2-3 FijiNet Business Requirements Evaluation *(Continued)*

Requirement	Analysis
Provide solution that has minimal up-front capital investment. Where appropriate, provide different cost models (for example, outsourcing) for cost-intensive services.	It is absolutely not economical for FijiNet to run all services in-house. We identified services that can be outsourced to reduce up-front costs. Services such as Internet news require an enormous amount of storage (for example, 300 GB plus 25% overhead of disk space) and up-keep. It is best outsourced to a UseNet provider. The billing system could be outsourced to an ASP. For a larger ISP with a large number of subscribers, it makes sense to manage such a service in-house. However, for small ISPs like FijiNet, this service is best outsourced to reduce up-front capital investment and maintenance costs.
May support broadband and wireless services in the future.	Broadband and wireless architectures are very different from traditional ISP architectures. Bandwidth demand for broadband is very high. To support broadband service, a network infrastructure must be able to handle high traffic loads. Many critical and specialized components are required for signal and protocol conversion. Due to cost and time-to-market constraints, we recommend that this requirement not be applicable.
Expand ISP services to national level in 5 years.	Scalability for 5 years is too far out. The constant changes in technology, business models, and usage patterns are very hard to predict that far from now. We recommended accommodating the next 12 to 18 months. Change is inevitable. However, planning for a shorter time frame is more predictable, less extreme, and more realistic.
Provide service responsiveness with the best possible level of performance within given cost constraints.	Conduct performance tuning on servers and applications to ensure the best possible level of performance with the given hardware and software.

Evaluating Functional Requirements

TABLE 2-4 provides our evaluation of functional requirements for FijiNet.

TABLE 2-4 FijiNet Functional Requirements Evaluation

Requirement	Analysis
System should be highly reliable, providing 99.99% uptime (four nines).	(See Business Requirement analysis in TABLE 2-3.)
System should be highly available, providing 24x7 service.	(See Business Requirement analysis in TABLE 2-3.)
Support at least 5000 concurrent active sessions (50% concurrency).	For 10,000 subscribers, 5,000 concurrent active sessions is 50% concurrency. It is not realistic or economical to support this many concurrent active sessions. Allocating 5,000 modems to handle 5,000 active users, as well as high-speed trunks (CT3s) for dial-up access, is expensive. The recommended percentage of concurrency for an ISP is 12.5% to 16.7%, based on an average industry usage. (These percentages correspond to ratios of 8:1 and 6:1.) Therefore, we recommend providing for 1,250 to 1,670 concurrent active sessions based on an estimate of 10,000 subscribers. Concurrency is important for sizing: the number of modems to be supported by access servers, the number of high-speed trunks to support dial-up, memory consumption by servers, etc.
Scalable to support 100,000 residential subscribers in 5 years.	(See Business Requirement analysis in TABLE 2-3.)
System should be modular and replicable to multiple sites.	To expand services from a regional to a national level, multiple POPs must be replicated to multiple geographical regions to handle a broader number of subscribers. To be replicable, the POP design must be modular and scale horizontally with minimum changes and efforts. Multisite configuration might be necessary to ensure availability in the event of a disaster.
Integrate new architecture with existing billing system and directory service.	(See Business Requirement analysis in TABLE 2-3.)

TABLE 2-4   FijiNet Functional Requirements Evaluation *(Continued)*

Requirement	Analysis
Automate subscriber care, registration, and billing.	Subscriber care, registration, and billing is time consuming when done manually, and implementing and maintaining a system is costly. Although a manual process might suffice for a small business as a short-term solution, it is not an effective long-term solution. Based on experience, a manual solution becomes un-manageable as the number of subscribers approaches 10,000 subscribers. In order for FijiNet to scale to 100,000 subscribers, automation must be implemented in the early stage. For FijiNet, operation and management of the infrastructure must be automated as much as possible to reduce on-going costs. We recommend this requirement be met by outsourcing it to an ASP who specializes in this area.
Central authentication and authorization.	A centralized directory approach is necessary to provide a seamless mechanism for authentication and authorization, and to provide integration with user and service provisioning throughout the entire infrastructure. If FijiNet already has a centralized directory implemented for telecommunication service, a cost-saving approach is to use the existing directory for authentication and authorization.

TABLE 2-4 FijiNet Functional Requirements Evaluation *(Continued)*

Requirement	Analysis
Provide initial service offering of email, web hosting, and Internet news.	**Email:** POP is the email service offered by most ISPs. It has modest demands on the mail server and low overhead on storage. We propose using POP for FijiNet's email service because it is usually the most economical way of providing email service to residential subscribers. IMAP is typically deployed in business environments. IMAP has many features and functions that POP does not have. Although IMAP is a better protocol than POP by design, it's not attractive to many ISPs. (The profit margin might diminish with the substantially larger investment in hardware demanded by the load of IMAP.) The value of POP is simplicity. It does one thing and one thing only—it enables users to download email messages to a local system on demand. For residential subscribers, the limitations of POP are acceptable. However, as more users become accustomed to the flexibility and power of IMAP in business environments, they're likely to start demanding the same from their residential service ISPs. The key in deciding which protocol is right for an ISP is user constituency. POP is an excellent solution for residential subscribers who typically access mail from a single computer. The biggest infrastructure difference between POP and IMAP-based servers is the impact of usage patterns on mail servers. **Web Hosting:** Web hosting of personal web pages can be done without any special consideration. **News Services:** For small- to mid-sized ISPs, news service is best outsourced to a UseNet provider. This approach is practical and cost effective because of the immensely large storage required for daily news articles and the intensive on-going management of newsgroups. It is not economical for small ISPs such as FijiNet to run Internet news in-house.
Scalable to handle addition of new value-added services such as address book, calendar, web mail, chat, and search engine in subsequent product and service releases.	Each new service requires different resources (CPU, memory, and storage) and behaves differently. To add services, the design must scale to handle a larger load and sustain an acceptable level of performance. For example, services such as streaming media exert very high demands on network bandwidth. For FijiNet to offer these value-added services in the future, capacity planning for these services must be done now to estimate resources required so that the architecture scales.

TABLE 2-4   FijiNet Functional Requirements Evaluation *(Continued)*

Requirement	Analysis
User data and service access must be highly secure through firewalls, authentication, and authorization features.	For FijiNet, because cost is the major constraint, a highly redundant N-tier architecture cannot be achieved without spending significant up-front capital investment. Therefore, IDS and multitier firewall layers will not be implemented. A firewall will be used to secure access between external networks and the internal network. Access will be allowed or denied based on firewall policies. Authentication and authorization will be done by directory service. A router ACL will provide front-end filtering.

Establish Assumptions for FijiNet

Based on our knowledge of FijiNet's requirements and our assessment of those requirements, now we need to fill in the gaps by making assumptions. (For detailed information about making assumptions in the design process, see "Establish Assumptions" on page 17.)

The architecture design we are forming is optimized for basic service offerings: email, web hosting, and Internet news. While some additional service offerings may be easily implemented, we will advise FijiNet that unspecified services may have implementation requirements that exceed the design.

TABLE 2-5 provides a list of assumptions and an evaluation of each assumption for the FijiNet design.

TABLE 2-5   Evaluation of Assumptions

Assumption	Evaluation
Email storage	We assume that email storage of 5 MB maximum per user account is sufficient for FijiNet's initial roll out. This storage estimate is based on an industry average among large-scale ISPs. The quota can be lowered or raised, depending on user demands.
Web page storage	Web page hosting is allowed a maximum of 5 MB per user account. This amount is based on industry average among large-scale service providers. This amount is sufficient for static content only.

TABLE 2-5 Evaluation of Assumptions *(Continued)*

News storage	Raw news articles need approximately 300 GB for daily storage. This amount may vary, depending on how FijiNet moderates its news groups. For example, if FijiNet actively moderates its news groups by removing stale news groups, restricting offensive materials, and filtering out duplicate news postings, less space is required. We recommend that FijiNet outsource news to a UseNet service provider.
Daily peak times	The two common peak usage times for business subscribers are 8 a.m. to 10 a.m. and 2 p.m. to 4 p.m. Users tend to access services, such as checking email, when they first get to work and again after lunch. For residential subscribers, the peak usage time is likely to be after hours, from 7 p.m. to 9 p.m. FijiNet is offering initial services only to residential subscribers, so we assume this peak time is applicable.
Concurrency percentage	The percentage of concurrency (number of active user sessions) is estimated to be 12.5%, which gives us 1,250 for FijiNet. We base this value on the industry average among large-scale service providers.
Modems	Based on the percentage of concurrency, we assume that 1,200 modems is sufficient for handling all active user sessions.
High-speed trunk for dial-up access	Two CT3s are sufficient to handle 1,250 to 1,670 concurrent active sessions. Multiple T1s could be used; however, the access server might not support a large number of T1s.
High-speed trunk for Internet access	One CT3 is sufficient for handling incoming and outgoing traffic to the Internet.

Note – For mathematical formulas to determine number of high-speed trunks, refer to Chapter 5.

Determine Design Trade-Offs for FijiNet

Because cost is the major design consideration for FijiNet, the design is constrained in areas such as scalability, availability, and reliability. We presented the trade offs and considerations to FijiNet, and their representatives accepted the trade offs and gave a green light to go forward. TABLE 2-6 lists the design considerations, what area they apply to, and our comments, including recommended design.

TABLE 2-6   Determining Design Trade-Offs for FijiNet

Design Consideration	Applies to	Comments
Use low-end network equipment.	Scalability	A lower-end switching router will be used. It uses an L2-L3 switch with a fixed port density. While the switching router can handle up to 100,000 subscribers, the switching router is not scalable to provide a higher level of port density or more WAN interfaces. For fixed chassis, the only way to scale vertically later is to replace the equipment. Horizontal scaling can be achieved by adding an additional switching router to increase availability and reliability.
Implement no redundancy.	Availability, Reliability	Redundant network equipment such as routers, switches, load balancers, and firewalls are not feasible. High availability is not mission critical for FijiNet; therefore, redundant network equipment is unnecessary at this time. FijiNet has no plans to offer reliability or SLAs for residential subscribers. Although redundancy can be added as needed, FijiNet is vulnerable to many single points of failure. A failure to any component can cause a partial or complete service failure. There is no way to ensure reliability to a single-chassis system unless redundancy is implemented. At a regional level, the implementation of availability is not feasible due to budget constraints. However, as FijiNet scales to a national level serving 100,000 subscribers or more, high availability will become critical to the business.

TABLE 2-6   Determining Design Trade-Offs for FijiNet *(Continued)*

Design Consideration	Applies to	Comments
Exclude HA and clustering.	Availability, Reliability	FijiNet's business case does not warrant high availability (HA) and clustering technology at this time. Implement a single-box configuration.
Implement minimum RAID.	Availability, Reliability	Implement redundant array of independent disks (RAID) 1 (mirroring) only where absolutely necessary, such as the boot disk. For user data storage, RAID 5 (stripping with parity) will be implemented to reduce overall cost. Because disks contain moving components, they are vulnerable to hardware failure. While service degradation is inevitable because data has to be rebuilt from parity, RAID 5 can ensure a higher level of reliability in the event of disk failure, at a lower cost than RAID 0+1.
Exclude IDS.	Security	Because FijiNet is a small ISP serving residential subscribers, IDS is excluded. The strategical business decision is based on IDS not being mission-critical to the business and IDS not fitting the budget constraint. This approach places FijiNet at a disadvantage, because they cannot be proactive in responding to breaches and break-in attempts in a timely manner.

Address Architectural Limitations for FijiNet

As the final task in formulating design requirements and evaluating them for FijiNet, we address major architectural limitations.

We identified the following limitations that should be communicated to FijiNet.

- **Scalability** – The architecture is designed to handle 10,000 subscribers on the initial rollout. It is scalable with the factor of 10 to support up to 100,000 subscribers. We request that FijiNet revise its plan from 5 years to 12 to 18 months to scale to 100,000 subscribers, because planning for 5 years from now is not realistic.

To scale above 100,000 subscribers would require major changes to the architecture. The network equipment would need to be replaced with a larger, higher-end chassis for vertical scalability; the 2-tier architecture would need to be expanded to an N-tier architectural model to enhance security, scalability, and performance; and redundancy would need to be implemented to ensure availability and reliability.

- **Performance** – The architecture is designed to offer only basic Internet services (email, web hosting, and Internet news). While the design is optimized for these services, the addition of new and/or unplanned services can cause performance degradation to the infrastructure.

- **Security** – Because cost is the major design constraint for FijiNet, IDS is excluded from the design. For FijiNet to be proactive and responsive to unauthorized access (both internal and external), an IDS would need to be implemented.

  Furthermore, the premise firewall is the single point of attack for intruders. And, it is the single point-of-failure to the architecture. If security is breached at the firewall, all servers in the infrastructure are vulnerable.

- **Availability and Reliability** – Because cost is the major design constraint for FijiNet, the architecture does not contain redundancy unless it is absolutely necessary and the cost is low. The absence of redundancy in some areas may render partial or complete service interruption in the event of hardware failure. The percentage of uptime is greatly dependent upon how long it takes to fix or replace failed hardware. Without redundancy, there is no way to remove single-points-of-failure within the infrastructure.

- **Open Source** – Because cost is the major design consideration for FijiNet, open source applications are favored over commercial products. Even though open source applications are free, they have disadvantages such as lack of features and support, unreliable performance, and unknown scalability. When FijiNet scales to 100,000 subscribers, the open source applications (where applicable) might need to be migrated to commercial products.

- **Broadband** – Architectures supporting broadband are very different from traditional ISP architectures. Bandwidth demand for broadband is very high. To support broadband service, a network infrastructure must be able to handle high traffic loads. Many critical and specialized components are required for signal and protocol conversion. Because FijiNet is uncertain about supporting it, we recommend that this requirement not be included.

- **Operation and Management** – For FijiNet, operation and management of the infrastructure must be automated as much as possible to reduce on-going costs. We recommend this requirement be outsourced to an ASP who specializes in this area.

## CHAPTER 3

Establishing an Architectural Model

This chapter introduces an architectural model as a framework for designing an ISP architecture. The model is based upon our experience and Sun best practices for designing ISP architectures. For architects who want it, the first two sections of this chapter provide background and definitions of concepts and components necessary for understanding an architectural model.

This chapter contains the following topics:

- "Understanding the Model" on page 44
- "Identifying Key Components" on page 45
- "Applying Architectural Principles" on page 51
- "Applying the Model to FijiNet" on page 60

Also, building upon the information in Chapter 2, this chapter shows how to apply the architectural model and principles to design requirements.

Understanding the Model

An ISP architectural model provides a design framework for ISP architectures, which are often complex and comprised of multiple components requiring careful consideration and design. When designing an architecture, it is helpful to use or create a model, then apply all the requirements, assumptions, and design trade offs.

The model presented here is from our point of view, based upon experience in design and resulting best practices. Although there are many other architectural models, principles, and ways of approaching a design, for purposes of demonstration we focus on selected key components and principles. We advise you to determine which attributes and principals are most appropriate for your design, from a larger pool of architectural design standards.

FIGURE 3-1 shows a sample architectural model. In the center of the model are key components. Surrounding these key components in smaller circles are architectural principles.

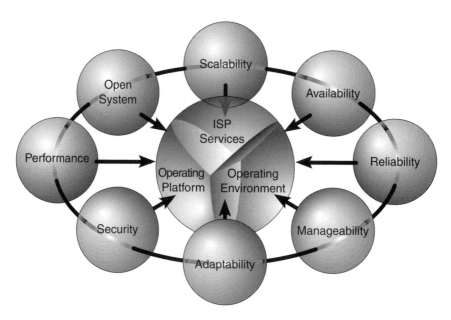

FIGURE 3-1   ISP Architectural Model

As shown in the figure, key components serve as the core for the architectural design. In the outer layer, architectural principles provide structure and considerations for making design decisions, then adhering to a design.

Identifying Key Components

After analyzing business and functional requirements (see Chapter 2), the initial step in modeling an ISP architecture is to identify key components.

In general, key components are uniform among most designs; at the minimum, there should be ISP services running within an operating environment on an operating platform. As shown in FIGURE 3-1, the core of this model consists of ISP services, operating environment, and operating platform.

Tip – The differences in a design are typically in the selection of services, an operating environment, and the operating platform, all of which are based on business requirements and preferences.

ISP Services

ISP services are usually categorized into four types: basic services, value-added services, infrastructure services, and operation and management services. The following paragraphs describe each of these.

Basic Services

Basic services are common services offered by ISPs to residential and business subscribers. As shown in FIGURE 3-2, basic services are email, web hosting, and Internet news. Although not listed, Internet access and FTP (file transfer protocol) are considered basic services; they are required for connectivity and content uploads, respectively.

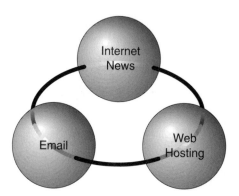

FIGURE 3-2   Basic Services

Internet News	Post news on the Internet
Web Hosting	Host personal web pages
Email	Send and receive email

Value-Added Services

Value-added services are special services offered to provide additional value to existing subscribers, to attract new subscribers, and to differentiate services from those offered by competitors. FIGURE 3-3 shows a sample of value-added services an ISP might offer.

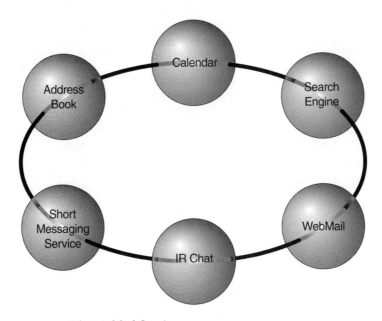

FIGURE 3-3   Value-Added Services

Calendar	Schedule appointments
Search Engine	Online search capabilities
WebMail	Email via web browser
IR Chat	Internet relay chat (IRC)
Short Messaging Service	Send text messages via short messaging service (SMS)
Address Book	Personal address book

What constitutes value-added services varies among ISPs and changes quickly as competitors follow leaders. Samples of value-added services are calendar, search engine, WebMail, IRC, SMS, and address book.

To add value, these services enhance a user's experience and provide tools that users want conveniently at their fingertips. Large ISPs today are aiming to be one-stop portals for everything from web surfing to online shopping.

As new services become more common, many ISPs subsequently convert value-added services to basic services.

Infrastructure Services

Infrastructure services are services that are absolutely critical to support other ISP services running within an infrastructure. These services run in the background and are transparent to users. Infrastructure services are the workhorses of infrastructure functions. FIGURE 3-4 shows the minimum required infrastructure services.

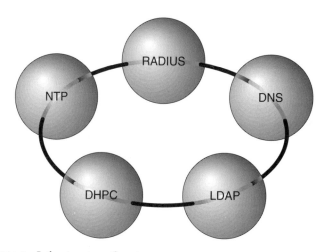

FIGURE 3-4 Infrastructure Services

DNS	Domain name system is for name resolution.
LDAP	Lightweight directory access protocol (LDAP) is for authentication and authorization
RADIUS	Remote access dial-in user service (RADIUS) is for remote access authentication.
NTP	Network time protocol (NTP) is for time synchronization.
DHCP	Dynamic host configuration protocol (DHCP) is for dynamic host configurations for client systems.

Operation and Management Services

Operation and management services are services that allow system administrators to maintain an environment and provide business continuity through uptime. These services are critical to the operation and management of an ISP. Routine tasks such as performing nightly backups, changing tapes, restarting services, installing software patches and upgrades, and monitoring ensure that the environment is working well.

FIGURE 3-5 shows operation and management services. Although these services are technically a form of infrastructure services and play a support role within an infrastructure, one or more of these services might not be an absolute requirement, depending upon an ISP's business requirements.

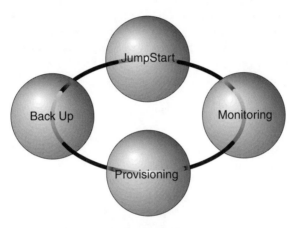

FIGURE 3-5 Operation and Management Services

JumpStart	Automates system installation and management tasks.
Monitoring	Monitors system utilization, intrusions, service availability, etc.
Provisioning	The two categories of provisioning are user and services. User provisioning consists of new user registration, care, and billing. Service provisioning consists of installing new software, patch updates, and software upgrades.
Back Up	Nightly backup for data protection and disaster recovery.

Operating Environment

An operating environment (OE) consists of an operating system (OS) and bundled tools and applications to provide a total solution with seamless integration. Most vendors offer a wide selection of packages for their OS, with different tools and applications.

Note – Most Internet tools are developed in UNIX before they are ported to other platforms, which may be a consideration when choosing an OE.

Most vendors include applications with an OE. These applications can be commercial, open source, or a combination of both. Commercial applications are usually high-end applications for enterprise environments, and licensing for these applications varies among vendors. Open source applications are usually lower-end applications with limited functionality and features, and licensing agreements are commonly provided under general public license (GPL).

Operating Platform

An operating platform is the underlying hardware platform that supports the operating environment. This hardware includes network equipment, enterprise servers, storage, etc.

Applying Architectural Principles

Supporting key components of the sample ISP architectural model are architectural principles, as shown earlier and again in FIGURE 3-6. Architectural principles are major design considerations that help you qualify advantages and disadvantages of each design option, so that you arrive at a solution that *best fits* business requirements, functional requirements, and available technology.

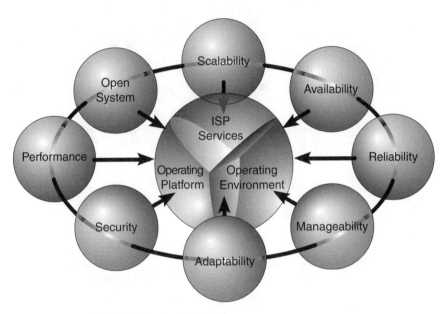

FIGURE 3-6 ISP Architectural Model

We categorize architectural principles into eight areas: scalability, availability, reliability, manageability, adaptability, security, performance, and open system. Although there are other design principles you might need to use or consider, we focus on these as most critical.

Consider each of these principles (and any others that apply) when evaluating design issues and trade-offs for key components. For example, apply scalability to different layers within an architecture. You could address it at the network, system, and application layers. Failing to address scalability at each layer could result in nonoptimal scalability for an architecture.

Ultimately, some architectural principles may not apply to your design. However, it's important initially to consider them as part of the design process, especially for large-scale environments with higher levels of complexity. For example, if cost is a significant design constraint, then adding expensive layers of redundancy to enhance availability is most likely not applicable.

Scalability

Scalability is the ability to add additional resources, for example, routers, switches, servers, memory, disks, and CPUs to an architecture without redesigning it. A good design takes into account the need for scalability so that, within reason, as a business grows and user demand increases, new computing resources can be added on demand. Some customers have a clear idea of their plans for growth and indicate such at the beginning, while others may need you to suggest and build in scalability, based upon your interpretation of their current and future business requirements.

When you address scalability, we recommend using the following scaling models, depending upon which one is applicable to your design. These are simplified models that address scaling for both hardware and software at the same time during the architecture design process.

TABLE 3-1   Scaling Model for Servers

Scaling Model	Vertical	Horizontal
System Type:	Single Large System	Multiple Small Systems
Software Type:	Multithreaded applications	Single-threaded applications
To Scale:	Add CPU, memory, disk, and I/O	Add additional systems

Both models apply to key components. Each major component within an infrastructure, for example, network, system, application, storage, etc., has its own scaling model.

Vertical Scalability

Multithreaded applications are more complex in their scaling model. Typically, the first line of scaling within a single system for a multithreaded application within a single system is to achieve the maximum vertical scalability by adding more resources such as CPU, memory, and I/O. Vertical scaling is appropriate for applications that scale well within a single large server, such as database servers.

Tip – Scale multithreaded applications vertically first. When maximum vertical scaling is achieved, scale the same applications using horizontal scaling techniques, for example, running the applications on multiple boxes behind a load balancer.

Horizontal Scalability

For single-threaded applications, the model for scaling is horizontal. In this model, a vertical scaling limitation of the server is replaced with a much more scalable load distribution paradigm. This technique is deployed at a system level by adding more servers to increase scalability.

Tip – Unlike multithreaded applications, single-threaded applications do not achieve optimal benefits from vertical scaling. For example, adding more memory benefits single-threaded applications; however, adding another CPU does not. Scaling horizontally can be done by running multiple instances on multiple boxes behind a load balancer.

In contrast to availability, which is designed for failover, the purpose of multiple system redundancy in scalability is to provide a model for adding resources to increase capacity.

Availability

Availability has many definitions within Internet architectures. In this book, it means that resources and access to those resources are available upon request. Availability design is predicated on the removal of any single point-of-failure within an architecture to ensure a desired level of uptime. This uptime is usually expressed in percentages and often referred as the "number of 9s." For example, most mission critical systems have a desired uptime of "five 9s," meaning that the system is available 99.999 percent of the time.

TABLE 3-2   Availability Levels

Uptime Percentage	Nines	Allowable Downtime Per Month
99.9999	6	0.043 minute
99.999	5	0.43 minute
99.99	4	4.30 minutes
99.9	3	43 minutes
99	2	7.2 hours

We determined allowable downtime by using the following formula:[1]

$$Availability = \frac{MTBF}{MTBF + MTTR}$$

where MTBF is mean time between failure and MTTR is mean time to repair.

For marketing reasons, many ISPs calculate the level of availability over a 12-month period instead of monthly. (This practice yields an overall higher average level of availability than calculating it monthly, because monthly calculations fluctuate from month to month.)

We calculate the availability monthly because system administrators typically perform maintenance monthly; therefore, monthly calculations are more beneficial for determining allowable downtime to perform maintenance and upgrades. This practice is fairly universal for system administrators of ISPs. Other reasons for calculating it on a monthly basis:

- Revenue, usage, stats, spending, etc. are done monthly.

- Waiting for one year to find out the level of availability is unrealistic.

1. Priscilla Oppenheimer, *Top-Down Network Design*, Cisco Press®, 1999.

A primary attribute of availability design is redundant hardware/software within the architecture, such as network, server, application, and storage.

Tip – Design in such a way that if a component fails, it does not cause the entire architecture to fail. To achieve this design objective, design using a modular approach, allowing components to be replaced at any time without affecting the availability of the system.

The four layers, covered in the following paragraphs, are as follows:

- Network layer
- System layer
- Application layer
- Data layer

Network Layer

At the network layer, availability can be achieved with redundant physical links to the Internet. This redundancy ensures that if there is a link failure, for example, due to hardware failure, access is still available via a surviving link. In addition, redundant network components such as routers, switches, load balancers, and firewalls are necessary to ensure access availability in the event of hardware failure. To enhance reliability at the network layer, remove all single points-of-failure from the network.

Note – For the Solaris Operating Environment (Solaris OE), IP multi-pathing (IPMP) can be used to achieve redundant network connections from the same server to multiple switches.

System Layer

At the system layer, availability is achieved with redundant servers in stand-alone or cluster configurations.

For front-end servers such as those deployed in web farms, you can use load balancers to ensure availability in the event that one or more servers fail to respond to service requests.

In a cluster environment, two or more servers are configured to provide high availability. The number of nodes configured in a cluster is dependent upon the software and hardware. If one server fails, one of the surviving servers takes over and responds to service requests.

A fundamental difference between stand-alone servers and clustered servers is the ability to maintain session states. If a stand-alone server fails while a session is active, the connection has to be reestablished from the client. However, if a clustered server fails, the session state and connection is maintained by a standby server.

Note – The cost of redundant servers and software licensing is extremely expensive for small- to mid-size ISPs. However, without it, ISPs may lose subscribers and revenue to competing ISPs because of subscriber dissatisfaction from service interruptions. Subscriber expectations for availability and reliability are usually high, and many competitors already offer high availability and reliability.

Application Layer

At the application layer, availability can be achieved with clustering and high availability software. You can configure applications with clusters or high availability to enhance availability in the event of service failure. Service failure and restart can be automatically invoked through service failure detection and monitoring. Also, you can enhance availability at the application layer by using a load balancer with multiple servers.

Data Layer

At the data layer, availability can be achieved with redundant storage arrays coupled with logical volumes. Redundant storage arrays allow data to be accessible in the event of a controller or storage array failure. Logical volumes and RAID (redundant array of independent disks) ensure data is accessible in the event of disk failure.

At the data layer, RAID 0+1 (stripping and mirroring) or RAID 5 (stripping with parity) achieves availability and reliability in case of disk failure. RAID 0+1 is a more expensive solution because twice the hardware (storage arrays and disks) is needed. However, the advantage is that no performance degradation occurs due to a disk failure. RAID 5 can have performance degradation if a disk fails, because data has to be rebuilt from parity.

Reliability

Reliability is best defined from the perspective of end users. Users want network services and servers to be available when they access them. Reliability for them is consistency of service uptime and availability. To users, a system is reliable when they do not frequently encounter busy signals on their modems, network connection error messages, etc.

From an architect's perspective, reliability is uptime and service response time for users, so that a system is available when users access services.

For businesses today, especially service providers, reliability of service has implications beyond customer satisfaction. Because service providers establish and maintain their reputations based on availability and reliability of their services, many of them require carrier-class grade high availability and reliability.

Tip – Reliability depends upon and is affected by the design for availability; therefore, your design for an ISP architecture should balance a customer's requirements for both availability and reliability, within any constraints imposed by customer or technology.

Dependent upon availability design, reliability is increased through an infrastructure based on redundant servers. Functionally componentized architecture results in more intrinsic redundancy and fewer inherent single points-of-failure. Furthermore, any damage to an individual service is unlikely to impact other services.

The constructs of redundancy are useful in achieving many aspects of reliability, scalability, and availability.

Manageability

Manageability addresses how an infrastructure can be managed during its life cycle. The key to manageability is to keep an architecture design simple, yet effective. Meet all functional and business requirements without adding complexity. If a design is too complex and difficult to manage, there is more likelihood for operation and management failure, and troubleshooting becomes more difficult and time consuming. Also consider management tools, management plans, and methods of monitoring services. Ensure that devices and components that need to be monitored are managed. If a system goes down and there is nothing monitoring the device or component causing the outage, customer satisfaction and subscriber satisfaction are at risk, in addition to associated costs and potential loss of revenue.

Adaptability

For any architecture, change during a life cycle is inevitable. An architecture must be adaptable enough to accommodate growth and changes in technology, business, and user needs. Within the customer's financial constraints and growth plans, design an architecture that allows for adaptability.

Modular architectures inherently support flexibility in two ways: individual components are themselves easily augmented, and, because components are independent, new components can be added without disturbing or revamping other components within an architecture.

Security

From a larger perspective, security is a combination of processes, products, and people. Security is achieved by establishing effective policies and implementing procedures that enforce policies. Security policies are useless without control over who has access to and can affect security on servers and services. Securing access requires establishing an appropriate authentication regime.

From an architecture perspective, security is access to network, system, and data resources.

- At the network layer, security can be achieved with an access control list (ACL) on routers, packet filters, firewalls, and network-based intrusion detection systems (IDS).
- At the system layer, security can be achieved with system hardening, access permission, host-based IDSs, scanners, and file checkers.
- At the data layer, security can be achieved with authentication and authorization.

Functional decomposition (separating functional components) contributes to security by making it easy to build security around different components. In addition, if one component is compromised, the security breach may be more easily contained.

Adapting to evolving threats is a never-ending cycle of processes. The strategy of responding to security threats has to evolve as potential intruders gain knowledge and discover new attack techniques.

We recommend designing security strategies with great flexibility in approaches to provide the best security against present and future threats.

Performance

Although performance has multiple definitions, in this book we relate it to the "expected" response time after a user requests a service. Depending upon an ISP's requirements, response time may be critical or noncritical, and these distinctions may be further refined by service type.

Individual services use system resources, for example, memory, CPU, and I/O, in different ways. A modular architecture provides the ability to independently monitor and tune each service.

The causes of slow response times are many. For example, some common causes are network latency, server degradation, and application responsiveness. Degradation at any of these layers can result in poor overall performance.

A system is easier to tune when it is running only a few applications. When many applications are running on a system, they must share resources, and tuning becomes complicated and challenging.

Tip – Two products available from Sun are useful in managing resources: Solaris Resource Manager (SRM) and Solaris Bandwidth Manager (SBM). SRM manages resources for users, groups, and enterprise applications. SBM controls bandwidth allocated to applications, users, and organizations.

Open System

Ideally, design using an open system approach so that an architecture is not dependent upon a single hardware or software vendor. An architecture is less flexible when built upon proprietary specifications. Building upon a set of open system standards that are accepted by a recognized consortium provides greater flexibility for business changes and growth, such as adding users and services and integrating new technology.

Applying the Model to FijiNet

In this section, we apply the architectural model to FijiNet. We combine the requirements, assumptions, and evaluation we formulated in Chapter 2 with the model and principles presented in this chapter.

Identify Key Components for FijiNet

After evaluating the business and functional requirements, we identify key components for FijiNet and find that they are in line with general design for ISP architectures. The core components consist of ISP services, an operating environment, and an operating platform.

ISP Services

FijiNet ISP services are basic, infrastructure, and operation and management services. While value-added services are not offered initially, they may be offered in the future.

Basic Services

FijiNet wants to offer basic services to residential subscribers. These services are email, web hosting, and Internet news. FTP is available for content uploads.

Value-Added Services

FijiNet is not offering value-added services initially; however, they might offer them in the near future.

Infrastructure Services

For FijiNet, all infrastructure services presented in the model apply (DNS, LDAP, RADIUS, DHCP, and NTP). These services represent the workhorse of FijiNet's infrastructure.

Operation and Management Services

Operation and management services for FijiNet are outsourced, including provisioning (billing, registration, and customer care).

Note – Operation and management services are beyond the scope of this book. Many resources are available, such as *OSS Essential: Support System Solutions for Service Providers*.

Operating Environment

The operating environment for FijiNet is a reliable operating system comprised of commercial and open source applications. To minimize cost, open source software is used as much as possible. TABLE 3-3 lists components for FijiNet's operating environment.

TABLE 3-3 Operating Environment for FijiNet

Product	Type	Description
Solaris 8 Operating Environment	Commercial	Operating system
Cisco® PIX®	Commercial	Firewall appliance
Solstice Backup*	Commercial	Backup software (bundled with Solaris 8); free usage for up to 200,000 entries
Amdocs Horizon (formerly Solect IAF Horizon)*	Commercial	Billing system for service providers
iPlanet™ Directory Server	Commercial	Directory software (bundled with Solaris 8); no charge for single server licenses
Steel-Belted Radius®	Commercial	RADIUS software for service providers
DNS	Open source	DNS software (free with Solaris 8)
DHCP	Open source	DHCP software (free with Solaris 8)
NTP	Open source	NTP software (free with Solaris 8)
sendmail	Open source	Mail software (free with Solaris 8)
WUftp	Open source	LDAP-compliant FTP software (free/bundled with Solaris 8)

TABLE 3-3   Operating Environment for FijiNet *(Continued)*

Product	Type	Description
WUimap	Open source	POP/IMAP (post office protocol/Internet mail access protocol) Internet mail software (free/ bundled with Solaris 8)
Apache	Open source	Web software (free/bundled with Solaris 8)
INN*	Open source	News software (free/bundled with Solaris 8)
OpenSSH	Open source	Secure SHell software

* These products are applicable if an ISP manages billing and news services internally. If an ISP chooses to out- source these services, then these software products are not needed.

Operating Platform

The operating platform for FijiNet is comprised of high-performance enterprise equipment (network, server, storage, etc.). Hardware was chosen based on FijiNet's requirements and cost constraints. The hardware supports an initial 10,000 subscribers and is scalable to 100,000 subscribers. TABLE 3-4 lists components for FijiNet's operating platform.

TABLE 3-4   Operating Platform for FijiNet

Product	Vendor	Description
Enterprise server	Sun Microsystems	Netra t1
Enterprise server	Sun Microsystems	Ultra 280R
Enterprise storage	Sun Microsystems	StorEdge D1000
Enterprise library	Sun Microsystems	StorEdge L280
Router	Cisco Systems®	Cisco™ 2651
Switch	Cisco Systems	Cisco 3512XL
Firewall	Cisco Systems	Cisco PIX 525
Access server	Cisco Systems	AS5400
Console server	Cisco Systems	AS2511

Note – The quantity for each component is provided with capacity planning in Chapter 6.

Apply Architectural Principles to FijiNet

We apply each of the principles to FijiNet's requirements, our interpretation and assumptions, and our evaluation. For detailed information supporting each of the principles applied, refer to Chapter 2.

Scalability

Due to cost constraints, we specify the smallest possible hardware that can handle the load. The architecture scales horizontally. Because of the smaller chassis size, the system has limited vertical scalability. For scaling from 10,000 to 100,000 subscribers, horizontal scaling is much more economical and flexible.

Availability

No redundancy is implemented, due to cost constraints. To provide a higher level of data availability at an affordable cost, we implement RAID 0+1. FijiNet's business plan and case do not warrant investment in redundancy for high availability at this time.

Reliability

The hardware we specify, enterprise server and storage, are very reliable. Although the hardware reliability is very high, we acknowledge that a single chassis component could fail, because there is no failover.

Manageability

We settle on a 2-tier architecture for FijiNet, to simplify the design. Due to cost, a single-box solution is the best fit. We acknowledge that if FijiNet wants to implement an N-tier architecture later, they need to implement a new architecture. A 2-tier architecture with a single-box solution cannot be retrofitted or scaled to be an N-tier architecture.

Adaptability

The architecture is based on open standards. We use no proprietary technology; therefore, the architecture should be adaptable and integrate with any open systems, standards-based technology. Also, the design is modular and should be adaptable to changes with no reconfiguration or rearchitecting.

Security

An ACL and packet filters provide a basic front-end filter at the router. We use a premises firewall for access control. At the host level, operating system hardening ensures proper file permission. For the Solaris OE, the Solaris Security Toolkit JumpStart™ Architecture and Security Scripts (JASS) is available from Sun Microsystems for OS hardening.

Performance

Based on benchmark results for various infrastructure services such as DNS and firewall, we are confident that FijiNet's server can be load tested with a simulated load. (Refer to Appendix F for benchmark data.) Note that without real user profile and usage pattern data, it's hard to predict actual load.

Open System

The architecture design for FijiNet uses open systems hardware and software based on recognized industry standards.

## CHAPTER 4

Creating a Logical Design

After evaluating an ISP's requirements and applying an architectural model, begin designing the architecture. To achieve all the architectural principles and arrive at an optimal architecture, start with a logical design, then move into the physical design (covered in the next chapter).

This chapter describes elements necessary for creating a logical design. It presents these elements in a high-level structure, showing how to design an architecture from the top-level down.

This chapter contains the following topics:

Note – For consistency in titles and text, we use the term topology for both network and service components. Network topology is hierarchical and service topology is not.

Creating a High-Level Framework

A high-level framework provides a logical structure within which you can define the major (top-level) elements of an architecture. Without a high-level framework, creating an optimal architecture design would be based more on trial-and-error than science and methodology.

Create a logical design by performing the following:

1. "Identify High-Level Topology" on page 66

2. "Identify Services Within the Topology" on page 70

3. "Define Service Flows" on page 86

4. "Define Networking Components" on page 96

Identify High-Level Topology

Start your logical design by identifying a high-level view of the topology. FIGURE 4-1 shows a generic topology for an ISP architecture. Depending upon your customer's requirements, the topology for your architecture may contain additional elements.

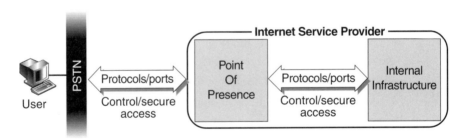

FIGURE 4-1   Generic ISP High-Level Topology

At a minimum, an ISP configuration usually consists of two key elements: point of presence (POP) and internal infrastructure.

As shown in this figure, a user connects to an ISP via a public switched telephone network (PSTN). Access between a user and POP is controlled and secured. Only infrastructure services and associated protocols/ports that are necessary to facilitate connectivities to an ISP are enabled.

The internal infrastructure represents an ISP's internal environment where services are run and physical servers reside. Services running on the internal infrastructure are basic services, infrastructure services, and value-added services (where applicable). After subscribers connect to an ISP, they can access internal services and the Internet.

POP Topology

POP is the access point where subscribers connect to an ISP via a PSTN. The POP ensures proper authentication and authorization for subscribers accessing an ISP's services. FIGURE 4-2 shows a typical POP topology and indicates which services are required for POP.

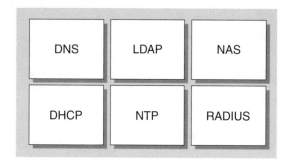

FIGURE 4-2   POP Topology

Services running at the POP are infrastructure services only. At a minimum, the infrastructure services necessary are domain name system (DNS), lightweight directory access protocol (LDAP), network access server (NAS), remote authentication dial-in user service (RADIUS), network time protocol (NTP), and dynamic host configuration protocol (DHCP). All of these infrastructure services are transparent to subscribers, yet absolutely necessary for providing seamless access to an ISP and its services. An ISP must have at least one POP as a point-of-access to the ISP and its services.

For a single-site configuration, a POP resides at the ISP's data center and provides subscribers with access to an ISP when they are within the local coverage area (local POP). Additional POPs usually reside outside of an ISP's data center at remote locations that are geographically dispersed (remote POPs). Adding more POPs enhance an ISP's capacity for supporting a larger number of concurrent subscribers.

POP structure for remote locations is very similar to local POP, with the addition of cache and one or more console servers. Because remote POP resides remotely from an ISP's data center, a cache server is typically necessary to cache frequently accessed data, thereby reducing network traffic between the remote POP and the ISP.

A remote POP requires one or more console servers for remote servers and network devices. A console server needs to be located close by the devices managed. This requirement is based on the fact that console server cabling has short signal attenuation. System administrators at an ISP can access a console server remotely through the network.

When additional POPs are added, they are typically remote POPs to support the subscriber population beyond local subscribers and to maintain low cost and convenient access for remote and nomadic subscribers. Adding remote POPs increases access points to an ISP and capacity for supporting more concurrent subscribers. To be successful and competitive, ISPs offer roaming access in addition to local access.

Internal Infrastructure Network Topology

Within an internal infrastructure, network topology is divided into logical tiers; access through each tier is secured by separate sets of firewalls. Network segmentation simplifies an architecture design, where various modules work together to form a complex design that is highly scalable and easy to manage.

As shown in FIGURE 4-3, network infrastructure is partitioned into seven layers: demilitarized zone (DMZ) network, services network, application network, content network, staging network, backup network, and management network.

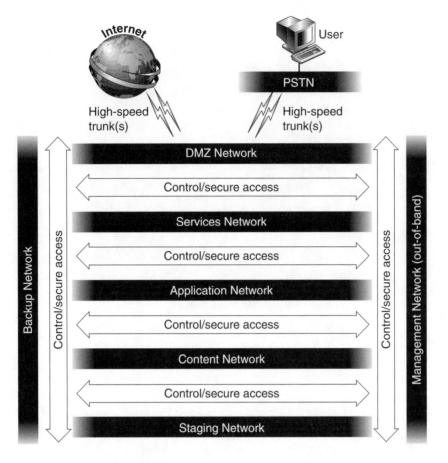

FIGURE 4-3 Logical Network Topology

Each network layer has its own function, and each service is strategically placed on one or more layers, based on its function. Depending on a service's function, a service runs on one or more layers, resulting in an intricate structure that facilitates optimal security and performance.

Also, network segmentation divides broadcast and collision domains. This structure isolates traffic types to enhance network response and reduce network latency. For example, a broadcast storm and resulting performance degradation are contained within a network segment so that other network segments are unaffected.

Divide network infrastructure into multiple layers to:

- Enhance network performance by segmenting collision and broadcast domains
- Enhance security through tier separation with multiple levels of secure firewalls
- Achieve N-tier architecture by functionally decomposing services
- Simplify management and troubleshooting through compartmentalizing tiers

---

Note – The model we present here is a simplified model. For more detail on other modeling approaches, we recommend referring to *Service Delivery Network (SDN): Reference Architecture*, a Sun white paper.

Identify Services Within the Topology

Based on the logical network topology identified in the previous section, identify the services within each layer. (As shown in FIGURE 4-3 on page 69, network infrastructure is partioned into seven layers of networks: DMZ, services, application, content, staging, backup, and management.)

Partition or functionally decompose services into multiple layers, whenever possible, to achieve an N-tier architecture. Isolating each layer allows architectural elements to be modular, and employing this approach enhances security and manageability. Depending on the services, you can partition some into two or more layers. For example, you can functionally decompose mail service into three layers:

- Mail relay at the DMZ network to accept incoming mail from the Internet and relay outgoing mail to the Internet
- Mail proxy at the services network for users to access email service
- Mail server at the content network to contain a MailStore (back-end server for email)

DMZ Network

The DMZ network is the intermediary network between the public Internet and an ISP's internal networks. It separates the "trusted" internal networks from the "untrusted" networks—those that are accessible to the public. FIGURE 4-4 shows a sample DMZ network.

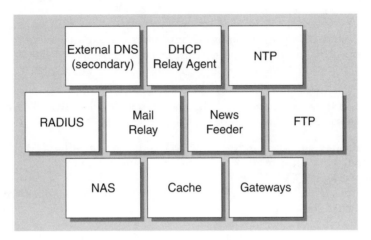

FIGURE 4-4 DMZ Network

Services running at the DMZ network are typically public services that require direct Internet access. For example, all of the services in the preceding figure require direct access because they are communicating with external services from the Internet.

For security reasons, servers from the Internet should not be able to directly connect to an ISP's internal servers.

POP services are often integrated on the DMZ network; acting as intermediaries between the Internet and ISP, they provide open communication channels to the Internet while maintaining secured and controlled access to ISP services.

The following paragraphs describe services that typically run at the DMZ network layer.

External DNS

The external DNS is required for name resolution of external hosts from the Internet. A traditional DNS configuration works well for most ISP environments; however, a better technique is a split DNS. This technique splits DNS into internal and external domains, and it is a fine example of separating tiers by dividing the line between internal and external access.

Separating DNS into internal and external domains has several advantages:

- A split DNS prevents internal host names and IP addresses from being revealed over the Internet. This functional characteristic allows a higher level of security, safeguarding internal hosts from some external attacks, such as denial of services (DoS).
- A split DNS enhances security and preserves public IP addresses where addresses are critically diminishing.

While having a primary external DNS server reside at the DMZ is common, we strongly recommend that you move the primary external DNS server to the content network or at least somewhere on the internal networks, because in those locations it is protected by multiple firewalls. Configure only secondary external DNS servers at the DMZ network.

All zone transfers can be one-way from a primary server to a secondary server. A list of secondary servers can be specified to ensure that only authorized servers are allowed for zone transfers.

Mail Relay

Mail relay is required for relaying incoming and outgoing mail messages between the Internet and an ISP. Its primary purpose is to accept inbound email from the Internet and send outbound email to the Internet.

For inbound mail, the mail relay plays an important role in enhancing security by functioning as an intermediary layer between the Internet and the MailStore.

Hardware required for mail relay servers is lightweight and is replicable horizontally with minimal configuration change and effort. Mail relay servers can be load balanced to provide a higher level of availability.

DHCP Relay Agent

DHCP is required for dynamic network configurations for client systems. At a minimum, configurations are hostname, IP address, netmasks, domain name, DNS server(s), and default gateway. Automatically configuring these parameters is important in maintaining a centralized administration environment.

The best location for a DHCP server is at the services network. You can place a DHCP server at the DMZ network; however, for security reasons, we recommend that you include a DHCP relay agent with this configuration.

DHCP at the DMZ network is typically configured with a DHCP relay agent. This configuration can be done two ways. One way is to have a dedicated server running DHCP relay agent software. The second and preferable way is to enable a DHCP relay agent on the router to forward DHCP messages. With this configuration, a router forwards DHCP messages to connected networks without needing a dedicated DHCP relay/server on every network.

News Feeder

News feeder is necessary to receive incoming feeds from UseNet providers or upstream news servers, as well as to propagate new articles and newsgroups to downstream news servers. For security reasons, the news feeder is typically configured at the DMZ network.

News feeders are responsible for content management and storage. Hardware requirements for news storage are extremely large. We recommend that you check the following web site for the most current storage estimate:

```
http://newsfeed.mesh.ad.jp/flow/size.html
```

Although it changes rapidly, a recent estimate for news storage is that approximately 300 Gbytes of storage is required for daily news from a full feed. Due to the sheer volume, most ISPs either outsource news service to a UseNet provider or filter news feeds and moderate newsgroups to keep content manageable and minimize cost.

RADIUS

RADIUS is required for authentication of remote users connecting to an ISP. RADIUS interfaces with a wide variety of NASs and authenticates remote users against various databases, including relational databases and LDAP. RADIUS is typically configured at the DMZ network, on the same network as NASs.

NTP

NTP is required for time synchronization with external clocks. The external clock can be a hardware clock or NTP server. A dedicated hardware clock is rarely configured for small ISPs. NTP is important in ensuring that time is accurate and synchronized between servers in an infrastructure. This synchronization is critical for firewalls to maintain proper access to an ISP, based on time of the day. Also, it is necessary for the NFS server to maintain proper file access for network file systems.

FTP

FTP (file transfer protocol) is required for uploading web content from a subscriber's system to an ISP. For security reasons, configure the FTP server at the DMZ network only.

NAS

NAS is a highly-concentrated digital modem pool with high-speed connections, such as T1 and channelized T3. Each T1 connection can provide 24 channels (23B+D), where each B channel provides 64 Kbit/sec and each D channel provides 16 Kbit/sec. The D channel is for signal provisioning and cannot be used for connection purposes.

A channelized T3, also known as CT3, is the multiplex of 28 T1s. For small ISPs, one or more T1s are sufficient, depending upon the number of concurrent users to be supported. For large ISPs, a CT3 is more economical because a single CT3 costs less than the equivalent multiplex of T1s. Because an access server provides access to an ISP for remote users, it is commonly configured at the DMZ network. However, NAS for larger sites is usually attached to a separate access network instead of the DMZ.

Cache

A cache server can be used to cache frequently accessed data such as web content, thereby enhancing performance by reducing network traffic.

Locate a cache server close to subscribers for optimal response time. You can omit a cache server for local POP, because data resides locally at the ISP. However, for remote POP, we recommend a cache server. For every remote POP, a cache server is critical to ensure an acceptable level of performance, because data resides remotely.

Gateways

A gateway is the point of interconnect between a data network and other networks that require protocol conversion. Interfacing networks can be voice or wireless networks, as well as legacy systems. For example, a wireless application protocol (WAP) gateway is used between a wireless network and a data network, where wireless markup language (WML) is converted to/from HTML format. (A WAP gateway is usually needed for serving wireless services.) Gateways typically are configured at the DMZ network. All access to an ISP's data network should be done at the point of interconnect to an ISP, that is, the DMZ network.

Services Network

The services network provides front-end access to ISP basic services for subscribers. Front-end servers at the services network are usually small, configured to replicate and scale horizontally with minimal changes. Front-end servers typically do not contain data and reside behind one or more load balancers, ensuring continuous services to subscribers through traffic distribution and redirection in the event of server failure.

You can install each service such as email, web, or news on separate servers; however, for management purposes, we recommend installing all services onto a single server. FIGURE 4-5 shows service components typically configured at the services network.

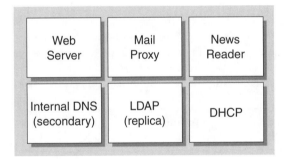

FIGURE 4-5   Services Network

Configuring all services on a single server provides the following advantages:

- Single configuration for all front-end servers
- Ease of replication for horizontal scalability
- Minimum configuration and effort required for replacement

Services running at the services network are basic services and some infrastructure services that are too vulnerable to be run at the DMZ network. The following paragraphs describe each service typically placed on the services network.

Web Server

A collection of web servers, called a web farm, are front-end servers that provide access to users' personal web pages. Web content can be either static or dynamic, depending on an ISP's service offering.

Static web content usually resides either locally on the same server as the web server or on a centralized content server, such as an NFS server. Dynamic web content does not reside locally. Instead, it is generated by an application server; the content can reside on an application server or a content server.

In general, hardware configurations for front-end web servers are lightweight and replicable horizontally with minimal configuration change and effort.

Mail Proxy

At the front-end of the DMZ network, one or more mail proxies interface with users for accessing email. For mail retrieval, post office protocol v3 (POP3) and Internet mail access protocol v4 (IMAP4) are offered to subscribers as methods for accessing email. Simple mail transfer protocol (SMTP) is offered for sending mail.

POP3 is popular among ISPs due to the simplicity of the protocol and the modest demand on the mail server (because most of the work is done on subscribers' systems). IMAP4 is increasingly popular among business users due to rich features and functionality, and it is becoming more common among ISPs. Similar to front-end server configuration, hardware required for mail proxies is lightweight and is replicable horizontally with minimal configuration change and effort.

Note – A mail proxy running an IMAP4 server requires more CPU and memory than POP3.

News Reader

The news reader is the front-end news server where subscribers read and post news articles. The news reader often does not have local content. It interfaces with the news feeder for news articles, history, and index. Although you can install both news reader and feeder on the same server, a more optimal approach is to functionally decompose the news service into two tiers.

News readers are responsible for service requests at the front end. The hardware required for news readers is lightweight and replicable horizontally with minimal configuration change and effort.

Internal DNS

The internal DNS is for name resolution of hosts on internal networks only. The tier separation of external and internal DNS enhances security.

You can configure internal DNS servers almost anywhere on an ISP's internal network. The most common configuration for internal DNS is placing a primary on the content network and one or more secondary servers on the services, application, or content network.

Tip – For security reasons, never place an internal DNS server on an external network such as the DMZ network.

Configure internal secondary DNS servers to be *forwarders*. All systems on internal networks should have resolvers point to internal secondary DNS servers for name resolution. If an external name needs to be resolved, the internal DNS server forwards the query to an external DNS server.

For systems on internal networks that don't require DNS, we recommend that they be configured to use a local hosts table. This configuration reduces the impact on DNS servers and limits security risks by only opening port 53 where required.

For reliability, strategically place multiple secondary servers on various networks to ensure service access. Couple these servers with front-end load balancers to assure availability, because DNS is critical to an ISP. If designed improperly, DNS service can cause a single point-of-failure to an entire architecture.

LDAP Replica

LDAP is a centralized method of authentication and authorization. All accesses are authenticated against LDAP, including, but not limited to, RADIUS, FTP, and email. Also, billing systems use LDAP for user provisioning, registration, and customer care.

LDAP is designed for read-intensive purposes; therefore, for optimal performance, direct all LDAP queries (read/search) to replica directory servers. We recommend using a replica for read-only purposes. Even though a master directory server can answer LDAP requests, its system resources are better used for LDAP writes, updates, and data replication.

Tip – You can have different directory indexes on the master and replicas. Indexing speeds up searches, but slows down updates. Indexes use more memory and disk.

Each replica directory server is capable of supporting millions of entries and thousands of queries per second. The directory service enables key capabilities such as single sign on (SSO) and centralized user/group management.

Most services access LDAP as read-only, such as email, FTP, and RADIUS. Very few services should access LDAP with read-write permission. Services that usually access LDAP with read-write permission are services such as calendar, webmail, billing, and directory replicas.

Similar to internal DNS servers, directory servers can be configured almost anywhere on an ISP internal network. For security reasons, always place the master directory server on the content network.

The most common configuration for directory replicas is to place them on the network where LDAP queries are intensive, such as the services and content networks. If you design multiple replicas, strategically place them on various internal networks to enhance reliability.

Tip – Avoid placing directory replicas on the DMZ network, because it is less secure than the services network or other internal networks, where firewalls provide additional security.

The hardware configuration for a directory replica is usually a multiprocessor system with a large amount of memory. For a directory master, CPU and RAM requirements can be less than directory replicas if the master is dedicated to perform only LDAP writes, updates, and data replication.

Although directory planning and analysis is beyond the scope of this book, we recommend that you approach planning for LDAP by using the following process:

1. Perform business and technical analysis.

2. Plan your directory data.

3. Plan your directory schema.

4. Plan your directory tree.

5. Plan your replication and referral.

6. Plan your security policies.

7. Plan your indexes.

8. Evaluate the plans.

For more information, refer to the following publications:

- *Solaris and LDAP Naming Services: Deploying LDAP in the Enterprise*
- *Understanding and Deploying LDAP Directory Services*
- *Implementing LDAP.*

DHCP

DHCP is required for dynamic network configurations for subscribers' systems. Minimal configurations are hostname, IP address, netmasks, domain name, DNS server, and default gateway.

The dynamic configuration of these parameters is important in maintaining a centralized administration environment.

For an ISP environment, DHCP only serves dial-up users. ISP servers do not require DHCP service, and static configuration is preferred.

For redundancy, it's a good idea to have a backup DHCP server on the internal network.

DHCP relay agents can be placed on various networks so that they relay DHCP messages to a DHCP server on the services network. For an ideal configuration, enabling DHCP relay agents at the router eliminates the need for having dedicated DHCP relay agents or servers on every network.

For security reasons, avoid placing a DHCP server on the DMZ network.

Application Network

For environments where content is dynamically generated when requested, an application server is required. It's common to place application servers on the content network; however, we recommend that you place application servers on their own network. This configuration is essential if an ISP wants to offer application service provider (ASP) services in the near future.

For smaller ISPs, you can omit the application network if web content is static and application servers are not required. This design approach applies to smaller ISPs offering basic services with personal home web page hosting. Another option for smaller ISPs is to combine the application network with the content network.

Content Network

The content network is considered the "pot of gold" by many ISPs because it is where all ISP content resides. This network must be highly secure. Design an architecture so that no servers or services from the Internet directly communicate with services or servers on the content network. Centralize content and data on this network to increase manageability and security. FIGURE 4-6 shows a sample content network.

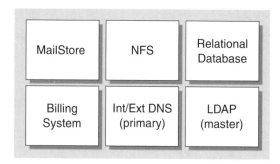

FIGURE 4-6   Content Network

The following paragraphs describe services that typically run on a content network.

MailStore

The MailStore is the back-end server for email. It contains email messages for all ISP subscribers. For medium-sized and large ISPs, we recommend that some form of high availability (HA) or clustering be implemented with MailStore to enhance reliability and availability.

The MailStore interfaces with front-end mail proxies (POP3 and/or IMAP4 servers) for subscriber access to email. Unlike web servers and news servers, large-scale mail servers do not use NFS servers for storage. Large-scale mail servers have their own methods of indexing and storing email messages.

Filesystems configured for MailStore are usually configured with very large numbers of inodes in the inode table. This configuration is due to the inherent characteristic of email, that is, a large number of small files.

NFS

The NFS allows file access across a network. NFS servers are commonly used for web content and news storage.

For ISP environments with static web content, storing content locally on every web server may not be economical or manageable. In these cases, we recommend centralized storage on an NFS server.

For large ISPs, NFS servers are often configured with HA or in clusters for reliability and availability. This design principle holds true for most, if not all, servers residing in a content network.

Relational Database

A database is a collection of related information, and databases come in many varieties. Inverted list, hierarchic, and network database models are older types of database systems. These are typically inflexible and difficult to work with. In today's world of information technology, relational databases dominate information management. Relational databases store and present information in tables and hide the complexity of data access from the user, making application development relatively simple.

For an ISP infrastructure, the relational database usually resides on the content network. This placement provides fast access to information by users and applications within the infrastructure, while maintaining a secure and centralized environment for data storage. A relational database is usually implemented in a large-scale environment where performance, availability, and manageability are critical to the business and dynamic content generation is required. For static content in a small-scale environment, an NFS server is sufficient.

Billing System

The billing system is one of the most critical infrastructure services. It facilitates new subscriber registration, customer care, user provisioning, and bill presentment.

To achieve a seamless integration, tightly integrate the billing system with the directory server. Also, relational databases are commonly needed for billing platforms and must be integrated with billing software. For small environments, the cost of the billing system can be too steep and not cost-effective to maintain in-house. Many small ISPs outsource this function to application service providers (ASPs).

Internal/External DNS

The primary DNS is required for zone transfers and zone updates. Place primary DNS servers for both internal and external domains on the content network. While having a primary external DNS server reside at the DMZ is common, we strongly recommend that you place it on the content network. Place only secondary external DNS servers on the DMZ network. (For the benefits of splitting the DNS in this manner, see "DMZ Network" on page 71.)

All zone transfers are one-way from a primary server to one or more secondary servers. A list of secondary servers can be specified to ensure that only authorized secondary servers receive zone data and dynamic updates.

When configuring DNS servers, use the following guidelines:

- Use primary DNS servers for zone updates and zone transfers only.
- Use secondary DNS servers for name resolution.
- To increase performance, point all systems to one or more secondary DNS servers for name resolution.
- For availability, use front-end load balancers for load distribution.

LDAP Master

The LDAP master directory is the core of authentication, authorization, and accounting for an ISP. Directory service is considered critical for an ISP. If not designed properly, it can be the single point-of-failure. Design the directory so that it is secure and highly available. The master directory server is usually configured with HA or clusters to ensure availability and reliability.

Replicate part or all of the directory information tree (DIT) to authorized replica servers. For optimal performance, point systems to the nearest replicas for LDAP searches and reads. They should not point to the master directory server directly for LDAP queries.

Staging Network

The staging network is for installing, developing, and testing services. Before a product, service, or upgrade is rolled out for production, it should be thoroughly tested for usability, functionality, and performance. The staging network usually consists of two main areas: an area for developing or installing software and an area for testing, as shown in FIGURE 4-7. Although they do not have to be on the same network, we place them on the same network, with different servers for each.

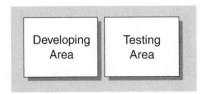

FIGURE 4-7   Staging Network

Developing Area

The area for developing software consists of one or more servers on which system administrators and engineers develop software for an ISP, whether it is for managing infrastructure or offering services.

The area for developing software usually does not require high-performance servers, but it must have adequate resources (CPU, memory, storage, etc.) and tools (compiler, content management, source code repository, version control, etc.). These resources are especially important when multiple administrators and engineers are modifying the same code.

Testing Area

The testing area is for simulating how an application performs under conditions representative of a production environment. Also, the testing area is necessary for use-case testing to verify that an application functions and works as expected in a scripted scenario.

We recommend that you configure the environment as closely as possible to the production environment, everything from hardware to software setup. This configuration ensures that all metrics, such as benchmarks, accurately represent and correlate with the production environment.

Management Network

The management network is a secure environment dedicated for systems, network, and security administration of an ISP. It is usually configured out-of-band, that is, the administration environment is isolated from the subscriber environment through secure access. Such segregation can be achieved through separate network switches residing behind a secure firewall. Restrict access to operations and management personnel only. FIGURE 4-8 shows a sample management network.

FIGURE 4-8   Management Network

The following paragraphs describe services typically configured on the management network.

Console

A console server is required for managing system and network device consoles. Access to consoles must be secure; access should only be from the administration network by authorized system administrators. Locate the console server in close proximity to the servers being managed by the console, because console server cabling has a distance limitation.

Log

The log server is for managing system logs. Direct all system logs from all servers to a centralized log server. Configure the log server with sufficient storage for logs. Automate scripts to rotate and archive old logs for later analysis when required.

Grant access to the log server only from the management network by authorized system administrators. Applications that are incompatible with syslogd(1m) can be logged to local systems, but log files must be transferred via secure copy or other secure mechanisms to a centralized log server for archiving.

Boot/Install

The boot/install server is required for network booting and installation. The install server contains boot images, software images, and install scripts.

Although the boot server is different from the install server, you can configure them on the same system.

When configuring a boot server, use one of the following configurations:

■ For small ISPs with few virtual local area networks (VLANs), configure a multi-homed boot server (a system with more than one network interface). This approach is better than having a boot server on each and every network. A boot server is required for each network because BOOTP packets cannot be forwarded beyond the first hop.

Caution – Small ISPs typically configure a multihomed boot server to keep costs down; however, be advised that it is a significant security risk. Other alternatives are available. For more information, refer to *JumpStart Technology*.

■ For large ISPs with a large number of VLANs, configure routers to relay BOOTP packets. This approach eliminates the need for having a boot server on every network segment.

Management

The management server is required for general-purpose systems and network management of an ISP. One or more management servers may be required, depending on the environment. Examples of management tasks are monitoring services, systems, and networks. Management software such as Tivoli®, PATROL® by BMC Software, Best/1®, and OpenView® may be helpful. Also, resource management software such as Solaris Bandwidth Manager (SBM), Solaris Resource Manager (SRM), and Sun Management Center (SunMC) may be helpful.

Backup Network

A backup network isolates backup traffic from other network traffic so that it doesn't affect response time and create network latency for other services.

For most ISPs, a dedicated backup network is necessary. If an ISP has relatively little data to back up and has sufficient network bandwidth for backup traffic, a dedicated backup network is unnecessary.

Where you place backup servers depends upon the following:

- For small ISPs that do not have a backup network, place a backup server on the management network. Access to the management network needs to be open to allow back-up traffic to traverse in and out of the management network. Be aware that this configuration may have potential security risks.

- For large ISPs, place the backup server on a backup network. Only back-up traffic should be allowed to traverse in and out of the backup network. Other services should not be allowed to access the backup network directly.

A backup network does not have to be out-of-band like the management network; however, access to the backup network should be limited to backup services only, such as communication between backup agents and backup servers.

Separating backup traffic from other ISP traffic alleviates potential network contention, ensuring appropriate response times for ISP services while minimizing network latency.

Define Service Flows

To implement architectural principles and achieve an optimal design, study and identify service flows for each service. Service flow is the interaction (communication) between a client and server. Also, service flow identifies the inbound traffic type and what's allowed and not allowed to flow into an ISP's network.

By fully understanding and identifying service flows, you can design an architecture that is modular and that optimizes integration, security, and availability. Additionally, it's important to understand service flow so that later you can establish firewall rules and security policies that are appropriate for the environment.

To understand communication and dependency between different services, detail the service flow for each service and document it. The following topics provide examples of service flow diagrams and descriptions of flows.

Domain Name Server (DNS)

FIGURE 4-9 shows the service flow for a split-DNS server.

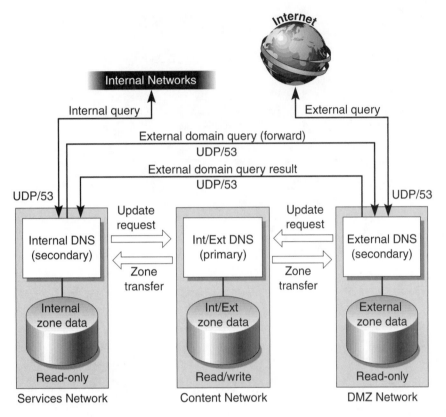

FIGURE 4-9 DNS Service Flow

An external secondary DNS server communicates with DNS servers on the Internet to provide name resolution for external host names. (External hosts should only be allowed to query an external secondary DNS server.)

An internal secondary DNS server serves only internal hosts. It provides name resolution for internal host names. When an internal DNS server needs to resolve an external Internet name, it forwards a query to the external secondary DNS server.

For security reasons, do not allow an external system on the Internet to be able to resolve internal names. Separate the environments of primary and secondary servers. Place secondary servers on networks where services reside. Place a primary server on a secure network such as the content network.

Content updates such as dynamic updates and zone transfers flow one-way. Secondary servers contain read-only data, whereas the primary server can read and write data. Requests for updates flow to the primary server. The primary server communicates zone data updates to secondary servers.

Lightweight Directory Access Protocol (LDAP)

FIGURE 4-10 shows the service flow for the LDAP server.

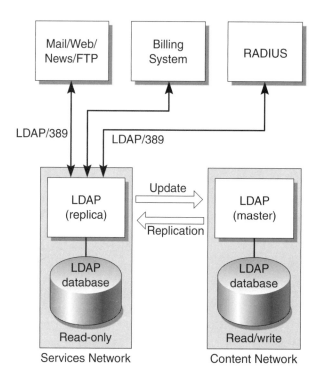

FIGURE 4-10 LDAP Service Flow

Applications such as email, web, news, FTP, RADIUS, and billing are designed to communicate with LDAP, which provides centralized authentication, authorization, and accounting (AAA).

All LDAP queries should be directed to replica servers, because LDAP servers are optimized for read-intensive applications. Replica directory servers are multi-threaded and capable of processing thousands of queries per hour. (Actual performance depends on specific software and hardware being benchmarked.)

Replicas can answer queries and accept requests for updates; any modifications to LDAP entries flow to the master directory server. If an update request flows to a replica, the replica forwards the request to the master.

Although you could have a master directory server answer queries, it's better for performance reasons to have the master only handle writes, updates, and data replications.

When the master updates the database, updates flow to replica servers based on how a system administrator set up the event. For example, updates may be sent to replicas on demand, on a regular schedule, or whenever an update is completed.

Dynamic Host Configuration Protocol (DHCP)

FIGURE 4-11 shows the service flow for a DHCP server.

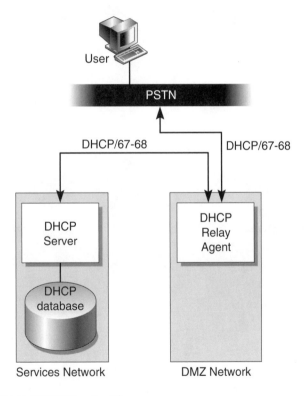

FIGURE 4-11 DHCP Service Flow

All DHCP requests flow into the DHCP relay agent. The DHCP relay agent relays messages to the DHCP server. Requests are typically for IP address leases and some common network configurations. A subscriber's system communicates with the DHCP relay agent server to request an IP address, and the DHCP server responds by assigning an address, usually assigned for one day (24 hours), depending upon the environment.

The DHCP relay agent server is usually configured on the DMZ network or the same network where the access server resides. The best location for a DHCP server is at the services network.

Remote Authentication Dial-In User Service (RADIUS)

FIGURE 4-12 shows the service flow for RADIUS.

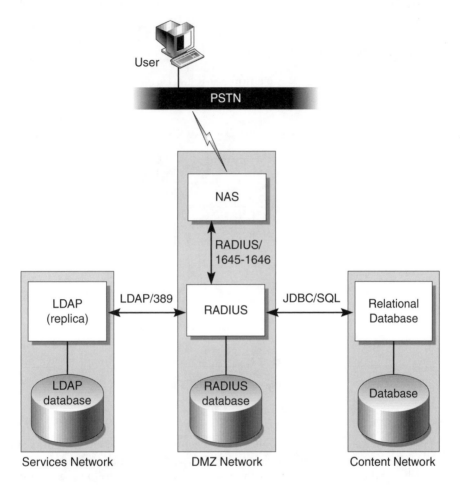

FIGURE 4-12 RADIUS Service Flow

When a subscriber dials in, the RADIUS server authenticates the user. The RADIUS server can have a local RADIUS database, a relational database, or LDAP for authenticating users. It can use any of these three. If you want a centralized AAA service, direct the RADIUS server to use LDAP. We recommend that you use the LDAP server for authentication because it is designed for read-intensive performance.

The access server's configuration tells it which RADIUS server to communicate with for authenticating users.

The RADIUS server communicates with only two services: it receives requests from the NAS, and it communicates with the directory server to authenticate users.

Network Time Protocol (NTP)

FIGURE 4-13 shows the service flow for the NTP.

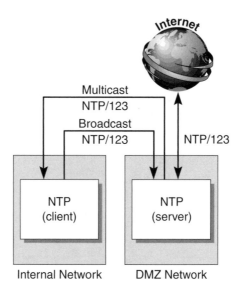

FIGURE 4-13 NTP Service Flow

All systems can be configured as NTP clients. An NTP client communicates with the NTP server periodically to determine if the clock is synchronized. When necessary, it adjusts the clock. The correct time is important for the following reasons:

- When users access an ISP, the firewall must have the correct time to allow or deny access based on the current time, if required.
- Servers such as the NFS server must have the correct time to maintain file handles for mounted file systems.
- An accurate time stamp must be maintained for all access recorded in log files.

Synchronization between NTP clients and an NTP server can be done by either broadcast or multicast. In general, multicast is preferred because it has a lower overhead than broadcast.

Refer to the following web site for a list of public NTP servers:

```
http://www.eecis.udel.edu/~mills/ntp/servers.html
```

Email Service

FIGURE 4-14 shows the service flow for email.

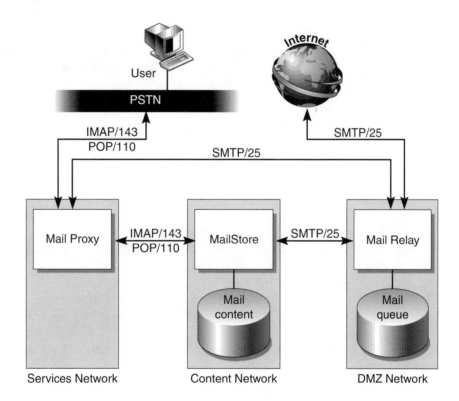

FIGURE 4-14 Email Service Flow

Users connect to a mail proxy server to send and retrieve email, using POP or IMAP.

The mail proxy talks to a mail relay to send mail.

The mail proxy talks to the MailStore to retrieve email for users.

For incoming email, the mail relay server relays mail to the MailStore. For outgoing mail, the mail proxy server relays email to the mail relay. For retrieving email, the mail proxy retrieves email from the MailStore for users. Users only communicate with the mail proxy for accessing email services.

Web Service

FIGURE 4-15 shows the service flow for web hosting.

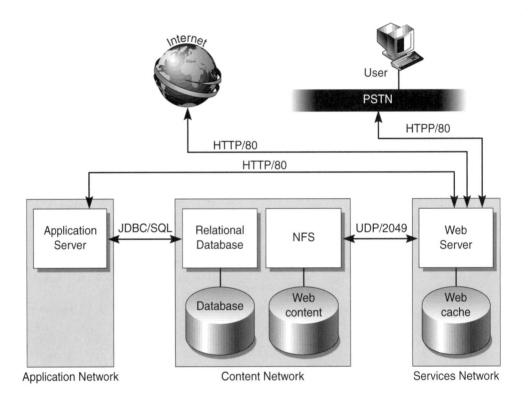

FIGURE 4-15 Web Hosting Service Flow

To access web pages, subscribers connect to a web server via browsers. For frequently accessed data, the web server retrieves data directly from cache. Static content can be local or NFS mounted. Dynamic content is usually generated by an application server from content residing in a relational database at the back end.

For small environments with static content, NFS mounting is common. Be aware that NFS mounting can create heavy overhead for network traffic. For large environments, content is usually dynamic and, therefore, a relational database is commonly used instead of NFS mounting.

News Service

FIGURE 4-16 shows the service flow for news service.

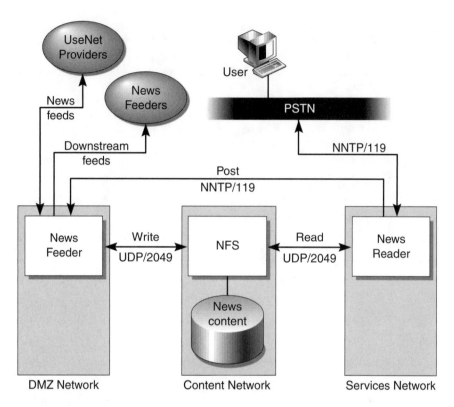

FIGURE 4-16 News Service Flow

To read or post news, subscribers connect to a news reader via browsers. The news reader communicates with the news feeder to retrieve the content. Also, the news feeder communicates with a UseNet provider for news feeds. Content can reside locally on the news feeder server or on an NFS mounted file system. Multiple news feeders can be load balanced for availability.

From a business perspective, it is usually not economical to run news service in-house. The resources (server and storage) required are expensive. We recommend that news service be outsourced to a UseNet provider.

If an ISP provides news service in-house, we recommend that the ISP moderate and filter newsgroups as much as possible. To maintain quality and performance, we recommend that the ISP remove stale news groups, restrict offensive materials (depending upon local and federal laws), and filter out duplicate news postings and expired articles.

Define Networking Components

After identifying services with the topology, define the networking components (routers, switches, load balancers, etc.) that best fit the services and overall logical design.

In the beginning of this chapter, we described an ISP network design methodology for developing an overall network topology using an N-tiered hierarchical model. In this model, the overall network structure is divided into multiple layers.

Each layer of the model has a function that is independent in purpose from other layers in the hierarchical model. However, each layer must be designed to be fully compatible and complementary to other layers. By using the hierarchical design method and keeping each layer separate, you can produce a highly flexible and scalable network. The same applies to your architectural design for networking components.

Each networking component layer provides the necessary functionality to the network. The layers do not need to be implemented as distinct physical entities. Each layer can be implemented with a combination of layer 2 (L2) switching and layer 3 (L3) routing devices. Although a layer can be omitted altogether, maintain the hierarchy to achieve optimum performance. The hierarchal network model has three layers, as shown in FIGURE 4-17.[1]

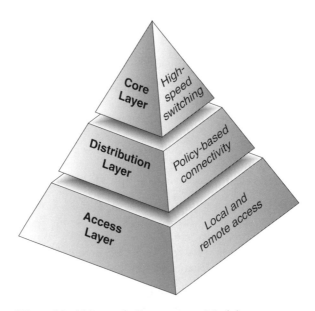

FIGURE 4-17 Hierarchical Network Components Model

1. Adapted from *Designing Cisco Networks*, Diane Teare, Cisco Press, 1999.

The *core layer* provides optimal communication between sites. The core layer is the high-speed switching backbone of the network, and this layer has the following characteristics:

- Reliability
- Redundancy
- Quick convergence
- Fault tolerance
- Low latency

The core layer primarily provides wide-area links between geographically remote sites, connecting data centers or network operation centers (NOCs).

Core links are usually point-to-point. Core services, for example, Optical Carrier-level 3 (OC-3), frame relay, asynchronous transfer mode (ATM), and so forth, are typically leased from network service providers (NSPs).

Systems rarely reside in the core layer, and we recommend not placing them there. The mission of core layer design is to focus on redundancy and reliability while bearing in mind the cost of downtime. The core layer's primary function is to provide optimal transport between remote sites. This layer is usually implemented as a high-speed wide area network (WAN), normally ATM, OC-3, or frame relay. The wide-area characteristic of the link may indicate a need for redundant paths, so that the network can withstand individual circuit outages; without redundant paths, links can create single points-of-failure. Rapid convergence of routing protocols are generally considered important core design features.

The *distribution layer* of the network is the demarcation point between the core and access layers. The distribution layer has many roles:

- Policy
- Security
- Media translation
- Routing between VLANs
- Broadcast and collision domain segmentation
- Demarcation between static and dynamic routing protocols

The distribution layer represents the distribution of network services to multiple VLANs within a network environment. This layer is where the backbone network is located and is typically based on fiber distributed data interface (FDDI), FastEthernet, or Gigabit Ethernet. The distribution layer is often where network policy is implemented.

Network evolution is occurring rapidly, and as newer and faster technologies emerge, existing technologies move downward in the hierarchical model. The distribution layer includes a network backbone with all its connecting routers. Typically, distribution layer devices serve a region by acting as a concentration point for many of its access tier sites. The big benefit of the hierarchal model is fast problem isolation due to network modularity.

The *access layer* usually consists of one or more VLANs that provide access to network services. The access layer is where almost all systems are attached to the network, usually via Ethernet, Token Ring, or FDDI. In ISP environments, including many corporate networks, the access layer is commonly where servers such as web server, email, proxy, and firewalls are located.

The principal functions of the access layer are to connect various local area networks (LANs) to the distribution layer, provide logical network segmentation, and isolate broadcast traffic between segments. The access layer is characterized by switched and shared bandwidth environment.

Routers and Switches

The decision to use L2 switching or L3 routing functionality in a network design depends on which problems you are trying to solve. These problems can be categorized as media or protocol.

Media problems occur when too many devices contend for access to a LAN segment, causing an excessive number of collisions and slow response time. Protocol problems are caused by protocols that do not scale well; they typically occur when a protocol that was designed for small networks is being used for larger networks. The general guidelines are as follows:

- If problems involve media contention, use switching.
- If problems are protocol related, use routing.

Broadcasts are used by many protocols as part of their normal operations. However, network performance can suffer from too many broadcasts. L2 switches forward broadcasts and multicasts. This approach becomes a scalability issue as flat networks become larger. If there are too many hosts on a LAN, broadcasts can cause performance degradation to the network. When broadcasts are more than approximately 20 percent of the traffic in the LAN, network performance degrades.

Tip – In a single flat network, a good rule-of-thumb is to avoid having more than 100 IP-based systems, due to broadcast radiation and performance degradation. The scalability of a switched network depends on a number of factors, the most important being the type of protocols used.

Routers

Routers, also known as L3 devices, are necessary for interworking communication. Routers offer the following services:

- Broadcast domain segmentation
- Hierarchal addressing
- Inter-VLAN communication
- Fast convergence
- Quality of service (QoS)

In the past, much emphasis was put on the packets-per-second (pps) forwarding rate of routers. Today, less emphasis is placed on pps because routers can process packets so quickly, especially with new switching technology provided by multilayer switches.

Like switches, routers use tables of addresses to forward packets to their proper destination. Unlike L2 switches, routers maintain tables of L3 logical addresses. Thus, router configuration is protocol-specific. Routers use specialized protocols to share information about routes and destinations among each other. With routers, broadcast packets are typically not forwarded.

Switches

Switches, also known as L2 devices, operate at the data link layer. (Refer to the OSI model for more information.) An excellent source for information is *TCP/IP Illustrated, Volume 1 - The Protocols*. However, in the last couple of years, LANs were revolutionized by the exploding use of switching at L2. LAN switches provide performance enhancements for new and existing data networking applications by increasing bandwidth and throughput.

The primary function of switches is to filter or forward frames. Switches work by examining frames seen on the network and by building a table that pairs the source hardware address of the frame with the switch port on which it was seen. By keeping local traffic local, switches can dramatically cut traffic on individual segments and improve overall network performance. Note that Ethernet collision packets are always filtered, but broadcast packets are always forwarded to all ports.

Ethernet is the most widely deployed LAN technology, and its use continues to grow because of its simplicity and low cost. Ethernet's main disadvantage is that it is based on Carrier Sense Multiple Access/Collision Detection (CSMA/CD), which is a bus arbitration scheme with the side effect of rapid degradation of available bandwidth in heavy traffic conditions.

A bus arbitration scheme defines the mechanism by which a system transmits data across the bus. However, this limitation can be overcome through switching. CSMA/CD is associated with the creation of a collision domain, a concept unique to the Ethernet environment.

Although collisions are normal events in Ethernet, an excessive number of collisions further reduces available bandwidth. In reality, the actual available bandwidth of Ethernet due to collisions is reduced to a fraction (about 40 percent) of the theoretical bandwidth (10 Mbit/sec, 100 Mbit/sec, or 1000 Mbit/sec). This reduction in bandwidth can be remedied by segmenting the network using switches or routers.

Segmentation is the process of splitting a single collision domain into two or more collision domains. L2 switching can be used to segment the logical bus topology and create separate collision domains. Therefore, more bandwidth is made available to individual systems. With switching technology, attached systems receive dedicated bandwidth rather than shared bandwidth, because each system is in its own collision domain. Ethernet switches are devices that microsegment a collision domain, eliminating the impact of packet collisions.

Multilayer Switches

Traditionally, L2 switching was provided by LAN switches, and L3 networking was provided by routers. Increasingly, these two networking functions are being integrated into one common platform with multilayer switches.

Mirroring the integration of L3 networking technology into LAN switching devices, most likely WAN switching equipment, will increasingly incorporate L3 networking capabilities. As traditional L3 routers gain support for higher capacity and bandwidth, the integration of L2 technologies enables routers to achieve optimum performance levels.

New features and technology are being added to switches, for example, switches can now perform load balancing. Switching sometimes results in nonoptimal routing of packets because packets only travel on paths that are included in the Spanning Tree Protocol (STP RFC 1493), which is running to prevent broadcast storms in a switched network.

When routers are used, the routing of packets can be controlled and designed for optimal paths. Routing and redundancy in switches can be done by allowing one instance of the STP per VLAN. Using STP ensures that the network doesn't have any loop. However, the drawback of using STP is that the convergence time can take much longer. A good network design eliminates loop where possible so that STP doesn't need to be used. In general, incorporate switches in network design to provide high bandwidth.

Load Balancers

Load balancers are network appliances with secure, real-time, embedded operating systems that intelligently load balance IP traffic across multiple servers. Load balancers optimize the performance of your site by distributing client requests across a cluster of multiple servers, dramatically reducing the cost of providing large-scale Internet services and accelerating user access to those applications.

Load-balancing solutions, in general, are successful because they provide three fundamental benefits in server-farm environments:

1. The ability to manage, scale, and reduce the variability of traffic loads.

2. A low-cost, easy-to-implement, high-availability strategy for managing server traffic.

3. An ability to intelligently manage connections between clients and servers.

Ideal for mission-critical applications, load balancers allow you to build a highly redundant and available server farm. Servers are automatically and transparently placed in and out of service, providing availability. Each load balancer itself is equipped with an optional hot-standby failover mechanism, which builds increased redundancy for the server farm system.

In today's high-speed computing environment, such as large ISP infrastructures, load balancing with solutions such as Cisco LocalDirector, Resonate Dispatch Manager®, Resonate Dispatch Monitor®, and F5's 3-DNS® Controller are no longer sufficient, because they represent a single point-of-failure within a large-scale infrastructure. This limitation is due to the inability of load balancers to support high bandwidth and fast switching. Load balancing is now done with multilayer switches with load balancing capabilities.

Firewalls

A firewall is defined as a single point between two or more networks through which all traffic must pass and where traffic can be controlled, secured, and logged. The earliest firewalls were routers where they segmented LANs and filtered traffic based on rules defined in access control lists (ACLs). As more businesses connected to the Internet, awareness of Internet security issues grew. The need for better security caused some vendors to develop their own solutions. Subsequently, some of these solutions were made into commercial products.

Firewalls can be network-based, host-based, or hybrid. Usually they are implemented to secure access to networks and systems that are connected to networks. While most firewalls today have many attractive features and qualities, keep in mind the fundamental tenet of security, that is, security and complexity are often directly proportional.

While some security experts debate that a firewall is just another packet filter with a pretty front-end GUI and it does not provide any substantial benefits other than packet-filtering routers, we strongly believe that security is a combination of people, technology, and processes. Admittedly, no single product or technology can provide the best optimal solution for every environment.

Nothing is absolute and there is always an uncertainty. There is uncertainty in every aspect of security. No security system is 100 percent secure. Someone, somewhere, will find a way to exploit vulnerabilities. We recommend the following guidelines:

- In addition to router ACLs and packet filters, use firewalls to control access to networks and systems.

- Use firewalls to segment and control access to network layers.

- Diversify different firewall products throughout an infrastructure. If any security exploits occur on a single firewall product, security isn't compromised on the entire infrastructure.

- Because firewalls can be a single point-of-failure within an infrastructure if not designed properly, implement high availability at firewalls.

- For large-scale environments where heavy throughput is required, implement firewall load balancing with multilayer switches.

Intrusion Detection Systems (IDSs)

Intrusion detection systems (IDSs) can be either network-based, host-based, or hybrid. Network-based IDSs are most commonly used to examine passing network traffic for signs of intrusion. Host-based IDSs examine user and system activity on local machines for signs of intrusion. Hybrid IDSs combine both hardware and software for an end-to-end solution. Each type of IDS has strengths and weaknesses. In the following sections, we provide strengths and weaknesses of network-based and host-based IDSs.

For small ISPs serving residential users, an IDS might not have any value or return on investment. Because there are no service level agreements (SLAs) for residential users, the data are not considered sensitive or classified, and capital investment on IDS might be too expensive.

For ISPs operating on a national level, supporting both residential and business users, the demand for service availability, reliability, and security are critical to business. To proactively respond to security incidents, large ISPs should implement an IDS.

> **Tip –** Creating a network diagram is an invaluable tool for planning intrusion detection. When reviewing the diagram, evaluate key network choke points (routers, switches, load balancers, and firewalls) or collections of systems that are sensitive to business operations. A detailed network diagram may provide intrinsic clues as to the right location for sensors, and it may be useful later for troubleshooting during the implementation phase.

If an IDS is going to monitor front-end web servers for penetrations, then the most useful position for the sensor is on the services network, where web servers reside. If web servers are compromised, the best chance of detecting an intrusion is the target network or system.

If you want the IDS to monitor internal servers such as application servers, then the best place for the sensor is inside the firewall on the application network. The logic behind this approach is that the firewall prevents the vast majority of attacks aimed at internal servers, and that regular monitoring of firewall logs identifies attacks. The IDSs on internal networks detect some attacks that manage to get through the firewall. Some organizations like to use IDSs to monitor internal resources that contain sensitive information. In this case, the most logical place for the sensor is on the choke point between those systems and internal networks.

Note that part of the security community advocates placing sensors *outside* the firewall to monitor intrusions from the Internet. The firewall itself should log any attacks it stops, assuming that one enables logging and monitors the logs. What value does an IDS provide in this scenario? Intrusions stop at the firewall; therefore, an IDS outside the firewall is redundant. It probably isn't a productive use of resources and time to install and monitor intrusions outside a firewall.

Network-Based IDSs

A network-based IDS examines passing network traffic for signs of intrusion. If you determine that a network-based IDS is the solution for your ISP customer, decide in advance where to place the sensor(s). The placement depends significantly on what kind of intrusion the ISP wants the system to detect.

A network-based IDS usually has two logical components: sensor and management station.

The sensor resides on a target network and monitors it for suspicious traffic. The sensors are usually dedicated systems that exist only to monitor the network. They have network interface in *promiscuous* mode, which means they receive all network traffic, not just that destined for their IP address, and they capture passing network traffic for analysis. If they detect something that looks unusual, they pass it back to the management station.

The management station resides on the management network (out-of-band), and receives alarms from sensors for analysis and response. The management station displays the alarms or performs additional analysis. Some displays are simply an interface to a network management tool, but some are custom graphical user interfaces (GUIs) designed to help system administrators analyze problems.

Strengths of network-based IDSs:

- Does not require modification of target systems. This advantage is helpful because installing additional software may exceed system capacities and degrade performance.

- Is not on a critical path for any service. IDS failure does not have a significant impact on the infrastructure.

- Tends to be more self-contained than host-based IDS. Network-based IDS runs on a dedicated system that is simple to install and configure.

Weaknesses of network-based IDSs:

- Only examines network traffic on the target network to which it is directly connected. This problem is particularly endemic in a switched Ethernet environment.

- Many sensors may be required to meet coverage on all critical network segments. Because each sensor costs money, broad coverage can become prohibitively expensive.

- Tends to use signature analysis to meet performance requirements, which means that it detects common attacks, but is inadequate for detecting more complex information threats.

- May need to communicate large volumes of data back to the management station. In many cases, monitored traffic generates a larger amount of analysis traffic.

  Many systems use aggressive data-reduction processes to reduce the amount of communicated traffic. They also push much of the decision-making process out into the sensor itself and use the management station as a status display or communications center, rather than for actual analysis. The disadvantage of this approach is that it provides very little coordination among sensors, that is, any given sensor is unaware that another has detected an attack. Such a system cannot normally detect synergistic or complex attacks.

- Is often limited on processing power (CPU) and memory. Processing engines for network-based IDSs are often not powerful enough to analyze traffic. Network-based IDSs are notorious for dropping packets if they do not have enough buffer and processing power to analyze the large amount of traffic.

- Might have a difficult time handling attacks within encrypted sessions.

Host-Based IDSs

A host-based IDS examines activity on the local server. These frequently use the system's audit and logging mechanisms as a source of information for analysis. IDS looks for unusual activity that is confined to the local host such as failed login, unauthorized file access, or system privilege alterations. The host-based IDS generally uses rule-based engines for analyzing activity.

A host-based IDS usually provides much more detailed and relevant information than a network-based IDS.

If you determine that a host-based IDS is the solution for your ISP customer, install it on a test/development system well in advance of planned installation on a production system. Even on a quiescent system, some files change regularly, so the IDS reports some changes. Some host-based systems report when a user process alters the system password file. This report would happen if an intruder added an account; however, it would also happen when an authorized user changed his or her password. System administrators need time to become familiar with the operation of IDS so that alarms can be properly diagnosed, before a production system is implemented.

Keep in mind that when using a host-based IDS, it should be monitored frequently. If the target system is compromised, an intruder can alter system logs and suppress alarms. Logging should not be logged locally to the target system. All logging should be directed to one or more dedicated log servers residing on the management network.

Strengths of host-based IDSs:

- Can be an extremely powerful tool for analyzing possible attacks. It can indicate exactly what an intruder did, which commands the intruder ran, what files were opened and/or modified, and what system calls were executed, rather than just rather vague guesses.

- Tends to have lower *false positive* rates than a network-based IDS. The range of commands executed on a specific target system are much more focused than the types of traffic flowing across a network. This property can reduce the complexity of host-based analysis engines.

- Can be used in environments where broad intrusion detection is not needed, or where the bandwidth is too high for sensors to handle the large volume of data to be analyzed.

- May be less risky to configure with an active response, such as terminating a service or logging off an unauthorized user. A host-based IDS is more difficult to spoof into restricting access from legitimate users and sources.

Weaknesses of host-based IDSs:

- Requires installation on the particular target system being protected. This approach can pose serious capacity and performance problems on the target system. In some cases, it can even pose security problems because the security personnel may not ordinarily have access to the target server.

- Another problem associated with host-based IDSs is that they tend to rely on the innate logging and monitoring capabilities of the target system. If the target system isn't configured to do adequate logging and monitoring, system administrators have to change the configuration, which can result in a higher level of complexity for change management.

- It is relatively expensive. Many ISPs do not have the financial resources to protect the entire network infrastructure using host-based IDS. These ISPs must very carefully choose which specific set of target systems to protect. These choices can leave wide gaps in coverage.

- Suffers to an even greater degree from isolation than a network-based IDS. It can be almost totally ignorant of the network environment. Thus, the analysis time required to evaluate damage from a potential intrusion increases linearly with the number of target systems covered.

Creating a High-Level Framework for FijiNet

In this section, we create a high-level framework for our ISP customer FijiNet. Combining requirements, assumptions, and evaluations formulated in Chapter 2 with the architectural model and principles developed in Chapter 3, we apply preferred practices for creating a logical design.

For descriptions of services and other elements of a high-level framework, refer to the previous section "Creating a High-Level Framework" on page 66.

The following information focuses on decisions we made to create a logical design for FijiNet, a small ISP entering the market. Where applicable, we explain the reasons for decisions and describe trade-offs.

We create a logical design for FijiNet by performing the following:

- "Identify High-Level Topology for FijiNet" on page 107
- "Identify Services Within the FijiNet Topology" on page 110
- "Define Service Flows for FijiNet" on page 113
- "Define Networking Components for FijiNet" on page 121

Identify High-Level Topology for FijiNet

Based upon FijiNet's requirements, we identified the high-level topology shown in FIGURE 4-18.

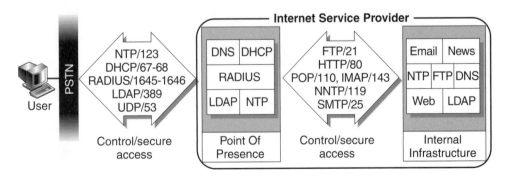

FIGURE 4-18 FijiNet Topology

POP is the access point where subscribers connect to FijiNet. Access to the POP is through a NAS with high-density terminations and digital modems.

Infrastructure services running at the POP to facilitate connectivity for subscribers are DNS, DHCP, LDAP, RADIUS, and NTP.

Basic services are email, web hosting, Internet news, and FTP. FijiNet is not offering any value-added services for the initial deployment.

For email service, both POPv3 and IMAP4 provide access, and SMTP provides mail delivery. Static web hosting is provided by Apache web server (part of Solaris 8 Operating Environment). Internet news is outsourced to a UseNet provider.

FijiNet POP Topology

The POP topology for most ISPs is consistent and does not vary greatly. As shown in FIGURE 4-19, FijiNet's POP topology is identical to the generic POP.

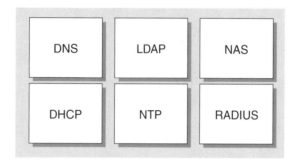

FIGURE 4-19 FijiNet POP Topology

Because FijiNet is a single-site configuration, content resides locally at the data center; therefore, a cache server is unnecessary.

FijiNet Internal Infrastructure Network Topology

In contrast to the generic logical network topology shown in FIGURE 4-3 on page 69, we partioned FijiNet's network infrastructure into three layers: internal network, external network, and management network, as shown in FIGURE 4-20. We chose this approach because of FijiNet's size, limited requirements, and cost constraints.

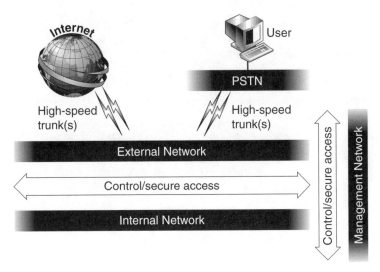

FIGURE 4-20 FijiNet Logical Network Topology

FijiNet's network topology is a 3-tier architecture model:

  The external network is for external services, and it closely matches the DMZ network.

  The internal network is for internal services, and it consolidates the services, application, and content networks.

  The management network for FijiNet is in-band (due to cost restrictions), compared to our generic model earlier, which is out-of-band. The management network for FijiNet is for systems, network, and security management.

FijiNet can add other tiers in the future to achieve an N-tier model, as their subscriber population increases or when their architecture requires modification to support new services.

Ideally, we would like to configure the internal and external networks on the same switch and the management network on a separate switch, so that it is out-of-band. However, due to FijiNet's cost constraints, we use a single-switch configuration. Consequently, we configure the management network in-band.

We use two T1s for Internet connectivity, and two CT3s for dial-up access. In the next chapter, we show how to calculate, for capacity planning, the number of modems and high-speed trunks needed for this configuration.

Identify Services Within the FijiNet Topology

Based on our 3-tier architectural model for FijiNet, we identify services within each network layer: internal, external, and management.

To meet FijiNet's requirements, we made the following changes from our generic model, presented earlier in this chapter:

- Email, web, and news services normally configured at the services network are on the internal network.
- The FTP server normally configured on the DMZ network is on the internal network.
- The NTP, external secondary DNS, RADIUS, mail relay, and NAS are on the external network.
- Network, security, systems management, log, backup, and console servers are on the management network.

FijiNet External Network

FIGURE 4-21 shows the services we place on FijiNet's external network.

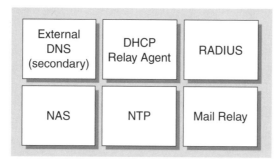

FIGURE 4-21 FijiNet External Network

The external network is for external services, such as infrastructure services that are required for POP. External name resolution and time synchronization require direct Internet access.

For security reasons, we place the DHCP server on the internal network. A DHCP relay agent relays DHCP messages to the DHCP server.

Our goal is to place as many services on the internal network as possible, unless they are absolutely required to reside on the external network.

FijiNet Internal Network

FIGURE 4-22 shows the services we place on FijiNet's internal network.

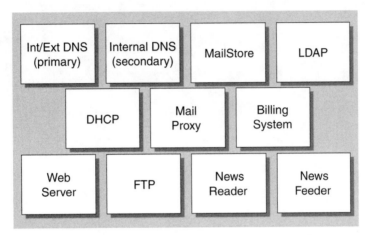

FIGURE 4-22 FijiNet Internal Network

Because we are using a modular approach with a single-server configuration, we place all basic services on a single server, which resides on the internal network.

We acknowledge that there are many design trade-offs in a single-server approach at each layer. Also, there are risks. All risks must be identified and mitigated. In the next chapter, we address the risks and how to mitigate them.

FijiNet Management Network

Services typically running on the management network are console server, log server, boot/install server, and management (system, network, security) server.

Because of cost constraints and initial subscriber population size, we place the backup server on the management network rather than having a separate network for it.

FIGURE 4-23 shows the services we place on FijiNet's management network.

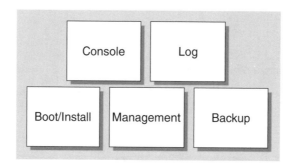

FIGURE 4-23 FijiNet Management Network

Define Service Flows for FijiNet

In Chapter 3, we applied architectural principles and a model to FijiNet's requirements. Here, we apply the principles and model to FijiNet's service flows to achieve an optimal design.

FijiNet DNS

As FIGURE 4-24 shows, we use a split-DNS configuration (internal and external) for FijiNet.

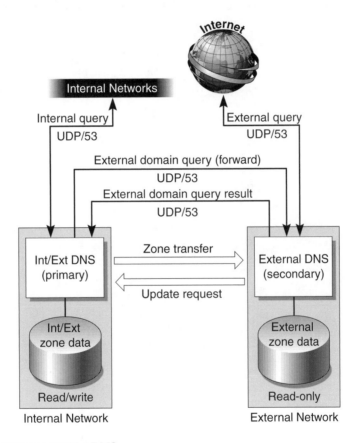

FIGURE 4-24 FijiNet DNS

The external secondary DNS server is on the external network, and the primary DNS server is on the internal network. The primary DNS server functions as the primary for both internal and external domains.

The external secondary DNS server communicates with DNS servers on the Internet for name resolution of hosts on the Internet. It periodically receives zone transfers from the primary DNS server on the internal network for zone data updates.

FijiNet LDAP

We place an LDAP server on the internal network, as shown in FIGURE 4-25. Because of cost constraints, we omit replica servers.

Note – We plan on using an iPlanet directory server, so we can configure multiple master directory servers.

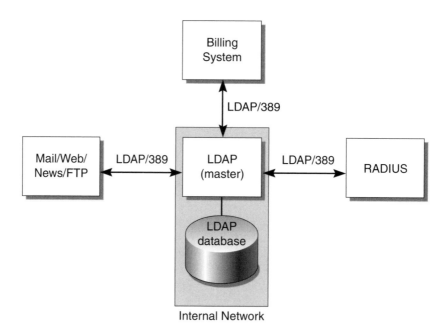

FIGURE 4-25 FijiNet LDAP

FijiNet DHCP

FIGURE 4-26 shows the flow of the DHCP service.

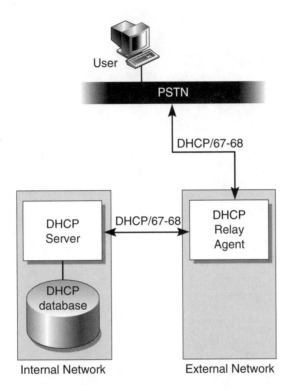

FIGURE 4-26 FijiNet DHCP Server

When users dial up, the NAS contacts the DHCP relay agent for dynamic configuration information. The DHCP relay agent relays DHCP messages to the DHCP server, which returns the information to users.

The DHCP relay agent is an intermediary between the DHCP server and users. The DHCP relay agent can be configured on a dedicated server or on a router.

For FijiNet, we decided that the best configuration was to enable the DHCP relay agent on the router. This configuration has two advantages. First, a DHCP server does not have to reside on the external network. By having the DHCP server on the internal network, we reduce security risk. Second, with DHCP relay agents enabled at the router, this allows the DHCP server to scale well, so that we do not need a DHCP server at each network because BOOTP/DHCP packets cannot be forwarded beyond the local network.

FijiNet RADIUS

FIGURE 4-27 shows the flow of the RADIUS service.

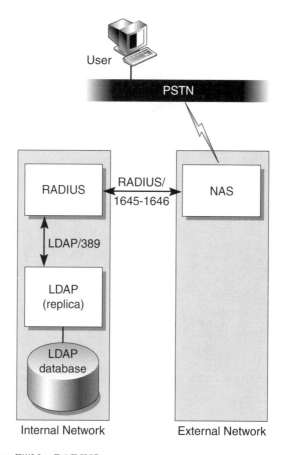

FIGURE 4-27 FijiNet RADIUS

All remote access from users is authenticated by the RADIUS server, which interfaces with the LDAP server.

To maintain a centralized authentication method, we decided not to use a local RADIUS database and/or external relational database. RADIUS queries the LDAP server for user information to authenticate users.

FijiNet NTP

FIGURE 4-28 shows the flow of the NTP service.

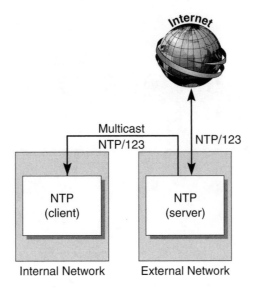

FIGURE 4-28 FijiNet NTP

For FijiNet, the NTP server synchronizes with external NTP servers' clocks on the Internet. It's not economical to maintain an external clock for a small ISP.

NTP servers frequently multicast to NTP clients to check the time. If a clock is not synchronized, NTP clients synchronize to the NTP server clock time.

The NTP server frequently multicasts to public Internet NTP servers, synchronizing with them if time drift is detected.

Refer to the following web site for a list of public NTP servers:

```
http://www.eecis.udel.edu/~mills/ntp/servers.html
```

FijiNet Email Service

FIGURE 4-29 shows the flow of Email service.

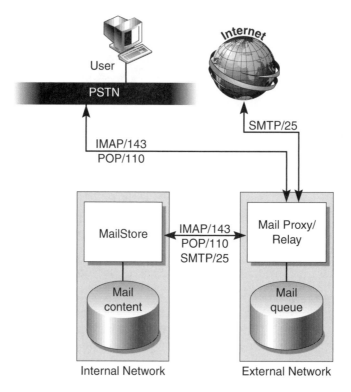

FIGURE 4-29 FijiNet Email Service

On the external network, a mail relay and mail proxy are configured. The mail relay is the intermediary that relays mail messages in and out of FijiNet. The mail proxy is configured for users to access and retrieve email, using POP and IMAP.

For the mail relay, there is dedicated disk space for incoming and outgoing mail queue. The mail relay does not contain mail messages. On the internal network, a MailStore contains all mail messages.

Users must not be able to connect to the MailStore directly from the Internet. Both POP3 and IMAP4 are available for retrieving mail at the front end.

FijiNet Web Service

FIGURE 4-30 shows the flow of web service.

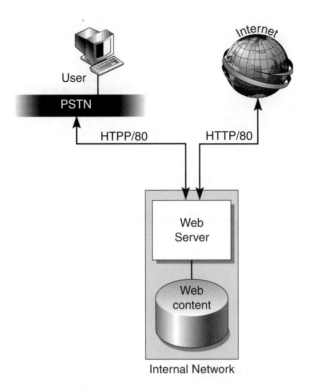

FIGURE 4-30 FijiNet Web Service

To access web pages, subscribers connect to a web server via browsers. The web server is on the internal network. Static web content resides on the same system as the web server. Due to cost constraints, there is not a centralized NFS server for content. Because there is no dynamic content, an application server is unnecessary.

FijiNet News Service

FIGURE 4-31 shows the flow of news service.

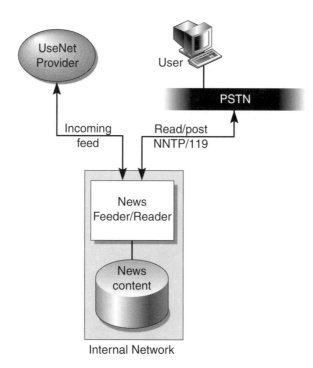

FIGURE 4-31 FijiNet News Service

Both news reader and news feeder are on the same physical server on the internal network. Users can read and post articles to the news reader. There is a single feed from the UseNet provider to FijiNet. There is not a downstream feed to any other news server.

For FijiNet, we could place the news reader/feeder on either the external or internal network. Because of the single-server configuration, which limits the flexibility of service decomposition, we place the news reader/feeder on the internal network. All news articles, spools, and histories are stored locally. An NFS server is not used as a centralized news content server.

Define Networking Components for FijiNet

After identifying topology, services within the topology, and service flows, we determine networking components for FijiNet that best fit the services and overall logical design.

Routers and Switches

For FijiNet's 10,000-subscriber environment, we determine that an L3 router with two WAN interfaces is needed for Internet connectivity, and at least one 10/100 Mbit/sec port is needed for internal connectivity.

For scalability, we suggest that two 10/100 Mbps are required if additional routers are added to provide availability. In Chapter 5, we provide information for capacity planning of WAN/LAN ports for routers.

We determine that an L2 switch with a sufficient number of 10/100 Mbit/sec ports is needed. To ensure that the ports can scale to support up to 100,000 users, we must design the architecture so that FijiNet can add ports on demand for additional network devices and servers. Because of their cost constraints, we start with a minimum configuration. FijiNet can then scale horizontally when needed. The aggregation of port density can be done by cascading or daisy chaining multiple switches. In Chapter 5, we provide information for capacity planning the ports on switches.

Load Balancers

Due to cost constraints, we accept that load balancers are not applicable to FijiNet's market-entry architecture of 10,000 subscribers. However, when FijiNet grows to 100,000 subscribers or higher and load distribution becomes critical to service availability, load balancers will be necessary. Therefore, it is important to plan for future traffic growth and how load balancing fits into the overall architecture, such as scalability, availability, performance, etc. described in the architectural model in Chapter 3.

Intrusion Detection System (IDS)

Because FijiNet's service offering is for residential users and no SLAs are being offered, an IDS is not required.

An IDS is not cost effective for a 10,000-subscriber environment. However, as FijiNet grows and adds different types of users (such as business subscribers) and services, security will become critical. When a higher level of security is required, an IDS will be important to protect unauthorized access to services and data.

## CHAPTER 5

Creating a Physical Design

After creating a logical design, create the physical design, which consists of constructing a high-level network design and planning for capacity. This chapter provides information to assist you in formulating estimates for how much capacity your design needs. Use it as a general sizing guideline for estimating storage and memory for services.

We suggest that you approach this part of the architecture process with the objective of performing initial capacity planning, based upon estimated usage or industry averages. Also, plan to scale to maximum capacity, based on the ISP's requirements.

Because of many unknown variables in an ISP's environment and ever-changing traffic, load characteristics, and subscriber usage patterns, it's unrealistic to calculate exact capacity amounts during the design phase. Aim for reasonable estimates that can later be refined using actual resource utilization data.

This chapter contains the following topics:

- "Creating a High-Level Network Design" on page 124
- "Planning Capacity" on page 132
- "Creating a Network Design for FijiNet" on page 164
- "Planning Capacity for FijiNet" on page 167

Creating a High-Level Network Design

Although there are many methods for creating a network design and addressing capacity planning, we suggest that you approach the process by creating a physical network design, then planning capacity for software and hardware.

We recommend the following *overall* process for creating a physical network design:

1. Start with a generic high-level network design that includes as many tiers or layers as needed. Identify all major network components within the infrastructure. We recommend that you create a diagram of your network design to document all components during this process.

2. Plan the capacity required for software and hardware.

3. For each tier or layer, determine the network components required, such as routers, switches, and load balancers.

4. Choose the level of redundancy and availability appropriate for the architectural design.

5. Determine the number of fire ridges required for separating tiers or layers.

6. For each fire ridge, determine the number of firewalls needed.

7. Decide if an Intrusion Detection System (IDS) is required. If IDS is required, determine the appropriate places to place the sensors.

8. Determine the number of modems and high-speed trunks for Internet connectivity and dial-up access.

9. Determine how many network access servers (NASs) are needed to handle concurrent users.

10. Determine if cache servers are required.

11. Place servers at appropriate layers, for example, web servers at the services network, database servers at the content network, and so on.

Note – Detailed content and tips for making decisions related to the steps in this process are in the preceding chapters. In this chapter, we build on that information and guide you through modeling capacity for software, servers, and network components. In the next chapter, we describe how to select software and hardware components to satisfy the physical design you create.

Build a Network Design Diagram

We recommend that before planning software and hardware capacity, you create a high-level network design diagram. Creating a diagram assists you in ensuring that your design satisfies all of an ISP's requirements. (Use the information you developed from reading Chapters 2 to 4.) Also, it assists you in capacity planning for components, because they are all identified and documented in the diagram.

In FIGURE 5-1, we show an ideal, fully redundant, highly scalable N-tier network architecture design. This generic design example details each layer, including components at each layer.

Some key characteristics of this design are as follows:

- The core routers have multiple Internet connections for availability in the event of link failure.

- All network devices, such as routers and switches, throughout the infrastructure are fully redundant to ensure availability and eliminate all single points-of-failure.

- Separating each layer is a fire ridge, which is a firewall complex consisting of two or more load-balanced firewalls. This approach ensures maximum security, availability, and scalability. The firewalls can be configured in stand-alone or in high availability (HA) mode and can be scaled horizontally to provide an overall aggregate throughput.

- If session state preservation is required, the firewalls can be configured in HA pairs or clusters with active-active configuration. In the event that any of the firewalls fail, session states are preserved.

- Multilayer switches (L2 to L7) are used throughout the infrastructure, eliminating all single points-of-failure from simple load-balancing devices. Multilayer switches are capable of wire-speed switching, gigabit performance, and traffic distribution based on load or content type.

- Caching engines are placed at the DMZ network for performance enhancement, especially for ISP environments with multiple POPs.

- IDS sensors can be strategically placed throughout the infrastructure for security monitoring.

- Management network is out-of-band.

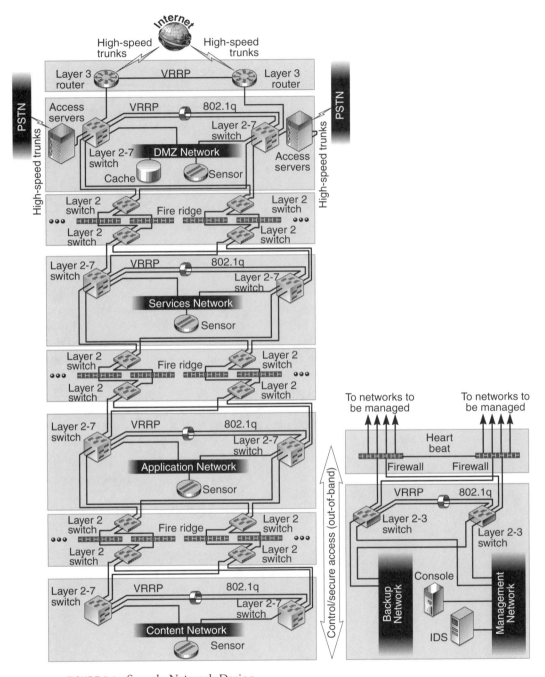

FIGURE 5-1 Sample Network Design

Create IP Address Schema

Create a well-designed IP address schema so that network addresses are scalable to handle growth.

Using the network design you created in the previous section, identify the types and ranges of IP addresses required for your design.

FIGURE 5-2 shows a sample IP address schema based on our generic ISP network design in FIGURE 5-1.

In any ISP network topology, an IP address schema usually consists of three different address ranges:

1. Small address ranges (/29 to /30 masking) for point-to-point connections between network devices for management purposes (*core layer*)

2. Medium address ranges (/26 to /28 masking) for connections between layers of network devices such as between a router and firewall (*distribution layer*)

3. Large address ranges (/24 masking) for servers connecting to the network (*access layer*)

For more information about these layers, see Chapter 4. For more information about IP address schema, refer to the following resources:

- *IP Fundamentals*
- *Internetworking with TCP/IP, Volume I*
- *TCP/IP Illustrated, Volume 1 - The Protocols.*

Core Layer

At the core layer, the 30-bit mask (/30 prefix) is often used for heartbeats, which is a point-to-point connection between two network devices of the same type, such as between two routers. This connection is required for link status checking in ensuring high availability. Traffic on this network is strictly for link management purposes only. Addresses used for this purpose are usually private addresses (RFC 1918). With this approach, the 30-bit masking yields up to 64 (2^6) possible subnets where each subnet can have up to three possible addresses, but only two addresses ($2^2-2=2$) are usable because one address is reserved for network numbers (all zeros) and one address is reserved for broadcasts (all ones).

In TABLE 5-1, we present sample address masking at the core layer.

TABLE 5-1   Sample Address Masking at Core Layer

VLANs	Subnets	Addresses	Broadcast	Netmask
A1	10.0.0.0	10.0.0.1-2	10.0.0.3	255.255.255.252
A2	10.0.0.4	10.0.0.5-6	10.0.0.7	255.255.255.252
A3	10.0.0.8	10.0.0.9-10	10.0.0.11	255.255.255.252
...	...	...	...	...
A62	10.0.0.244	10.0.0.245-246	10.0.0.247	255.255.255.252
A63	10.0.0.248	10.0.0.249-250	10.0.0.251	255.255.255.252
A64	10.0.0.252	10.0.0.253-254	10.0.0.255	255.255.255.252

Note – For Class A address space, there are 128 (2^7) possible networks. However, only 126 networks are usable ($2^7-2=126$) because all zeros and all ones are reserved and may never be used for actual network numbers. For Class A address space, network 0.0.0.0 is reserved for default route and network 127.0.0.0 is reserved for loopback.

Distribution Layer

At the distribution layer, the 28-bit mask (/28 prefix) is often used for interconnecting network devices between layers, such as between routers and firewalls or between firewalls and switches. With this approach, the 28-bit masking yields up to 16 (2^4) possible subnets where each subnet can have up to 16 possible addresses, but only 14 (2^4-2=14) addresses are usable, because one address is reserved for network numbers (all zeros) and one address is reserved for broadcasts (all ones).

For large-scale environments where high availability and multiple load-balanced firewalls are needed, we recommend that you mask a lower number of bits, such as 27 bits, to ensure enough IP addresses are allocated. The type of addresses used at the distribution layer depends upon the topology. Public addresses are typically used on the distribution layer adjacent to the core layer. This approach ensures that addresses used at the DMZ network are registered addresses. For all other networks, (for example services, content, etc.) private addresses can be used for security enhancement and public address preservation.

TABLE 5-2   Sample Address Masking at Distribution Layer

VLANs	Subnets	Addresses	Broadcast	Netmask
B1	10.0.0.0	10.0.0.1-14	10.0.0.15	255.255.255.240
B2	10.0.0.16	10.0.0.17-30	10.0.0.31	255.255.255.240
B3	10.0.0.32	10.0.0.33-46	10.0.0.47	255.255.255.240
...	...	...	...	...
B14	10.0.0.208	10.0.0.209-222	10.0.0.223	255.255.255.240
B15	10.0.0.224	10.0.0.225-238	10.0.0.239	255.255.255.240
B16	10.0.0.240	10.0.0.241-254	10.0.0.255	255.255.255.240

Note – For Class B address space, there are 16,384 (2^{14}) possible networks. Only 16,382 (2^{14}-2=16,382) networks are usable.

Access Layer

At the access layer, the default Class C address with 24-bit mask (/24 prefix) is often used for interconnecting servers to a network. With this approach, the 24-bit masking yields up to 256 (2^8) possible subnets where each subnet can have up to 256 possible addresses, but only 254 (2^8-2=254) addresses are usable, because one address is reserved for network numbers (all zeros) and one address is reserved for broadcasts (all ones).

Addresses used at the access layer are usually private addresses (RFC 1918), with the exception of the DMZ network. This approach conserves IP addresses and enhances security.

For environments with a large number of hosts on a single network, a higher order of masking, such as 25 bits or higher, can be beneficial in preventing broadcast storms, thereby creating a more manageable network.

TABLE 5-3   Sample Address Masking at Access Layer

VLANs	Subnets	Addresses	Broadcast	Netmask
C1	10.0.0.0	10.0.0.1-254	10.0.0.255	255.255.255.0
C2	10.0.1.0	10.0.1.1-254	10.0.1.255	255.255.255.0
C3	10.0.2.0	10.0.2.1-254	10.0.2.255	255.255.255.0
...	...	...	...	...
C254	10.0.253.0	10.0.253.1-254	10.0.253.255	255.255.255.0
C255	10.0.254.0	10.0.254.1-254	10.0.254.255	255.255.255.0
C256	10.0.255.0	10.0.255.1-254	10.0.255.255	255.255.255.0

Note – For Class C address space, there are 2,097,152 (2^{21}) possible networks, but only 2,097,150 (2^{21}-2=2,097,150) networks are usable.

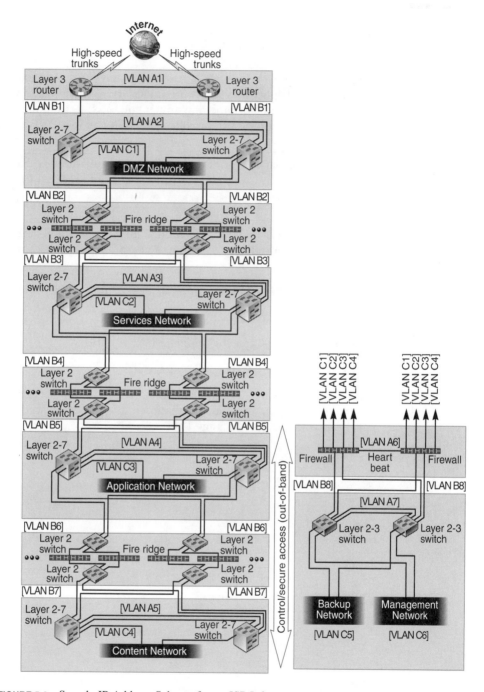

FIGURE 5-2 Sample IP Address Schema for an ISP Infrastructure

Planning Capacity

Planning for appropriate levels of capacity ensures that all design requirements are met, such as scalability and resource availability, as described in Chapter 2. Capacity planning helps you determine how much your architecture needs to scale, and it helps you select appropriate software and hardware (network, servers, and storage).

Tip – Perform capacity planning *before* selecting software and hardware. A common pitfall is to select hardware and software, then try to make it fit your capacity requirements.

In modeling capacity planning, formulate initial capacity planning based upon estimated usage or industry averages, and plan to support scaling for maximum capacity.

We recommend that you perform capacity planning in the following order:

1. "Estimate Software Capacity" on page 133.

2. "Estimate Server Capacity" on page 156.

3. "Estimate Network Capacity" on page 157.

If you have not created a high-level network design of your physical design, we recommend that you read the information in the preceding section "Creating a High-Level Network Design" on page 124.

Estimate Software Capacity

Estimate the software capacity, including the operating environment, before planning capacity for servers and network equipment.

Refer to the following sections:

- "Basic Services" on page 133
- "Infrastructure Services" on page 143
- "Operation and Management Service" on page 149
- "Operating Environment" on page 153

Note – In the "Estimate Software Capacity for FijiNet" on page 167, we use these formulas with data to show how the numbers are calculated.

Basic Services

Estimate capacity for basic services such as email, web, news, and FTP. Refer to the following sections:

- "Email Service" on page 133
- "Web Service" on page 136
- "News Service" on page 138
- "FTP Service" on page 142

Note – Your architecture design may have other basic services. Here, we cover the most common basic services.

Email Service

To plan capacity for email, estimate the storage and memory by using the information in TABLE 5-4 and TABLE 5-5.

Storage for email software and other plug-ins (antivirus, antispamming, etc.) is usually negligible in comparison to storage for MailStore and mail queue.

The mail queue is the temporary storage area for outgoing email messages that cannot be sent immediately and need to be queued until the next retry. We recommend that you configure the mail queue on the MailStore and the mail relay. (Mail proxy does not need mail queue.)

Tip – We strongly recommend you allocate the email queue to be approximately 20 percent of the email storage. While this value varies with environments, 20 percent is sufficient for an initial sizing, and can be adjusted accordingly as needed. In most ISP environments, approximately 40 percent of subscribers are active mail users.

The mail proxy usually requires a large amount of memory and sufficient CPU to handle post office protocol (POP) and Internet mail access protocol (IMAP) connections when users retrieve email. The mail relay usually does not require as much memory or CPU as the mail proxy. The message store requires large CPU and memory for email storage and management.

TABLE 5-4   Estimating Storage for Email Service

Variable	Value	Description
T	Environment dependent	Total number of subscribers
P_{act}	Environment dependent	Percentage of active email users
S_{ave}	Environment dependent	Average email message size
N_{rev}	Environment dependent	Average email messages received per user per day
S_{msa}	$T \times P_{act} \times S_{ave} \times N_{rev}$	Average storage for active email users
S_{msp}	Environment dependent	Average storage for email queue
S_{msm}	Environment dependent	Maximum email storage quota per subscriber
S_{msq}	Environment dependent	Maximum storage for email queue
S_{mss}	Application dependent	Storage requirement for email software and various plug-ins

$$S_{ms(proxy)} = S_{mss}$$

$$S_{ms(relay)} = S_{msp} + S_{mss}$$

$$S_{ms(average \cdot mailstore)} = S_{msa} + S_{msp} + S_{mss}$$

$$S_{ms(maximum \cdot mailstore)} = (T \times S_{msm}) + S_{msq} + S_{mss}$$

TABLE 5-5 Estimating Memory for Email Service

Variable	Value	Description
T	Environment dependent	Total number of subscribers
P_{con}	Environment dependent	Percentage of concurrency
P_{act}	Environment dependent	Percentage of active email users
P_{pop}	Environment dependent	Percentage of POP users
P_{ima}	Environment dependent	Percentage of IMAP users
M_{msi}	Application dependent	Memory footprint per IMAP connection
M_{msp}	Application dependent	Memory footprint per POP connection
M_{mst}	Application dependent	Memory footprint per simple mail transfer protocol (SMTP) connection
M_{msb}	Application dependent	Memory requirement for email server

$$M_{mp} = T \times P_{con} \times P_{act} \times P_{pop} \times M_{msp}$$

$$M_{mi} = T \times P_{con} \times P_{act} \times P_{ima} \times M_{msi}$$

$$M_{mt} = T \times P_{con} \times P_{act} \times M_{mst}$$

$$M_{ms(proxy)} = M_{mp} + M_{mi} + M_{msb}$$

$$M_{ms(relay)} = M_{mt} + M_{msb}$$

$$M_{ms(mailstore)} = M_{mp} + M_{mi} + M_{mt} + M_{msb}$$

Web Service

To plan capacity for web service, estimate the storage and memory by using the information in TABLE 5-6 and TABLE 5-7.

Storage for the web server is minor in comparison to storage required for web content. Additionally, the storage requirement is dependent on software selected, additional modules or plug-ins required, and online documentation. The sizing depends upon the vendor's recommendation. After selecting software, refer to the vendor's installation manual for web storage sizing recommendations.

It has been estimated that approximately 25 percent of ISP subscribers have personal web pages. The average web storage size per user is estimated to be 250 Kbytes.

In large-scale ISPs with multiple POPs, cache server can be used to cache data that are frequently accessed, especially in environments where content is static. Web caching can also be done at the web server. Storage for web cache is estimated to be 20 percent of the overall web page storage. While this value varies in different environments, it is sufficient for initial sizing and can be adjusted accordingly.

TABLE 5-6   Estimating Storage for Web Service

Variable	Value	Description
T	Environment dependent	Total number of subscribers
P_{act}	Environment dependent	Percentage of active users with web pages
S_{ave}	Environment dependent	Average web storage size per user
S_{wsa}	$T \times P_{act} \times S_{ave}$	Average storage for active users with web pages
S_{wsd}	Environment dependent	Average storage for web cache
S_{wsw}	Environment dependent	Maximum web storage quota per subscriber
S_{wsc}	Environment dependent	Maximum storage for web cache
S_{wss}	Application dependent	Storage requirement for web software and various plug-ins

$$S_{ws(average)} = S_{wsa} + S_{wsd} + S_{wss}$$

$$S_{ws(maximum)} = (T \times S_{wsw}) + S_{wsc} + S_{wss}$$

There are two sizing models for web servers: threads and fork/exec model. The difference between the two models is how memory is initially allocated when a web server is instantiated.

For more information about multi-threaded process architecture and modeling for web servers, refer to the following sources:

- For details on multi-threaded process architecture, see *Solaris Internals: Core Kernel Architecture* and *Threads Primer: A Guide to Multithreaded Programming*.

- For the list of common web servers and their associated models, refer to:

  `http://www.acme.com/software/thttpd/benchmarks.html`

- For detail modeling for web servers, see *Capacity Planning for Web Performance: Metrics, Models, & Methods*.

TABLE 5-7   Estimating Memory for Web Service

Variable	Value	Description
T	Environment dependent	Total number of subscribers
P$_{con}$	Environment dependent	Percentage of concurrency
N$_{web}$	Environment dependent	Number of web servers
N$_{par}$	1	Number of parent processes
N$_{pro}$	Environment dependent	Number of child processes (fork/exec model)
N$_{thr}$	Environment dependent	Number of threads (thread model)
N$_{con}$	Environment dependent	Peak number of HTTP connections
M$_{wsc}$	Application dependent	Memory footprint per HTTP connection
M$_{wss}$	Application dependent	Memory footprint per child process (fork/exec model)
M$_{wst}$	Application dependent	Memory footprint per thread (thread model)

$$M_{wm(thread)} = (N_{web} \times N_{thr} \times M_{wst}) + (N_{con} \times M_{wsc})$$

$$M_{wm(fork)} = (N_{web} \times (N_{par} + N_{pro}) \times M_{wss}) + (N_{con} \times M_{wsc})$$

News Service

To plan capacity for news service, estimate the storage and memory by using the information in TABLE 5-8 and TABLE 5-9.

Storage for news service is extremely large, and growing exponentially. News service is often outsourced to a UseNet provider, such as UUnet, to reduce an ISP's up-front and on-going costs.

As of June 2001, it was estimated that 300 Gbytes of storage is required for a full feed for daily news articles. It has been estimated that storage for daily news feed will reach approximately 550 Gbytes by the end of 2001. For more information, refer to:

```
http://newsfeed.mesh.ad.jp/flow/size.html
```

Currently, approximately 1.5 million articles are generated per day. Thus, to have enough storage to handle a large number of files, the file system must be designed with a sufficient number of inodes. See FIGURE 5-3 for a sample graph of daily news articles, indicating the steady rise in the number of news articles and showing a current value of 1.5 million articles per day.

FIGURE 5-4 shows the current storage requirements for a full news feed. Estimating based on 300 Gbytes of disk and 1.5 million news articles, the file system must have at least 200,000 inodes per gigabyte of disk space.

In FIGURE 5-5, we show sample trends for storage over the next 12 months, based upon current usage.

Note – The sample data in these figures is actual data from a UseNet provider.

News spooler, history, and index is estimated to be 10 percent of news storage. This value varies in different environments and depends upon many factors, such as how newsgroups are moderated, how stale newsgroups are managed, and how many upstream and downstream feeds are made. We recommend that you adjust overhead accordingly.

TABLE 5-8   Estimating Storage for News Service

Variable	Value	Description
S_{nsa}	Time dependent	Storage requirement for daily news articles for a full feed
S_{nsh}	Environment dependent	Storage requirement for news spooler, history, and index
S_{nss}	Application dependent	Storage requirement for news software

$$S_{ns} = S_{nsa} + S_{nsh} + S_{nss}$$

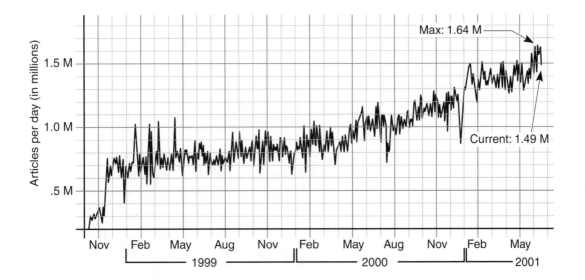

FIGURE 5-3   Daily Number of News Articles

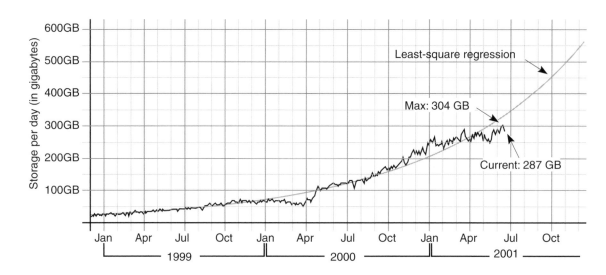

FIGURE 5-4   Storage Requirements for Full Feed

Note – LSQ (Least SQuare) is a mathematical model for estimating future growth of news storage, based on current trends.

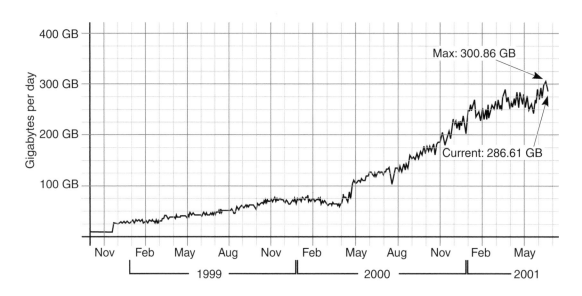

FIGURE 5-5   Future Storage Estimate

The Internet Software Consortium (ISC) (`http://www.isc.org`) recommends that systems with less than 256 Mbytes of RAM use a tagged hash table for history database. This approach, although somewhat slower, consumes less memory. How much RAM is required for the news server depends on several factors:

- Is the news feed received from a UseNet provider a full feed or partial feed?

- Are there any downstream feeds?

- How are newsgroups moderated, filtered, maintained, etc?

InterNetNews[SM] (INN) administrators recommend 1 Gbyte of memory for the news reader. If the history hash doesn't fit in memory, article expiration takes longer. The news feeder requires a lot of memory, because of the high number of sockets open to handle the volume of data.

Note – For information on INN mailing lists, refer to `http://www.isc.org/ services/public/lists/inn-lists.html`. INN mailing list archives are located at `http://www.isc.org/ml-archives/inn-workers`.

TABLE 5-9   Estimating Memory for News Service

Variable	Value	Description
T	Environment dependent	Total number of subscribers
P_{con}	Environment dependent	Percentage of concurrency
P_{act}	Environment dependent	Percentage of active news users
M_{nss}	Application dependent	Memory footprint per news server
N_{nfd}	Environment dependent	Number of downstream feeds
M_{nfd}	Application dependent	Memory requirement per downstream feed
N_{nco}	$T \times P_{con} \times P_{act}$	Peak number of news connection
M_{nco}	Application dependent	Memory footprint per news connection

$$M_{nm} = M_{nss} + (N_{nfd} \times M_{nfd}) + (N_{nco} \times M_{nco})$$

FTP Service

To plan capacity for FTP (file transfer protocol) service, estimate the storage and memory by using the information in TABLE 5-10 and TABLE 5-11.

How much storage is required for a spooler varies greatly in different environments. An FTP spooler usually doesn't have to be very large, but it must be cleared regularly, for example, with shell scripts and cron jobs.

Content updates for subscribers' personal web pages are infrequent, and concurrency for FTP sessions is very low, because only a small percentage of subscribers have web pages and a smaller number of those subscribers update their web pages. Memory required for FTP is minimal. Each FTP process is approximately 400 Kbytes.

TABLE 5-10 Estimating Storage for FTP Service

Variable	Value	Description
S_{fss}	Application dependent	Storage requirement for FTP software
S_{fsu}	Environment dependent	Storage requirement for FTP spool

$$S_{fs} = S_{fss} + S_{fsu}$$

TABLE 5-11 Estimating Memory for FTP Service

Variable	Value	Description
M_{ftp}	Application dependent	Memory footprint per FTP process
N_{ftp}	Environment dependent	Number of concurrent FTP connections

$$M_{fs} = M_{ftp} \times N_{ftp}$$

Infrastructure Services

Estimate the capacity needed for infrastructure services such as domain name system (DNS), remote authentication dial-in user service (RADIUS), lightweight directory access protocol (LDAP), dynamic host configuration protocol (DHCP), and network time protocol (NTP). Refer to the following sections:

- "DNS Service" on page 143
- "RADIUS Service" on page 144
- "LDAP Service" on page 145
- "DHCP Service" on page 147
- "NTP Service" on page 148

Note – Your architecture design may have other infrastructure services. Here, we cover the most common and minimum required services.

DNS Service

To plan capacity for DNS service, estimate the storage and memory by using the information in TABLE 5-12 and TABLE 5-13. In general, DNS consumes very little CPU and memory resources.

TABLE 5-12 Estimating Storage for DNS Service

Variable	Value	Estimation
S_{dns}	Application dependent	Storage requirement for DNS software
S_{dnd}	Environment dependent	Storage requirement for DNS zone databases

$$S_{dn} = S_{dns} + S_{dnd}$$

TABLE 5-13   Estimating Memory for DNS Service

Variable	Value	Description
M_{dns}	Application dependent	Memory requirement per DNS server
M_{zon}	Environment dependent	Memory requirement for zone database

$$M_{dn} = M_{dns} + M_{zon}$$

RADIUS Service

To plan capacity for RADIUS service, estimate the storage and memory by using the information in TABLE 5-14 and TABLE 5-15.

In general, RADIUS usually does not require a large amount of memory. Allowing for variances based on the software and the vendor's recommendation, use the following guidelines:

- 64 Mbytes of RAM for a small- to mid-sized ISP
- 128 Mbytes for a large ISP

TABLE 5-14   Estimating Storage for RADIUS Service

Variable	Value	Description
T	Environment dependent	Total number of subscribers
S_{rse}	Application dependent	Average size for a RADIUS database entry
S_{rsd}	$T \times S_{rse}$	Storage requirement for RADIUS database
S_{rss}	Application dependent	Storage requirement for RADIUS software
S_{rsl}	Environment dependent	Storage requirement for RADIUS log

$$S_{rs} = S_{rsd} + S_{rss} + S_{rsl}$$

TABLE 5-15   Estimating Memory for RADIUS Service

Variable	Value	Description
T	Environment dependent	Total number of subscribers
P_{con}	Environment dependent	Percentage of concurrency
N_{rsc}	$T \times P_{con}$	Peak number of RADIUS authentication
M_{rse}	Application dependent	Memory footprint per RADIUS authentication
M_{rsa}	$N_{rsc} \times S_{rse}$	Memory requirement for RADIUS authentications
M_{rss}	Application dependent	Memory requirement for RADIUS server

$$M_{rs} = M_{rsa} + M_{rss}$$

LDAP Service

To plan capacity for directory service, estimate the storage and memory by using the information in TABLE 5-16 and TABLE 5-17.

The storage requirement for directory software is usually quite large, because of the complexity of the application and availability of support for various platforms and applications. The size of the directory application is dependent upon the vendor. The LDAP database can be large; however, the size depends on the number of entries in the database, number of fields populated per LDAP entry, and complexity of directory schema.

TABLE 5-16   Estimating Storage for Directory Service

Variable	Value	Description
T	Environment dependent	Total number of subscribers
S_{dse}	Environment dependent	Average size for a directory database entry
S_{dsd}	$T \times S_{dse}$	Storage requirement for directory database
S_{dsi}	$2 \times S_{dsd}$	Storage requirement for directory index
S_{dss}	Application dependent	Storage requirement for directory software

$$S_{ds} = S_{dsd} + S_{dss} + S_{dsi}$$

Index databases can get very large, depending on what attributes are indexed and what type of indexing is used. You can easily have index databases that are equal to or larger than the entry database. In most cases you can figure out how much space the entries take up and double it to allow for indexing, which is what we recommend in the formula in the preceding table. Note that this calculation affects memory requirements too.

A typical configuration for directory servers is putting more memory on LDAP replicas, because these servers are used for LDAP searches and queries. If the LDAP master is dedicated for replication only, you can configure less memory for it.

For more information on LDAP, see *Understanding and Deploying LDAP Directory Services*.

TABLE 5-17   Estimating Memory for Directory Service

Variable	Value	Description
T	Environment dependent	Total number of subscribers
M_{dss}	Application dependent	Memory requirement for directory server

$$M_{ds} = M_{dss}$$

DHCP Service

To plan capacity for DHCP service, estimate the storage and memory by using the information in TABLE 5-18 and TABLE 5-19.

Storage for DHCP is usually very small. Even for a large ISP, the storage requirement is minor compared to other services. An average entry in the DHCP database is approximately 256 bytes.

TABLE 5-18 Estimating Storage for DHCP Service

Variable	Value	Description
T	Environment dependent	Total number of subscribers
S_{dhe}	Application dependent	Average size for a DHCP database entry
S_{dhd}	$T \times S_{dhe}$	Storage requirement for DHCP database
S_{dhs}	Application dependent	Storage requirement for DHCP software

$$S_{dh} = S_{dhd} + S_{dhs}$$

Memory sizing for DHCP is quite different from other services, because it is allocated up-front for leases. How much memory is required depends upon how many leases are allocated in the lease table. The size of the DHCP database doesn't dictate the amount of memory required for DHCP. Allocate enough memory for the lease table to serve the number of concurrent users. Anything larger than that provides no additional benefit.

According to the ISC, the average memory consumption per lease is approximately 256 bytes. A small single-CPU system with 32 Mbytes of RAM can efficiently be configured as a DHCP server for small- to mid-sized ISPs.

TABLE 5-19 Estimating Memory for DHCP Service

Variable	Value	Description
T	Environment dependent	Total number of subscribers
P_{con}	Environment dependent	Percentage of concurrency
N_{dhc}	$T \times P_{con}$	Peak number of DHCP leases
M_{dhl}	Application dependent	Memory footprint per DHCP lease
M_{dhd}	$N_{dhc} \times M_{dhl}$	Memory requirement for DHCP leases
M_{dhs}	Application dependent	Memory footprint for DHCP server

$$M_{dh} = M_{dhd} + M_{dhs}$$

For more information on DHCP, refer to *The DHCP Handbook: Understanding, Deploying, and Managing Automated Configuration Services*.

NTP Service

To plan capacity for NTP service, estimate the storage and memory by using the information in TABLE 5-20 and TABLE 5-21.

Storage and memory for NTP is very small and negligible. There are no special considerations for NTP service and no extra storage and memory requirements other than for the software.

Tip – In a Solaris environment, memory use for NTP can be estimated from looking at the output of the following command: `pmap -x <PID>`.

TABLE 5-20 Estimating Storage for NTP Service

Variable	Value	Description
S_{nts}	Application dependent	Storage requirement for NTP software

$$S_{ns} = S_{nts}$$

TABLE 5-21 Estimating Memory for NTP Service

Variable	Value	Description
M_{nts}	Application dependent	Memory requirement for NTP server

$$M_{ns} = M_{nts}$$

Operation and Management Service

Estimate the capacity needed for operation and management services such as backup, firewalls, and logging. Refer to the following sections:

- "Backup Service" on page 149
- "Firewall Service" on page 151
- "Log Service" on page 152

Note – Operation and management services are beyond the scope of this book. Many resources are available, such as *OSS Essential: Support System Solutions for Service Providers*, Kornel Terplan, John Wiley and Sons, Inc., 2001.

Backup Service

To plan capacity for backup service, estimate the storage and memory by using the information in TABLE 5-22 and TABLE 5-23.

For backup servers such as Sun Solstice Backup™, VERITAS NetBackup Datacenter™, or Legato NetWorker®, the major storage required is for backup *index*. The index is used to track files that are backed up online.

The *browse policy* determines how long files are kept on index for online browsing. Each entry in the browse policy takes approximately 220 bytes. The size of the backup index depends on the following factors:

- Volume of data being backed up
- Level of backup
- Frequency of backup
- Browse and retention policies

To conserve disk space, your ISP may need to establish a shorter browse policy. Complementing the browse policy is the *retention policy,* which tracks save sets stored on each backup volume, thus, consuming less storage for indexing.

Tip – For ease of administration, we recommend that the browse and retention policies be set equally.

TABLE 5-22 Estimating Storage for Backup Service

Variable	Value	Description
S_{bsi}	Environment dependent	Storage requirement for backup indexes
S_{bss}	Application dependent	Storage requirement for backup software

$$S_{bs} = S_{bsi} + S_{bss}$$

In general, memory requirements are dictated by the number of backup instances and the number of clients backed up simultaneously. After selecting software, refer to the vendor's recommendation for memory sizing for backup.

TABLE 5-23 Estimating Memory for Backup Service

Variable	Value	Description
M_{bsd}	Application dependent	Memory requirement for backup server

$$M_{bs} = M_{bsd}$$

Firewall Service

To plan capacity for firewall service, estimate the storage and memory by using the information in TABLE 5-24 and TABLE 5-25.

Note – If your design uses a network-based firewall, you can omit storage for firewall software. Storage for firewall logs is still required. Logs are usually directed to a log server, because there is no local storage.

TABLE 5-24   Estimating Storage for Host-Based Firewall Service

Variable	Value	Description
S_{fws}	Application dependent	Storage requirement for firewall software, objects, and policy
S_{fwl}	Environment dependent	Storage requirement for firewall logs

$$S_{fw} = S_{fws} + S_{fwl}$$

How much memory is required for a firewall server depends upon the following:

- Graphical remote administration
- Short or long logging
- Encryption
- Network address translation
- Firewall state table size

After selecting software, refer to the vendor's recommendation for memory sizing.

TABLE 5-25   Estimating Memory for Firewall Service

Variable	Value	Description
M_{fws}	Platform dependent	Memory requirement for firewall

$$M_{fw} = M_{fws}$$

Log Service

To plan capacity for log service, estimate the storage and memory by using the information in TABLE 5-26 and TABLE 5-27.

The log spooler is the temporary storage area for new logs that have not been archived. Storage for the log spooler is usually small compared to storage for log archives. How much storage is required for archives is dependent on the volume of logs and how long logs are kept.

There are no special considerations for memory for log service. Sufficient memory must be present to support the underlying operating environment, with some overhead.

TABLE 5-26 Estimating Storage for Log Service

Variable	Value	Description
S_{lss}	Environment dependent	Storage requirement for log spooler
S_{lsa}	Environment dependent	Storage requirement for log archive

$$S_{ls} = S_{lss} + S_{lsa}$$

TABLE 5-27 Estimating Memory for Log Service

Variable	Value	Description
M_{lss}	Environment dependent	Memory requirement for log server

$$M_{ls} = M_{lss}$$

Operating Environment

Model the capacity planning for the file system layout for system disk, file system layout for data, and system disk storage. Refer to the following sections:

- "Storage Capacity" on page 153
- "Filesystem Layout for System Disk" on page 154
- "Filesystem Layout for Data" on page 155

Storage Capacity

Estimate the storage capacity for the operating system (root file system, swap space, log archive, and applications) by using the information in TABLE 5-28.

A special consideration for sizing the system disk is allocating enough disk space for swap and log archive. The rule of thumb for swap space is twice the amount of physical memory or RAM.

Keep in mind that swap space does not necessarily always equal twice the amount of physical memory, especially for systems that have a very large amount of memory where swap is never needed. In such cases, you can set swap space less than twice the amount of physical memory; for example, you can set it to equal the amount of memory.

Tip – It is important that you never set swap below the amount of physical memory, so that in the event of system crash, a complete core dump is saved. In general, at a minimum, set swap space to at least equal physical memory.

Based upon the environment, the amount of log archive storage needed is dependent on how many logs are generated, the type of logging that is performed, and how long logs are kept.

In general, you need much less disk space for applications than for logs.

TABLE 5-28 Estimating Storage for System Disk

Variable	Value	Description
S_{oss}	Vendor dependent	Storage requirement for operating system
S_{swp}	Recommend at least twice the amount of RAM	Storage requirement for swap space
S_{osl}	Environment dependent	Storage requirement for log archive
S_{app}	Environment dependent	Storage requirement for native and third-party applications

$$S_{os} = S_{oss} + S_{swp} + S_{osl} + S_{app}$$

Filesystem Layout for System Disk

Plan the file system layout for the system disk by using the information in TABLE 5-29.

It's important to plan the file system layout to ensure availability and scalability. If there is not enough room for growth, the system could run out of disk space. For example, if the /var partition were to run out of disk space, the system would freeze because logs could not be saved.

In UNIX, you can partition any disk up to eight partitions. Partition numbering is from 0 to 7.

- Partition 0 is always root partition.
- Partition 1 is usually swap.
- Partition 2 to 7 is operating system dependent.

We recommend spreading multiple swap partitions, if available, across multiple physical disks for performance enhancement.

Tip – For optimal performance, we recommend that you allocate partition 1 for swap. You can allocate partitions 2 to 7 for /usr, /var, /export, etc. in no particular order. The /usr/local is commonly configured for open source applications. For Solaris environments, we recommend using /opt for native and third-party applications.

Be aware that some vendors prefer a different scheme for partitioning and allocating disk space. After selecting an operating environment (refer to Chapter 6), consult the vendor's documentation for recommendations applicable to the operating environment.

TABLE 5-29 Filesystem Layout for System Disk

Partition	Filesystem	Description
0	/	Root (the first partition is always the root partition).
1	swap	Swap (the second partition is usually the swap partition)
2-7	Operating system dependent	/usr (binaries and libraries), /var (logs and patches), and /export (home directories)

Filesystem Layout for Data

Plan the file system layout for data by using the information in TABLE 5-30.

For management purposes, it is important to separate data from the system disk. Isolating data from the system disk ensures that if the system disk fails, data are not affected. Additionally, if data become corrupted, we don't want corrupted data to affect the system disk.

TABLE 5-30 Filesystem Layout for Data

Variable	Value	Description
/data	Environment dependent	Data (MailStores, web contents, news articles, etc.)

Tip – If you are planning to use VERITAS Volume Manager™ (VxVM), then plan to have data reside separately from the root diskgroup (*rootdg*). The rootdg is a disk group that contains system volumes only for VxVM. The rootdg is specific to each system and cannot be exported from one system and imported to another system. Separating data from rootdg allows you to export data from one system and import data to another system, when necessary, for example, in case of a system failure.

Estimate Server Capacity

After planning software capacity, determine what kind of server is appropriate to support the software design.

A benefit of server capacity planning is that it helps you understand application usage and resource utilization required, which will help you select the applicable hardware in the next chapter.

For an ISP's infrastructure, enterprise servers are the servers of choice. These servers vary in size, depending on the usage purpose. They are designed for scalability, performance, NEB-compliance, and rack-mounting. To estimate the size of enterprise servers for your ISP customer, use the information in TABLE 5-31.

TABLE 5-31 Sizing an Enterprise Server

Type	Size	Specification
Front-End Servers (DNS, DHCP, NTP, RADIUS, firewalls, mail relays, mail proxies, news readers, web servers, boot/install, etc.)	Small (horizontal scalability only)	Uniprocessor (1 CPU, ≤ 1 GB RAM)
Mid-Size Servers (application, backup, LDAP replicas, management, etc.)	Medium (horizontal and limited scalability)	Multiprocessor (≤ 4 CPU, ≤ 4 GB RAM)
Back-End Servers (NFS, MailStore, database, LDAP master, billing system, etc.)	Large (horizontal and high scalability)	Multiprocessor (≥ 4 CPU, ≥ 4 GB RAM)

Front-end servers are usually small and lightweight, such as web servers, mail relays, and mail proxies. These are typically uniprocessor with sufficient RAM and are coupled with front-end load balancers for load distribution. Front-end servers scale horizontally; therefore, multiprocessor systems are not required.

Servers for middle tier, such as application, management, and LDAP replica servers, are multiprocessor systems with limited scalability. While application servers can take advantage of a multiprocessor system, they don't require as much vertical scalability as that of back-end servers.

Back-end servers, such as the MailStore, NFS, database, and LDAP master, are large-scale multiprocessor systems with maximum vertical scalability. How much scalability is required depends on the environment and customer requirements.

Estimate Network Capacity

Estimate network capacity for the infrastructure so that the design provides bandwidth to support traffic load and sufficient modems and high-speed trunks are available for Internet connectivity and dial-up access.

Calculate the average utilization per user, and use that value in estimating bandwidth, modem, and trunk capacity.

Refer to the following sections:

- "Bandwidth" on page 157
- "Modems and High-Speed Trunks" on page 158
- "Network Components" on page 160

Bandwidth

On average, dial-up ISPs estimate that each user consumes approximately 1.7 Kbit/sec of network bandwidth. For example, if you have 1,250 concurrent users (total 10,000 subscribers with 12.5 percent concurrency), the network must be able to sustain 2.04 Mbit/sec.

Estimate the network bandwidth capacity for users by using the information in TABLE 5-32.

TABLE 5-32 Estimating Network Bandwidth for Users

Variable	Value	Description
T	Environment dependent	Total number of subscribers
P_{con}	Environment dependent	Percentage of concurrent users
B_{usr}	Environment dependent	Average network bandwidth consumption per user
B_{the}	Hardware dependent	Theoretical network bandwidth
B_{sat}	$40\% \times B_{the}$	Network bandwidth saturation level
B_{ove}	$10\% \times B_{the}$	Network bandwidth overhead

$$B = (T \times P_{con} \times B_{usr}) + B_{ove}$$

Modems and High-Speed Trunks

Determine the total number of modems to support the projected number of concurrent users. Using this number, you can then determine the number of high-speed trunks needed for dial-up and Internet access.

Modems

Based upon the projected number of concurrent users, estimate how many modems are required for dial-up access. Calculate it by using the information in TABLE 5-33.

Percentage of concurrency is often calculated from modem-to-user ratio. This value represents how many users a single modem can support. Traditionally, ISPs used 1:10 as the modem-to-user ratio, that is, 10 percent concurrency, which is one modem for every 10 active subscriber sessions.

Today, most ISPs use a 1:8 modem-to-user ratio, which is 12.5 percent concurrency. However, it is becoming difficult for ISPs to sustain their levels of concurrent users because more users are online and they stay online longer. More and more ISPs are increasing ratios to 1:6 (16.7 percent) to support the same number of subscribers.

If you do not have an estimate for number of concurrent users, base the number on industry usage for ISPs. A minimum ratio of 1:8 is industry usage for most ISPs, which represents a 12.5 percent concurrency.

TABLE 5-33 Estimating Modems Needed for Dial-up Access

Variable	Value	Description
T	Environment dependent	Total number of subscribers
P_{con}	Environment dependent	Percentage of concurrency

$$N_M = T \times P_{con}$$

High-Speed Trunks

To estimate trunk capacity, determine links needed for Internet connectivity and dial-up access.

Estimate Links for Internet Connectivity – Estimate the size of bandwidth required for Internet connectivity by using the information in TABLE 5-34.

The simplest approach is to determine the average bandwidth that will be consumed by concurrent users. The number of Internet connections required is dependent on the environment. Multiple links are usually required to ensure availability.

TABLE 5-34   Estimating Links Needed for Internet Connectivity

Variable	Value	Description
T	Environment dependent	Total number of subscribers
P_{con}	Environment dependent	Percentage of concurrent users
B_{usr}	Environment dependent	Average bandwidth consumption per user
L	Hardware dependent	Bandwidth supported per high-speed trunk

$$N_L = \frac{T \times P_{con} \times B_{usr}}{L}$$

Estimate Links for Dial-Up Access – Estimate the size of links for dial-up access by using the information in TABLE 5-35.

Many network access servers support multiple T1 links and one channelized T3 (CT3) link. If your link estimate is a small number of T1 links, it is probably cost effective to use T1 links. However, if your link estimate requires many T1 links, it is more cost effective to use one CT3 link.

CT3 links are best for large-scale environments where a large number of channels are required to support a large number of concurrent users. A single CT3 supports up to 672 channels, where each channel supports 64 Kbit/sec.

TABLE 5-35 Estimating Links Needed for Dial-up Access

Variable	Value	Description
T	Environment dependent	Total number of subscribers
P_{con}	Environment dependent	Percentage of concurrent users
C	Hardware dependent	Number of channels supported per high-speed trunk

$$N_L = \frac{T \times P_{con}}{C}$$

Network Components

If you have not already done so, identify the major network components of your network design. Identifying components helps you ensure that the network is scalable and performs at the level desired.

Estimate the port capacity for routers, switches, and consoles. Refer to the following sections:

- "Routers" on page 161
- "Switches" on page 162
- "Console Servers" on page 163

Routers

Capacity planning for routers is different from switches. When planning for routers, consider the following:

- Number of WAN interfaces
- Type of high-speed trunks
- Number of fixed LAN ports

Planning WAN interfaces and associated high-speed trunks ensures that the appropriate bandwidth is achieved for WAN backhaul with corresponding types of high-speed trunks. In addition, planning support for WAN interfaces ensures that redundant Internet connections can be achieved for HA in the event of link failure.

In addition to planning for WAN interfaces, plan for LAN interfaces. When multiple routers and switches are interconnected for availability, planning for LAN interfaces becomes critical.

Estimate the port capacity for routers by using the information in TABLE 5-36.

TABLE 5-36   Estimating Ports for Routers

Variable	Value	Description
N_{wan}	Environment dependent	Number of WAN interfaces slots (T1, T3, etc.)
N_{lan}	Environment dependent	Number of fixed LAN ports (10/100 Mbps)

$$P_R = N_{wan} + N_{lan}$$

Switches

It is important to plan for the number of network ports (10/100 Mbit/sec) needed, plus overhead for immediate and future growth. We recommend adding 20 percent overhead for immediate growth. For future growth, plan for overall scalability of the switches. Estimate the network port for switches by using the information in TABLE 5-37.

All switches have at least one dedicated port for uplink, usually Fast Ethernet (FE) for small switches and Gigabit Ethernet (GE) for large switches. The serial port is usually for failover, but you can use 10/100 Mbps as well. We recommend that the uplink port be large enough to handle upstream and downstream traffic.

Perform your capacity planning for switches by network layer. Depending on the role of each network layer, your total number of network ports vary. For example, switches at the services network might require a larger number of network ports than switches at the content network, because the services network has many small servers compared to the content network, which has a few large servers.

TABLE 5-37 Estimating Network Ports for Switches

Variable	Value	Description
N_{ser}	Environment dependent	Number of servers connected to the switch (mail relays, mail proxies, web servers, application servers, DNS servers, etc.)
N_{apl}	Environment dependent	Number of network appliances connect to the switch (firewalls, load balancers, cache engines, IDS sensors, console servers, access servers, etc.)
N_{adm}	Environment dependent	Number of network ports required for administrative purposes (trunking, heartbeats, failover, etc.)
N_{ove}	Environment dependent	Number of network ports required for immediate growth.

$$P_S = N_{ser} + N_{apl} + N_{adm} + N_{ove}$$

Console Servers

Capacity planning for console ports is simple and straightforward. Start by using the same number as the total number of devices to be managed by the console server. Then, add an appropriate amount of overhead for immediate growth. Estimate the port capacity for console servers by using the information in TABLE 5-38.

TABLE 5-38 Console Port Estimation for Console Servers

Variable	Value	Description
N_{ser}	Environment dependent	Number of servers connected to the console server (mail relays, mail proxies, web servers, application servers, DNS servers, etc.)
N_{apl}	Environment dependent	Number of network appliances connected to the console server (firewalls, load balancers, cache engines, IDS sensors, access servers, routers, switches, etc.)
N_{ove}	Environment dependent	Number of console ports required for immediate growth

$$P_S = N_{ser} + N_{apl} + N_{ove}$$

Creating a Network Design for FijiNet

We create a high-level network design for FijiNet, using the approach detailed in the general section and using the requirements established in earlier chapters.

Build a Network Design Diagram for FijiNet

In FIGURE 5-6, we show an illustration of the physical design we created for FijiNet's architecture.

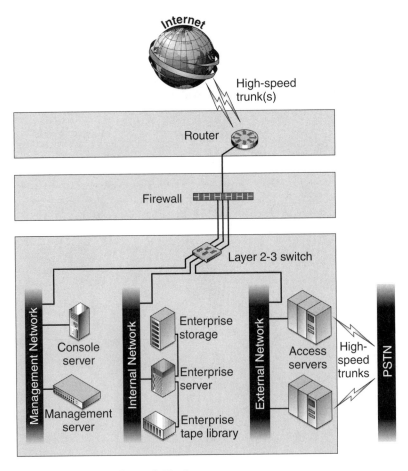

FIGURE 5-6   FijiNet Network Design

Create IP Address Schema for FijiNet

For FijiNet, we apply the general IP address schema for ISP infrastructures (presented earlier in this chapter), and adjust it accordingly. To satisfy FijiNet's requirements, we consider the following.

- Because FijiNet is forgoing redundant network devices, there is no need to plan for heartbeats between redundant components. Therefore, all virtual local area networks (VLANs) of type A (A1, A2, A3, etc.) do not apply to FijiNet.

- A single VLAN B1 will be used for FijiNet's network between router and firewall. This subnet yields up to 14 usable addresses for connections between the core router and the premises firewall.

  Although FijiNet only uses two addresses on the initial configuration, we need the network to scale to support a 100,000-user environment with full redundancy and high availability. Full redundancy may mean that more addresses are needed to support additional routers, switches, and heartbeats. High availability may mean that more addresses are needed for multiple connections from servers to switches.

- For three access networks, three VLANs (C1, C2, and C3) will be used. VLAN C1 is for the external network; VLAN C2 is for the internal network; and VLAN C3 is for the management network.

  The address for each VLAN is a full Class C address range. Addresses for the external network are public addresses. Addresses for the internal and management networks are private addresses (RFC 1918). While a full Class C address space is over allocated, it is implemented to ensure scalability to support more servers and virtual addresses as FijiNet grows toward a 100,000-user environment.

TABLE 5-39 shows the schema we created for FijiNet. See FIGURE 5-7 for an illustration of the IP address schema for FijiNet.

TABLE 5-39 IP Address Schema for FijiNet

VLANs	Subnets	Hosts	Broadcast	Netmask
B1	129.153.47.0	129.153.47.1-14	129.153.47.15	255.255.255.240
C1	129.153.48.0	129.153.48.1-254	129.153.48.255	255.255.255.0
C2	10.0.0.0	10.0.0.1-254	10.0.0.255	255.255.255.0
C3	10.0.1.0	10.0.1.1-254	10.0.1.255	255.255.255.0

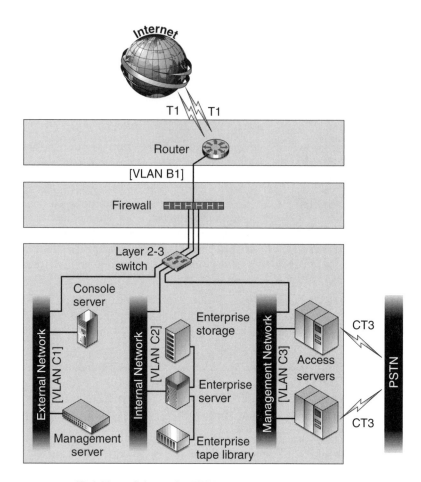

FIGURE 5-7 IP Address Schema for FijiNet

Planning Capacity for FijiNet

Based on the information we developed in earlier chapters about our sample ISP customer FijiNet, we model capacity planning by performing the following tasks:

1. "Estimate Software Capacity for FijiNet" on page 167

2. "Estimate Server Capacity for FijiNet" on page 186

3. "Estimate Network Capacity for FijiNet" on page 187

For each component, we provide the customized formula we used to estimate capacity based on FijiNet's requirements.

Estimate Software Capacity for FijiNet

Before planning for servers and network components, we perform capacity planning for software.

Refer to the following sections:
- "FijiNet Basic Services" on page 168
- "FijiNet Infrastructure Services" on page 175
- "FijiNet Operation and Management Services" on page 180
- "FijiNet Operating Environment" on page 184

FijiNet Basic Services

We estimate the capacity for basic services FijiNet plans to offer for their initial deployment: email, web, news, and FTP.

Refer to the following sections:

- "FijiNet Email Service" on page 168
- "FijiNet Web Service" on page 171
- "FijiNet News Service" on page 172
- "FijiNet FTP Service" on page 174

FijiNet Email Service

We determine the email storage and memory needed for FijiNet, as shown in TABLE 5-40 and TABLE 5-41.

TABLE 5-40   FijiNet: Estimating Storage for Email Service

Variable	Value	Description
T	10,000	Total number of subscribers
P_{act}	40%	Percentage of active email users
S_{ave}	25 KB	Average email message size
N_{rev}	20	Average email messages received per user per day
S_{msa}	$T \times P_{act} \times S_{ave} \times N_{rev}$	Average storage for active email users
S_{msp}	$20\% \times S_{msa}$	Average storage for email queue
S_{msm}	5 MB	Maximum email storage quota per subscriber

TABLE 5-40 FijiNet: Estimating Storage for Email Service *(Continued)*

Variable	Value	Description
S_{msq}	$20\% \times S_{msm}$	Maximum storage for email queue
S_{mss}	8 MB	Storage requirement for email software (sendmail, POP3, and IMAP4) and various plug-ins

$$S_{ms(proxy)} = S_{mss} = 8MB$$

$$S_{ms(relay)} = S_{msp} + S_{mss} = 405MB$$

$$S_{ms(mailstore)} = S_{msa} + S_{msp} + S_{mss} \approx 2.4GB$$

$$S_{ms(maximum)} = (T \times S_{msm}) + S_{msq} + S_{mss} \approx 60GB$$

TABLE 5-41 FijiNet: Estimating Memory for Email Service

Variable	Value	Description
T	10,000	Total number of subscribers
P_{con}	12.5%	Percentage of concurrency
P_{act}	40%	Percentage of active mail users
P_{pop}	90%	Percentage of POP users
P_{ima}	10%	Percentage of IMAP users
M_{msi}	1 MB	Memory footprint per IMAP connection
M_{msp}	200 KB	Memory footprint per POP connection

TABLE 5-41   FijiNet: Estimating Memory for Email Service *(Continued)*

Variable	Value	Description
$\mathbf{M}_{mst}$	300 KB	Memory footprint per SMTP connection
$\mathbf{M}_{msb}$	1 MB	Memory requirement for email server

$$M_{mp} = T \times P_{con} \times P_{act} \times P_{pop} \times M_{msp} = 90MB$$

$$M_{mi} = T \times P_{con} \times P_{act} \times P_{ima} \times M_{msi} = 50MB$$

$$M_{mt} = T \times P_{con} \times P_{act} \times M_{mst} = 150MB$$

$$M_{ms(proxy)} = M_{mp} + M_{mi} + M_{msb} = 141MB$$

$$M_{ms(relay)} = M_{mt} + M_{msb} = 151MB$$

$$M_{ms(mailstore)} = M_{mp} + M_{mi} + M_{mt} + M_{msb} \approx 291MB$$

FijiNet Web Service

We determine the web storage and memory needed for FijiNet, as shown in TABLE 5-42 and TABLE 5-43.

With 5 Mbytes quota per subscriber for web storage, we calculate that the maximum storage required is 60 Gbytes. However, planning for this amount is not realistic, nor it is economical. We recommend that storage planning be based on active users who have web pages. For FijiNet, we use an ISP average usage for the percentage of active users with web pages, and the average web storage per user.

TABLE 5-42   FijiNet: Estimating Storage for Web Service

Variable	Value	Description
T	10,000	Total number of subscribers
P_{act}	25%	Percentage of active users with web pages
S_{ave}	500 KB	Average web storage size per user
S_{wsa}	$T \times P_{act} \times S_{ave}$	Average storage for active users with web pages
S_{wsd}	$20\% \times S_{wsa}$	Average storage for web cache
S_{wsw}	5 MB	Maximum web storage quota per subscriber
S_{wsc}	$20\% (T \times S_{wsw})$	Maximum storage for web cache
S_{wss}	6 MB	Storage requirement for web software and various plug-ins

$$S_{ws(average)} = S_{wsa} + S_{wsd} + S_{wss} \approx 1.5GB$$

$$S_{ws(maximum)} = (T \times S_{wsw}) + S_{wsc} + S_{wss} \approx 60GB$$

For FijiNet, the peak number of HTTP connections is assumed to be equal to the number of concurrent users (12.5 percent), which is 1,250 HTTP operations per second. Also, our memory calculation for FijiNet is based on our plan to use an Apache web server.

Note – Resident memory is the sum of private memory and shared memory. All web processes share the same shared memory segment. Additional web processes forked require private memory; however, they do not require additional shared memory.

TABLE 5-43 FijiNet: Estimating Memory for Web Service

Variable	Value	Description
T	10,000	Total number of subscribers
P_{con}	12.5%	Percentage of concurrency
N_{web}	1	Number of web servers
N_{par}	1	Number of parent process
N_{pro}	5	Number of child processes (fork/exec model)
N_{con}	$T \times P_{con}$	Peak number of HTTP connections
M_{wsc}	10 KB	Memory footprint per HTTP connection
M_{wss}	2 MB	Memory footprint per child process (fork/exec model)

$$M_{wm(fork)} = (N_{web} \times (N_{par} + N_{pro}) \times M_{wss}) + (N_{con} \times M_{wsc}) = 24.5MB$$

FijiNet News Service

We determine the news storage and memory needed for FijiNet, as shown in TABLE 5-44 and TABLE 5-45. We base the calculation on one day of storage for news articles.

Note – If FijiNet wants to store news for more than one day, we would need to calculate the delta (rate of changes between expired and new articles) so that additional storage could be planned.

For FijiNet, there will be no downstream feeds, and there is only one upstream feed to FijiNet from a UseNet provider.

Memory footprint for news connection is similar to IMAP connection, where only message headers are downloaded. Message content is not downloaded unless specifically requested. Thus, we assume that approximately 1 Mbyte of memory is required per news connection. While this assumption might not be accurate, depending on the news server being used and the environment in question, it is sufficient for an initial estimate.

TABLE 5-44 FijiNet: Estimating Storage for News Service

Variable	Value	Description
S_{nsa}	300 GB (as of May 2001)	Storage requirement for daily news articles for a full feed
S_{nsh}	$10\% \times S_{nsa}$	Storage requirement for news spooler, history, and index
S_{nss}	25 MB	Storage requirement for news software

$$S_{ns} = S_{nsa} + S_{nsh} + S_{nss} \approx 330 GB$$

TABLE 5-45 FijiNet: Estimating Memory for News Service

Variable	Value	Description
T	10,000	Total number of subscribers
P_{con}	12.5%	Percentage of concurrency
P_{act}	10%	Percentage of active news users
M_{nss}	1 MB	Memory footprint per news server
N_{nco}	$T \times P_{con} \times P_{act}$	Peak number of news connection
M_{nco}	1 MB	Memory footprint per news connection

$$M_{nm} = M_{nss} + (N_{nco} \times M_{nco}) = 126 MB$$

FijiNet FTP Service

We determine the FTP storage and memory needed for FijiNet, as shown in TABLE 5-46 and TABLE 5-47.

For FTP spool, there is no fixed amount that must be set. The amount depends upon an ISP's environment. For FijiNet, we allocate approximately 15 percent of the average web storage (250 Mbytes) for FTP spool area. Depending on the environment, the FTP spool can be allocated to whatever amount is appropriate.

TABLE 5-46 FijiNet: Estimating Storage for FTP Service

Variable	Value	Description
S_{fss}	2 MB	Storage requirement for WU-FTP software
S_{fsu}	250 MB	Storage requirement for FTP spooler

$$S_{fs} = S_{fss} + S_{fsu} \approx 252MB$$

We estimate each FTP process to be approximately 400 Kbytes. A new process is spawned for every FTP session. While FTP service must be made available for content uploads, the service usage is minor compared to other basic services. For FijiNet, we assume that 10 concurrent FTP sessions are sufficient. This number can be set to an amount appropriate to the environment.

TABLE 5-47 FijiNet: Estimating Memory for FTP Service

Variable	Value	Description
M_{ftp}	400 KB	Memory footprint per FTP process
N_{ftp}	10	Number of concurrent FTP connections

$$M_{fs} = M_{ftp} \times N_{ftp} = 4MB$$

FijiNet Infrastructure Services

We estimate the capacity needed for infrastructure services: DNS, RADIUS, LDAP, DHCP, and NTP.

Refer to the following sections:

- "FijiNet DNS Service" on page 175
- "FijiNet RADIUS Service" on page 176
- "FijiNet LDAP Service" on page 177
- "FijiNet DHCP Service" on page 178
- "FijiNet NTP Service" on page 179

FijiNet DNS Service

We determine the DNS storage and memory needed for FijiNet, as shown in TABLE 5-48 and TABLE 5-49.

TABLE 5-48   FijiNet: Estimating Storage for DNS Service

Variable	Value	Description
S_{dns}	29 MB	Storage requirement for BIND/DNS software
S_{dnd}	1 MB	Storage requirement for BIND/DNS zone databases

$$S_{dn} = S_{dns} + S_{dnd} = 30MB$$

TABLE 5-49   FijiNet: Estimating Memory for DNS Service

Variable	Value	Description
M_{dns}	3 MB	Memory requirement for BIND v9 server
M_{zon}	1 KB	Memory requirement for BIND v9 server

$$M_{dn} = M_{dns} + M_{zon} \approx 3MB$$

FijiNet RADIUS Service

We determine the RADIUS storage and memory needed for FijiNet, as shown in TABLE 5-50 and TABLE 5-51.

On average, a RADIUS local database entry is approximately 1 Kbyte. Thus, the overall storage for RADIUS local database is negligible for FijiNet.

If a local database is maintained for RADIUS for authentication, approximately 10 Mbytes of storage is required for 10,000 users in addition to storage required for software.

For FijiNet, authentication is done by the directory server. Therefore, storage for RADIUS database is not required. However, some storage might be needed for the local database of system administration accounts. Note that storage for a local database of system administration accounts is negligible.

We estimate approximately 250 Mbytes for RADIUS logs initially. We recommend that FijiNet monitor RADIUS logs to determine the actual level of utilization.

TABLE 5-50 FijiNet: Estimating Storage for RADIUS Service

Variable	Value	Description
T	10,000	Total number of subscribers
S_{rse}	1 KB	Average size for a RADIUS database entry
S_{rsd}	$T \times S_{rse}$	Storage requirement for RADIUS database
S_{rss}	105 MB	Storage requirement for Steel-Belted RADIUS/SPE software
S_{rsl}	250 MB	Storage requirement for RADIUS log

$$S_{rs} = S_{rsd} + S_{rss} + S_{rsl} = 365MB$$

RADIUS does not utilize much memory; however, we advise that you adhere to the amount of memory recommended by a vendor. RADIUS does require storage for logs. How much storage is needed depends on how long logs are kept and the level of logging performed.

Based on a recommendation from Funk Software™, we estimate that 64 Mbytes of RAM is needed for RADIUS.

TABLE 5-51   FijiNet: Estimating Memory for RADIUS Service

Variable	Value	Description
M_{rss}	64 MB	Memory requirement for RADIUS server

$$M_{rs} \approx 64MB$$

FijiNet LDAP Service

We determine the directory storage and memory needed for FijiNet, as shown in TABLE 5-52 and TABLE 5-53.

Our memory estimate is based on the number of LDAP data interchange format (LDIF) entries in the database.

TABLE 5-52   FijiNet: Estimating Storage for Directory Service

Variable	Value	Description
T	10,000	Total number of subscribers
S_{dse}	10 KB	Average size for a directory database entry
S_{dsd}	$T \times S_{dse}$	Storage requirement for directory database
S_{dss}	2 GB	Storage requirement for directory software

$$S_{ds} = S_{dsd} + S_{dss} = 2.1GB$$

In general, memory calculation is based on the number of entries in the LDAP database. The following memory calculation for FijiNet is based on iPlanet recommendations.

- For 10,000 to 250,000 entries, use 2 Gbytes of disk and 256 Mbytes of RAM.
- For 250,000 to 1,000,000 entries, use 4 Gbytes of disk and 512 Mbytes of RAM.
- For 1,000,000+ entries, use 8 Gbytes of disk and 1 Gbyte of RAM.

Roughly 256 Mbytes of RAM is required for FijiNet, so we plan 256 Mbytes to 1 Gbyte of RAM for best performance on their production system.

TABLE 5-53   FijiNet: Estimating Memory for Directory Service

Variable	Value	Description
T	10,000	Total number of subscribers
M_{dss}	256 MB	Memory requirement for directory server

$$M_{ds} = M_{dss} \approx 256MB$$

For more information on LDAP, refer to *Solaris and LDAP Naming Services - Deploying LDAP in the Enterprise*, Tom Bialaski and Michael Haines, Sun Microsystems, Inc., 2001.

FijiNet DHCP Service

We determine the DHCP storage and memory needed for FijiNet, as shown in TABLE 5-54 and TABLE 5-55. On average, each DHCP entry in the database is approximately 1 Kbyte. On average, memory footprint for each DHCP lease is approximately 256 bytes.

TABLE 5-54   FijiNet: Estimating Storage for DHCP Service

Variable	Value	Description
T	10,000	Total number of subscribers
S_{dhe}	1 KB	Average size for a DHCP database entry
S_{dhd}	$T \times S_{dhe}$	Storage requirement for DHCP database
S_{dhs}	1 MB	Storage requirement for DHCP software

$$S_{dh} = S_{dhd} + S_{dhs} \approx 10MB$$

TABLE 5-55   FijiNet: Estimating Memory for DHCP Service

Variable	Value	Description
T	10,000	Total number of subscribers
P_{con}	12.5%	Percentage of concurrency
N_{dhc}	$T \times P_{con}$	Peak number of DHCP connections
M_{dhl}	220 bytes	Memory footprint per DHCP lease
M_{dhd}	$N_{dhc} \times M_{dhl}$	Memory requirement for DHCP leases
M_{dhs}	736 KB	Memory requirement for DHCP server

$$M_{dh} = M_{dhd} + M_{dhs} \approx 1MB$$

FijiNet NTP Service

We determine the NTP storage and memory needed for FijiNet, as shown in TABLE 5-56 and TABLE 5-57.

There is no memory sizing available for NTP. The resident memory (sum of shared and private memory) is approximately 2128 Kbytes. The shared memory is 1272 Kbytes, and the private memory is 856 Kbytes. This memory estimate is based on NTP server running on Solaris 8 Operating Environment (Solaris 8 OE).

TABLE 5-56   FijiNet: Estimating Storage for NTP Service

Variable	Value	Description
S_{nts}	2 MB	Storage requirement for NTP software

$$S_{ns} = S_{nts} \approx 2MB$$

TABLE 5-57   FijiNet: Estimating Memory for NTP Service

Variable	Value	Description
$\mathbf{M}_{nts}$	2128 KB	Memory footprint for NTP server

$$M_{ns} = M_{nts} \approx 2MB$$

FijiNet Operation and Management Services

We estimate the capacity needed for operation and management services for backing up data, providing security via firewalls, and logging.

Refer to the following sections:

- "FijiNet Backup Service" on page 181
- "FijiNet Firewall Service" on page 182
- "FijiNet Log Service" on page 183

Note – Operation and management services are beyond the scope of this book. Many resources are available, such as *OSS Essential: Support System Solutions for Service Providers*, Kornel Terplan, John Wiley and Sons, Inc., 2001.

FijiNet Backup Service

We determine the backup storage and memory needed for FijiNet, as shown in TABLE 5-58 and TABLE 5-59.

For FijiNet, we estimate 1 Gbyte storage total for Solstice Backup software and indexes, with a 6 to 12 month browsing policy.

For memory, we estimate that approximately 256 Mbytes of RAM is required for backup software.

TABLE 5-58 FijiNet: Estimating Storage for Backup Service

Variable	Value	Description
S_{bsi}	900 MB	Storage requirement for indexes
S_{bss}	75 MB	Storage requirement for backup software

$$S_{bs} = S_{bsi} + S_{bss} \approx 1\,GB$$

TABLE 5-59 FijiNet: Estimating Memory for Backup Service

Variable	Value	Description
M_{bsd}	256 MB	Memory requirement for backup server

$$M_{bs} = M_{bsd} = 256MB$$

FijiNet Firewall Service

We determine the firewall storage and memory needed for FijiNet, as shown in TABLE 5-60 and TABLE 5-61.

We estimate 1 Gbyte is needed for firewall log storage. The size of the firewall log depends on the type of logging and how much log is generated. We recommend that FijiNet monitor the storage for firewall and adjust it accordingly.

TABLE 5-60 FijiNet: Estimating Storage for Firewall Service

Variable	Value	Description
S_{fws}	0 MB	Storage requirement for firewall software, objects, and policy
S_{fwl}	1 GB	Storage requirement for firewall logs

$$S_{fw} = S_{fws} + S_{fwl} \approx 1 GB$$

TABLE 5-61 FijiNet: Estimating Memory for Firewall Service

Variable	Value	Description
M_{fws}	12 MB	Memory requirement for firewall

$$M_{fw} = M_{fws} = 128MB$$

FijiNet Log Service

We determine the log storage and memory needed for FijiNet, as shown in TABLE 5-62 and TABLE 5-63.

For FijiNet, we estimate that approximately 250 Mbytes is required for spooling daily logs, and 750 Mbytes for archiving logs for 12 months. Logs older than 12 months are rotated and recycled.We recommend that storage for log archive be monitored and storage adjusted, where applicable.

The amount of storage required depends on the number of systems logged, how much logging is generated by each system, type of logs (normal or debug), and how long logs are kept.

TABLE 5-62 FijiNet: Estimating Storage for Log Service

Variable	Value	Description
S_{lss}	250 MB	Storage requirement for log spooler
S_{lsa}	1 GB	Storage requirement for log archive

$$S_{ls} = N_{lss} \times S_{lsa} \approx 1,25GB$$

TABLE 5-63 FijiNet: Estimating Memory for Log Service

Variable	Value	Description
M_{lss}	32 MB	Memory requirement for log server

$$M_{ls} = M_{lss} \approx 32MB$$

FijiNet Operating Environment

We model the capacity planning for the file system layout for system disk, file system layout for data, and system disk storage. Refer to the following sections:

- "FijiNet Storage" on page 184
- "FijiNet Filesystem Layout for System Disk" on page 185
- "FijiNet Filesystem Layout for Data" on page 186

FijiNet Storage

We determine the capacity for the operating environment (OE), swap space, log archive, and applications, as shown in TABLE 5-64.

Our calculation shows that a system disk with a capacity of 6 Gbytes or more is required. For FijiNet, a 9-Gbyte disk (10,000 RPM) is sufficient for all system disks.

TABLE 5-64 FijiNet: Estimating Storage for System Disk

Variable	Value	Description
S_{oss}	2.4 GB	Storage requirement for OE
S_{swp}	At least $2 \times$ RAM	Storage requirement for swap space
S_{osl}	2 GB	Storage requirement for log archive
S_{app}	1 GB	Storage requirement for native and third-party applications

$$S_{os} = S_{oss} + S_{swp} + S_{osl} + S_{app} \approx 6GB$$

FijiNet Filesystem Layout for System Disk

We plan the file system layout for the system disk, as shown in TABLE 5-65.

TABLE 5-65   Filesystem Layout for System Disk

Partition	Filesystem	Description
0	/	Root partition
1	swap	Swap partition
2	-	Reserved (entire disk)
3 to 7	(empty)	Available for future use

For every system, we partition the system disk into two partitions: root and swap. We could partition /usr, /var, /export, and /opt as individual file systems. However, for better storage management and utilization, we use a single root file system and collapse everything under root. This approach has no negative impact on performance.

Note – If we want to use VxVM, we must reserve partitions 3 and 4 for public and private regions for VxVM database, to encapsulate the system disk. In addition, two cylinders must be reserved at the end of the disk. Most likely, we will use Solstice DiskSuite™ logical volume management, because it is part of Solaris 8 Operating Environment.

For system availability, we use two internal disks. For consistency and ease of administration, we use disks of the same size/type. One disk is the system disk and the other is a spare disk. For consistency, we partition both disks exactly the same. To better utilize the spare disk, we can configure the system to take advantage of the swap partition on the spare disk. Thus, the primary swap partition resides on the system disk and the secondary swap partition is on the spare disk.

FijiNet Filesystem Layout for Data

We plan the file system layout for the system disk, as shown in TABLE 5-66.

TABLE 5-66   Filesystem Layout for Data

Variable	Value	Description
/data	See capacity planning section	Data (MailStores, web contents, news articles, etc.)

It is important to separate data from the system disk, so that FijiNet can export and import data, for example, in case of system failure. Depending on FijiNet's system and its purpose, /data file system can be created for data such as MailStore, web content, news articles, etc. For front-end systems such as web servers, no data resides on the system. Front-end servers only handle incoming transactions and interface with user requests. We can place /data on back-end servers on the content network.

We recommend that FijiNet configure /data file system with a logical volume, for example, Solstice DiskSuite, so that disk space can grow automatically. We would also configure RAID 0+1 (redundant array of independent disks, stripping and mirroring) to provide data protection against disk failure.

Estimate Server Capacity for FijiNet

After formulating the software capacity planning, we determine what kind of servers are appropriate for FijiNet, as shown in TABLE 5-67.

TABLE 5-67   FijiNet: Estimating Server Sizing

Type	Size	Specification
Front-end server	Small	Uniprocessor (1 CPU, < 1 GB RAM)
Back-end server	Medium	Multiprocessor (< 4 CPU, < 4 GB RAM)

Estimate Network Capacity for FijiNet

We estimate capacity planning for FijiNet's infrastructure so that there is enough bandwidth to support local traffic loads, and that enough modems and high-speed trunks are available for Internet connectivity and dial-up access.

Refer to the following sections:

- "FijiNet Bandwidth" on page 187
- "FijiNet Modems and High-Speed Trunks" on page 188
- "FijiNet Network Components" on page 190

FijiNet Bandwidth

Using industry figures and FijiNet's requirements, we determine the ports needed for bandwidth, as shown in TABLE 5-68.

TABLE 5-68 FijiNet: Estimating Network Bandwidth for Users

Variable	Value	Description
T	10,000	Total number of subscribers
$\mathbf{P}_{con}$	12.5%	Percentage of concurrent users
$\mathbf{B}_{usr}$	2 Kbps	Average network bandwidth consumption per user
$\mathbf{B}_{the}$	10 Mbps (10BaseT) 100 Mbps (100BaseT or FE) 1000 Mbps (1000BaseT or GE)	Theoretical network bandwidth
$\mathbf{B}_{sat}$	40% × $\mathbf{B}_{the}$	Network bandwidth saturation point
$\mathbf{B}_{ove}$	10% × $\mathbf{B}_{the}$	Network bandwidth overhead

$$B_{(100BaseT)} = (T \times P_{con} \times B_{usr}) + B_{ove} = 12.5 Mbps$$

FijiNet Modems and High-Speed Trunks

Using FijiNet's projected subscriber base, we estimate the total number of modems to support concurrent users. From the modem calculation, we then estimate the number of high-speed trunks needed.

Refer to the following sections:

- "FijiNet Modems" on page 188
- "FijiNet High-Speed Trunks" on page 188

FijiNet Modems

We estimate that 1,250 modems are required initially for FijiNet's architecture, as shown in TABLE 5-69.

TABLE 5-69   FijiNet: Estimating Modems for Dial-Up Access

Variable	Value	Description
T	10,000	Total number of subscribers
P_{con}	12.5%	Percentage of concurrent users

$$N_M = T \times P_{con} = 1250$$

This result is from the assumption of 1:8 modem-to-user ratio.

FijiNet High-Speed Trunks

We determine the links needed for Internet connectivity and dial-up access, as shown in TABLE 5-70 and TABLE 5-71.

We estimate that 1.62xT1 is required for FijiNet's Internet connectivity. Thus, two T1 interfaces are required. Only a single 10/100 Mbit/sec is required for LAN connection to the firewall. We recommend that FijiNet plan for two LAN ports, so that redundant routers and switches can be added later to provide higher availability. (The additional LAN port is necessary to facilitate redundant connections.)

TABLE 5-70 FijiNet: Estimating Links for Internet Connectivity

Variable	Value	Description
T	10,000	Total number of subscribers
P_{con}	12.5%	Percentage of concurrent users
B_{usr}	2 Kbps	Average bandwidth consumption per user
L	T1=1.544 Mbps T3=44.736 Mbps	Bandwidth supported per high-speed trunk

$$N_L = \frac{T \times P_{con} \times B_{usr}}{L} = 1.62 \times T1 = 0.06 \times T3$$

TABLE 5-71 FijiNet: Estimating Links for Dial-Up Access

Variable	Value	Estimation
T	10,000	Total number of subscribers
P_{con}	12.5%	Percentage of concurrent users
C	24 channels per T1 672 channels per CT3	Number of channels supported per high-speed trunk

$$N_L = \frac{T \times P_{con}}{C} \approx 52.08 \times T1 = 1.86 \times CT3$$

FijiNet Network Components

Based on the FijiNet network design diagram in FIGURE 5-6, we identify the network components needed for FijiNet's architecture. For each component, we decide whether to use a router or switch. Next, we estimate the port capacity for routers, switches, and consoles.

Refer to the following sections:

- "FijiNet Routers" on page 190
- "FijiNet Switches" on page 191
- "FijiNet Console Servers" on page 192

FijiNet Routers

We determine the ports needed for routers, as shown in TABLE 5-72. We need two WAN interfaces for FijiNet. Each interface will be connected to a T1 high-speed trunk, so that 1,250 concurrent users are supported (based upon the estimates for link connectivity in TABLE 5-70).

Only one 10/100 Mbit/sec port is needed for FijiNet; however, two ports are required for redundancy to achieve high availability as the architecture scales to support projected growth of 100,000 subscribers.

TABLE 5-72 FijiNet: Estimating Ports for Routers

Variable	Value	Description
N_{wan}	2 (T1)	Number of WAN interface slots (T1, E1, etc.)
N_{lan}	2 (10/100 Mbps)	Number of fixed LAN ports (10/100 Mbps)

$$P_R = N_{wan} + N_{lan} = 4$$

FijiNet Switches

For FijiNet, a minimum of 8 network ports is required. In addition, we are planning for 50 percent overhead for immediate growth. Thus, a total of 12 ports is needed (see TABLE 5-73), and an L2 switch for FijiNet's initial environment. As FijiNet grows toward 100,000 subscribers, multiple switches can be cascaded to aggregate a higher port density.

TABLE 5-73   FijiNet: Estimating Network Ports for Switches

Variable	Value	Description
N_{ser}	1 enterprise server 1 management server	Number of servers connected to the switch (mail relays, mail proxies, web servers, application servers, DNS servers, etc.)
N_{apl}	3 firewall interfaces 2 access servers 1 console server	Number of network appliances connected to the switch (firewalls, load balancers, cache engines, IDS sensors, console servers, access servers, etc.)
N_{adm}	0	Number of network ports required for administrative purposes (trunking, heartbeats, failover, uplink, etc.)
N_{ove}	4 (50% overhead)	Number of network ports required for immediate growth

$$P_S = N_{ser} + N_{apl} + N_{adm} + N_{ove} = 12$$

FijiNet Console Servers

For FijiNet, we need a console server with a minimum of 7 ports to support network devices and servers. With the addition of overhead for immediate growth, a total of 10 ports is required, as shown in TABLE 5-74.

TABLE 5-74   FijiNet: Estimating Ports for Console Server

Variable	Value	Description
N_{ser}	1 enterprise server 1 management server	Number of servers connected to the console server (mail relays, mail proxies, web servers, application servers, DNS servers, etc.)
N_{apl}	1 firewall 2 access servers 1 router 1 switch	Number of network appliances connected to the console server (firewalls, load balancers, cache engines, IDS sensors, access servers, routers, switches, etc.)
N_{ove}	3 (50%)	Number of console ports required for immediate growth

$$P_S = N_{ser} + N_{apl} + N_{ove} = 10$$

## CHAPTER 6

Selecting Components

This chapter provides general guidelines for selecting software, server, and network components for an architecture design. As part of this chapter, we provide tables listing commonly used commercial and open source products appropriate for ISP infrastructures.

Note – Product versions change and new products are released; therefore, the products listed in this chapter are not comprehensive. We list a sampling of products from various vendors to give you an idea of how to select products that meet your ISP's requirements.

This chapter contains the following topics:

Selecting Software

Based upon the requirements you arrived at in Chapter 2, select the applications and operating software appropriate for your services and the underlying operating environment (OE) and operating platform.

- "Choose Software for Basic Services" on page 195
- "Choose Software for Value-Added Services" on page 198
- "Choose Software for Infrastructure Services" on page 200
- "Choose Software for Operation and Management Services" on page 204
- "Choose an Operating Environment" on page 205

Tip – Identify and select the software for each service first, before selecting hardware. Limitations and oversights typically result when hardware is selected before software.

Use the following guidelines when selecting software:

- *Available solutions* – Does a vendor offer a commercial off-the-shelf product? If so, does the product meet all or most of the requirements without a complex development or integration effort?
- *Success stories* – Research the references for successful implementations. How successful are the implementations? Is there continuing development of the product? Is the product designed well?
- *Expertise in market* – Does the vendor have a good track record for working with customers in this market segment? Does the vendor understand the business requirements for the market? Does the product support the required features and functions?
- *Global presence* – Does the vendor have a global presence? Is the product supported in other languages? Does the vendor partner with system integrators?
- *Support* – Does the vendor provide support after the purchase and throughout the product life cycle? Does the vendor provide training to make customers self-sufficient?
- *Integration* – Are the APIs available for integration with other products? Is the product interoperable with other products and/or operating platforms?
- *Scalability* – Does the application scale to support a large number of subscribers (from hundreds of thousands to millions)?
- *Performance* – Does the vendor conduct benchmarks to test and demonstrate the product's performance?

- *Manageability* – Is the product manageable, yet flexible? Is the web interface supported for ease of management? Is this interface integrated with the management server?

- *Internationalization* – Does the vendor provide the product in all the languages that you need?

- *Quick time-to-market* – How long does it usually take for implementation?

Choose Software for Basic Services

To support basic services, select software for the following:

- "Mail Servers" on page 195
- "Web Servers" on page 196
- "News Servers" on page 197
- "FTP Servers" on page 198

Mail Servers

TABLE 6-1 lists popular commercial and open source mail servers. The product sendmail® is available both as a commercial product and as open source.

TABLE 6-1   Mail Servers

Name	Vendor
iPlanet Messaging Server (iMS)	iPlanet
Openwave® Email mx (formerly Intermail®)	Openwave Systems Inc. (formerly Software.com)
sendmail	sendmail.com, open source (sendmail.org)
Qmail®	Open source (qmail.org)

Commercial mail servers usually have post office protocol/Internet mail access protocol (POP/IMAP) servers integrated with the enterprise software. Open source sendmail and Qmail do not have POP/IMAP server integrated. If you choose a mail server that does not have POP/IMAP servers built-in, choose one of the POP/IMAP servers listed in TABLE 6-2.

TABLE 6-2   POP/IMAP Servers

Name	Vendor
UW IMAP	open source (University of Washington)
Cyrus	open source (Carnegie Mellon University)
Qpopper™	open source (Eudora/Qualcomm)
Pop3d	open source (gnu.org)

Web Servers

TABLE 6-3 lists web servers. Some are designed based on a fork/exec model, while others are designed based on a threaded model. Refer to `http://www.acme.com/software/thttpd/benchmarks.html` for more information about web servers and their associated models. Although the data are out dated, they are informative.

TABLE 6-3   Web Servers

Name	Vendor
iPlanet Web Server	iPlanet
Apache	open source (apache.org)
WebSphere®	IBM

Note – iPlanet Web Server is the web server commonly chosen for commercial solutions. It provides powerful web software essential for enterprises moving their business to the Internet. By offering high-performance, reliability, and manageability, iPlanet Web Server solves business-critical needs of some of the world's busiest web sites. iPlanet Web Server enables rapid development and deployment of web-based applications that can enhance communication, streamline processes, and reduce costs.

News Servers

TABLE 6-4 lists news servers. Typhoon™ is a carrier-class UseNet solution that scales to support thousands of simultaneous readers accessing hundreds of gigabytes of news, while keeping up with multiple full UseNet feeds.

Breeze™ News Server is a perfect choice for small- to medium-sized ISPs on a budget. It has a 1/2 Terabyte spool capacity and can support up to 50 concurrent news clients per license.

Breeze™ and Typhoon are considered the best commercial news servers by many ISPs, and InterNetNews (INN) is considered the best open source news server.

If your ISP is outsourcing news service, choose a UseNet provider. TABLE 6-5 lists some UseNet providers. Their service offerings and pricing varies; contact them for information.

TABLE 6-4   News Servers

Name	Vendor
Breeze	Openwave
Typhoon	Software.com (formerly bCandid)
INN	open source (isc.org)
DNews	NetWin

TABLE 6-5   UseNet Providers

Name	Vendor
Supernews®	CriticalPath
NewsGuy® News Services®	NewsGuy.com
Randori News	Randori News
NewsFeeds.com	NewsFeed.com

FTP Servers

TABLE 6-6 lists FTP (file transfer protocol) servers. UNIX operating systems usually include one or more FTP servers. Many other popular FTP servers are available. After features and functionality, the most important consideration in choosing an FTP server is LDAP-compatibility.

Select a server that supports LDAP for centralized authentication. The most commonly used FTP server by ISPs is WU-FTP. Both WU-FTP and ProFTPD are LDAP-enabled. Both of these FTP servers are bundled with Solaris 8 Operating Environment (Solaris 8 OE).

TABLE 6-6 FTP Servers

Name	Vendor
WU-FTP (part of Solaris 8 OE)	open source (University of Washington)
ProFTPD (part of Solaris 8 OE)	open source (proftpd.org)
NcFTPd	NcFTP Software

Choose Software for Value-Added Services

What constitutes value-added services varies among ISPs and changes quickly as competitors follow leaders. Samples of value-added services are calendar, address book, search engine, short messaging service (SMS), IR chat (IRC), and WebMail.

If your ISP identified value-added services, choose software to meet the customer's requirements.

If an ISP plans to roll out value-added services within the next 12 months, select appropriate software and make recommendations to the customer for planning purposes.

For guidelines in choosing software for value-added services, refer to the list under "Selecting Software" on page 194.

To support value-added services, select software for the following:

- "Application Servers" on page 199
- "Database Servers" on page 199

Application Servers

TABLE 6-7 lists application servers for value-added services. Contact the vendors for more information on product features and pricing.

TABLE 6-7   Application Servers

Name	Vendor
iPlanet Application Server (iAS)	iPlanet
BEA® WebLogic®	BEA
Vignette®	Vignette
PeopleSoft	PeopleSoft

Database Servers

Database servers are usually only required for large-scale environments. TABLE 6-8 lists database server vendors. Check with vendors for features, performance, pricing, and other information.

TABLE 6-8   Database Servers

Name	Vendor
Oracle 9i™	Oracle
IBM® DB2®	IBM
IBM Informix® OnLine	IBM (formerly Informix)
Sybase™ Adaptive Server™	Sybase, Inc.

Choose Software for Infrastructure Services

To support infrastructure services, select software for the following:

- "Domain Name System (DNS) Servers" on page 200
- "Lightweight Directory Access Protocol (LDAP) Servers" on page 201
- "Dynamic Host Configuration Protocol (DHCP) Servers" on page 202
- "Remote Access Dial-In User Service (RADIUS) Servers" on page 202
- "Network Time Protocol (NTP) Servers" on page 203

Domain Name System (DNS) Servers

TABLE 6-9 lists domain name system (DNS) servers. Berkeley Internet name domain (BIND) has been the *de facto* standard for domain name services, and is freely available from Internet Software Consortium (ISC). Also, commercial solutions are available for domain name service, such as Check Point Meta IP™ and Shadow IPserver™ from Efficient Networks™ (formerly Network TeleSystems). Check with vendors for product features, performance, and pricing.

Tip – Be aware of performance differences in BIND versions, which may affect your decision about the version that best suits your architecture design.

BIND v8 is single-threaded, while v9 is multithreaded. Note that our initial results found that BIND v9 may not scale linearly with multiprocessor systems. On the same system architecture, performance for BIND v9 is almost identical for a uniprocessor versus a multiprocessor system.

The three primary factors that affect BIND performance are processor speed, system board speed, and RAM. Processor speed has the greatest effect on BIND performance. RAM has the least effect.

The major design trade-offs between BIND v8 and v9 are performance and functionality. Refer to Appendix F for a DNS benchmark of Sun Enterprise™ servers.

TABLE 6-9   DNS Servers

Name	Vendor
BIND v8	open source (isc.org)
BIND v9	open source (isc.org)
MetaIP	Checkpoint
Shadow IPserver	Efficient Networks (formerly Network TeleSystems)

Lightweight Directory Access Protocol (LDAP) Servers

TABLE 6-10 lists lightweight directory access protocol (LDAP) solutions.

TABLE 6-10   LDAP Servers

Name	Vendor
iPlanet Directory Server (iDS)	iPlanet
Novell® eDirectory® Server	Novell
OpenLDAP℠	open source (openldap.org)
Active Directory™	Microsoft

Dynamic Host Configuration Protocol (DHCP) Servers

TABLE 6-11 lists dynamic host configuration protocol (DHCP) servers. There are many DHCP software products available, and the following table lists only the most common ones. Most OEs, such as Solaris 8 OE, have DHCP integrated. If you select an OE that does not have DHCP server integrated with the operating system, select a DHCP server from the following table.

TABLE 6-11   DHCP Servers

Name	Vendor
DHCP	open source (isc.org)
MetaIP	Checkpoint
Shadow IPserver	Efficient Networks
IOS® DHCP	Cisco Systems

Remote Access Dial-In User Service (RADIUS) Servers

TABLE 6-12 lists remote access dial-in user service (RADIUS) servers. When choosing a RADIUS server, select one that is LDAP-enabled. All of the RADIUS servers in the following table are LDAP-enabled.

TABLE 6-12   RADIUS Servers

Name	Vendor
Steel-Belted RADIUS	Funk Software
NAVISRADIUS™	Lucent Technologies
AAA RADIUS Server	Interlink Networks
freRADIUS	open source (freRADIUS)

Network Time Protocol (NTP) Servers

TABLE 6-13 lists network time protocol (NTP) servers. Note that Xntpd software is part of Solaris 8 OE.

For a list of public NTP servers, refer to:

    http://www.eecis.udel.edu/~mills/ntp/servers.html.

For a comprehensive list of hardware and software solutions for NTP, refer to:

    http://www.eecis.udel.edu/~ntp.

TABLE 6-13   NTP Servers

Name	Vendor
Xntpd	open source (University of Delaware)
Præcis™ Cntp	EndRun Technologies LLC
CoBox®	Lantronix

Choose Software for Operation and Management Services

To support management services, select software for the following servers:

- "Backup Servers" on page 204
- "System Management Servers" on page 204

Note – Detailed coverage of operation and management processes required are beyond the scope of this book.

Backup Servers

There are many backup products available; however, the solutions in TABLE 6-14 are commonly used for large-scale infrastructures and service providers.

TABLE 6-14   Backup Servers

Name	Vendor
Solstice Backup	Sun Microsystems
Legato Networker®	Legato
NetBackup products	VERITAS

System Management Servers

TABLE 6-15 lists commercial products for system management.

TABLE 6-15   Management Software

Name	Vendor
Sun Management Center (SunMC)	Sun Microsystems
Tivoli	Tivoli
hp OpenView®	Hewlett-Packard (HP)
PATROL by BMC Software, Best/1	BMC

TABLE 6-15 Management Software *(Continued)*

Name	Vendor
Netcool®	MicroMuse
TeamQuest® Performance Software	TeamQuest
BMC Patrol	BMC Software

Choose an Operating Environment

For Internet infrastructure, UNIX is predominantly used. There are many UNIX flavors available from vendors; TABLE 6-16 lists the most common. They range from Solaris (Sun Microsystems) to Linux® (open source). Approximately 65 percent of all Internet servers are Sun Enterprise servers, running Solaris Operating Environment (Solaris OE).

TABLE 6-16 Operating Environments for Service Providers

Operating Environment	Vendor
Solaris	Sun Microsystems
AIX®	IBM
HP-UX™	Hewlett-Packard (HP)
Compaq True64™ UNIX	Compaq
Linux (Red Hat®, Slackware®, Caldera®, Corel®, Debian™, Mandrake™, SuSE®, etc.)	open source (linux.org)
BSD (FreeBSD, NetBSD™, OpenBSD)	open source (bsd.org)

Note – For a list of Linux distributors, refer to `http://www.linux.org/dist/english.html`.

We purposely omitted a section on choosing the operating platform, because it is essentially the underlying network and servers that support the OE.

Selecting Servers

After selecting software, select the server components. Choose servers that support the OE and services in such a manner that components integrate to deliver the desired reliability, availability, scalability, and performance as in your architectural model arrived at in Chapter 3.

- "Determine Server Types" on page 206
- "Choose Enterprise Servers" on page 207
- "Choose Storage Equipment" on page 207

Determine Server Types

To support services, determine server type and tier for each class of server: front-end servers, mid-range servers, and back-end servers. TABLE 6-17 lists servers, specifications, and associated tiers.

TABLE 6-17 Server Types and Tiers

Type	Specification	Associated Tier
Front-end	Uniprocessor (1 CPU, ≤1 GB RAM)	DMZ and services networks
Mid-size	Multiprocessor (≤ 4 CPU, ≤ 4 GB RAM)	Application, backup, and management networks
Back-end	Multiprocessor (≥ 4 CPU, ≥ 4 GB RAM)	Content network

Choose Enterprise Servers

To support services, select enterprise servers. TABLE 6-18 lists enterprise servers.

TABLE 6-18 Enterprise Servers

Name	Vendor
Sun Enterprise servers	Sun Microsystems
HP Enterprise servers	Hewlett-Packard (HP)
IBM Enterprise servers	International Business Machines (IBM)
Compaq Enterprise servers	Compaq

Choose Storage Equipment

To support backup, recovery, and storage services, select hardware for the following:

- Data storage
- Tape libraries

Data Storage

TABLE 6-19 lists storage solutions. Key features to consider when choosing storage are the following:

- Scalability (storage capacity)
- Availability (multipathing, alternate pathing, redundant hardware controllers, redundant power supplies, hot-swap disks)
- Performance (UltraSCSI, Fibre Channel, disk access speed)
- Manageability (rack-mountable, FRU components)

Most storage arrays used for ISP environments are high-performance RAID with UltraSCSI (40 MB/s) or Fibre Channel (200 MB/s full-duplex) support.

Disk drives used in a storage array are usually high-speed 10,000 RPM drives. Some storage arrays have an integrated hardware-RAID controller, while other storage arrays rely on a server's RAID software.

When selecting the appropriate type of storage for an application, it is important to understand the nature of the application and its needs, for example, read-intensive, write-intensive, high I/O rate, etc. FIGURE 6-1 shows sample services and characteristics. For your ISP, determine which applications require fast disk access for storage.

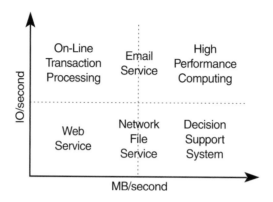

FIGURE 6-1 Sample Application Characteristics

TABLE 6-19 Data Storage

Name	Vendor
Sun StorEdge™	Sun Microsystems
Hitachi® SAN	Hitachi SAN Technology Laboratory
MetaStor® SAN	LSI Logic Corporation
EMC® Networked Storage	EMC

Tape Library

Look for the following key features when selecting an enterprise tape library:

- *Reliability* – Tape drives are moving components within tape libraries and usually the first components to fail. The reliability of the tape library directly correlates to how reliable the internal tape drives are.

- *Manageability* – Management interface, heterogeneous client support, technical support, etc. are important to manage large-scale environments.

- *Functionality* – Product features supported are important in choosing a product, for example, compression rate, tape drive read/write speed, number of slots, media types, indexes, snap-shot image, parallelism, etc.

- *Scalability* – The library permits adding backup servers and/or storage nodes to back up a larger volume of data.

TABLE 6-20 lists tape libraries.

TABLE 6-20 Tape Library

Name	Vendor
Sun StorEdge libraries	Sun Microsystems
Exabyte® autoloaders	Exabyte
DynaTek autoloaders	DynaTek
Quantum® tape libraries	ATL Products (subsidiary of Quantum Corporation)
Qualstar® tape libraries	Qualstar

Selecting Network Components

After selecting software and servers, select the networking components. Choose equipment that supports the OE, services, and servers in such a manner that all components work together to deliver the desired reliability, availability, scalability, and performance as in your architectural model arrived at in Chapter 3.

To support networking services, select equipment for the following:

- "Choose Routers and Switches" on page 210
- "Choose Load Balancers" on page 211
- "Choose Firewalls" on page 211
- "Choose Intrusion Detection System (IDS)" on page 212
- "Choose Console Servers" on page 213
- "Choose Network Access Servers" on page 213

Choose Routers and Switches

TABLE 6-21 lists major networking vendors in the telecommunication and service provider market. These vendors produce a wide range of networking products, including routers and switches.

TABLE 6-21 Networking Vendors

Vendor	Web Site
Foundry Networks®	http://www.foundrynet.com
Cisco Systems	http://www.cisco.com
Extreme Networks®	http://www.extremenetworks.com
Alteon WebSystems™ (Nortel)	http://www.alteonwebsystems.com
Nortel Networks™	http://www.nortel.com
Arrowpoint™ Communication	http://www.arrowpoint.com
Lucent Technologies®	http://www.lucent.com
Juniper Networks™	http://www.juniper.net

Choose Load Balancers

TABLE 6-22 lists some load balancers. They can be software-based, hardware-based, or switch-based solutions. For large-scale infrastructures with heavy traffic, switch-based balancers are strongly recommended for performance and scalability and are often used to minimize single points-of-failure.

TABLE 6-22   Load Balancers

Name	Vendor
Resonate Central Dispatch® and Resonate Global Dispatch® (software)	Resonate
RainWall™ (software)	Rainfinity
Local/Distributed Director (appliance)	Cisco Systems
Big-IP® and 3-DNS® (appliances)	F5 Networks
ServerIron™ (switch)	Foundry Networks
ACEdirector (switch)	Alteon Websystems

Choose Firewalls

TABLE 6-23 lists firewalls. Many commercial solutions are available today, and they have matured and are very comparable based upon performance and support features. A firewall can be either software-based or hardware-based. For specific features and pricing, contact the vendors.

TABLE 6-23   Firewalls

Name	Vendor
Check Point™ Firewall-1® (software)	Check Point Software Technologies, Inc.
Gauntlet® Firewall (software)	Network Associates, Inc. (formerly PGP Security)
Raptor® Firewall (software)	Symantec

TABLE 6-23   Firewalls *(Continued)*

Name	Vendor
PIX® Firewall (appliance)	Cisco Systems
VPN Firewall Brick™ (appliance)	Lucent Technologies
Firebox® (appliance)	Watchguard Technologies

Choose Intrusion Detection System (IDS)

TABLE 6-24 lists intrusion detection system (IDS) vendors. An IDS solution can be software-based, hardware-based, or a hybrid. An IDS solution can be expensive, and is usually not applicable to small environments such as those providing services only to residential subscribers. An IDS is more applicable to large-scale environments or environments providing services to business subscribers where security, confidentiality, and service level agreements (SLAs) are a high priority.

TABLE 6-24   Intrusion Detection Systems

Name	Vendor
NetRecon®, NetProwler™ (network-based)	Axent Technologies, a subsidiary of Symantec
Secure IDS (network-based)	Cisco Systems
Real Secure™ (hybrid)	Internet Security Systems (ISS), Inc.
Cybercop™ (hybrid)	Network Associates Technology, Inc.
Network Flight Recorder™ (network-based)	Network Flight Recorder, Inc.

Choose Console Servers

TABLE 6-25 lists console servers. Choose console servers that have enough port density to support the number of servers you want to manage.

TABLE 6-25   Console Servers

Name	Vendor
Access Server	Cisco Systems
Console Server™	Lantronix, Inc.
Secure Console Server™	Lantronix, Inc.
Perle™ Console Server	Perle Systems, Inc.

Choose Network Access Servers

TABLE 6-26 lists network access servers (NASs). A NAS is only required when an ISP is offering dial-up access to subscribers.

TABLE 6-26   Access Servers

Name	Vendor
Network Access Servers	Cisco Systems
Remote Access Servers	Lucent Technologies
Nortel™ Access Servers	Nortel Networks Limited Corporation
SuperStack® 3	3COM® Corporation

Selecting Hardware Rack Equipment

Select rack equipment to hold the hardware. TABLE 6-27 lists universal hardware racks that are commonly used in data center environments.

TABLE 6-27   Hardware Racks

Name	Vendor
Sun Racks (http://www.sun.com)	Sun Microsystems
SharkRack® (http://www.sharkrack.com)	SharkRack, Inc.
Server Racks (http://www.swdp.com)	SouthWest Data Products
Server Racks (http://www.lanstar.com)	LanStar

Selecting Software for FijiNet

Following the general model for selecting software, and using the requirements arrived at in Chapter 2, we select software appropriate for FijiNet's services.

- "Choose Software for FijiNet's Basic Services" on page 215
- "Choose Software for FijiNet's Infrastructure Services" on page 217
- "Choose Software for FijiNet's Operation and Management Services" on page 218
- "Choose Operating Environment for FijiNet" on page 220

Choose Software for FijiNet's Basic Services

To support basic services, we select software for the following:

- "Mail Servers" on page 215
- "Web Servers" on page 216
- "News Server" on page 216
- "FTP Servers" on page 216

Mail Servers

We choose sendmail for FijiNet to provide a reliable and scalable foundation for delivering messaging services to subscribers. Using sendmail reduces the overall cost for FijiNet's environment. Note that sendmail is the mail transfer agent (MTA) and is part of Solaris 8 OE. It sends and receives email via simple mail transfer protocol (SMTP).

We choose UW IMAP to provide accessibility to email messages for subscribers, because sendmail does not have POP/IMAP servers integrated. UW IMAP supports both POP and IMAP and is integrated with Solaris 8 OE. For more information on UW IMAP, refer to `http://www.washington.edu/imap`.

Web Servers

We choose Apache for FijiNet to provide web hosting services. Apache is integrated with Solaris 8 OE. Apache is light, fast, and freely available on the Internet at no cost. For more information on Apache, refer to `http://www.apache.org`.

Note – Apache is the web server of choice for a 10,000-user environment because it is open source (free). As FijiNet scales to a 100,000-user environment, a commercial solution for enterprise environment is recommended.

News Server

Based upon our earlier recommendation in Chapter 2, FijiNet is outsourcing news service to a UseNet provider.

FTP Servers

We choose WU-FTP for its features and functionality, especially security features and the ability to be authenticated via directory service. WU-FTP is part of Solaris 8 OE and is LDAP-compliant.

Choose Software for FijiNet's Infrastructure Services

To support infrastructure services, we select software for the following:

- "DNS Servers" on page 217
- "LDAP Servers" on page 217
- "DHCP Server" on page 218
- "RADIUS Server" on page 218
- "NTP Server" on page 218

DNS Servers

We choose BIND v8 for FijiNet. BIND v8 is part of Solaris 8 OE. If FijiNet needs additional features in the future, such as dynamic update, they can migrate to BIND v9. (The migration process is basic.)

Sun Netra™ t1 (1x440MHz) with 1 Gbyte of RAM running BIND v8.2.2 handles up to 5,800 requests per second and sustains an average of 5,600 requests per second. BIND v9.1.0 running on the same server handles up to 2,100 requests per second and sustains an average of 2,000 requests per second. In general, BIND v9 is more CPU-bound than v8.

LDAP Servers

We choose the iPlanet Directory Server (iDS) for FijiNet's directory services. The iDS is part of Solaris 8 OE. The license is free for up to 200,000 entries in the LDAP database. The iPlanet Directory server fits well in FijiNet's environment, supporting the initial base of 10,000 users and is scalable to 100,000 users.

Although we could use Open LDAP, we choose iDS for future scalability and performance. iDS delivers a user-management infrastructure for enterprises that manage high volumes of user information. iDS integrates with existing systems and acts as a central repository for the consolidation of information. It provides flexible, personalized user profiles, preferences, and authentications. Additionally, it helps reduce internal administration costs and ensures accurate, up-to-date information.

iDS is based on industry-standard LDAP. It supports all major platforms and system requirements. It supports flexible replication models and standards-based hierarchical naming and advanced security features, is easy to administer, and is cost-efficient.

DHCP Server

We choose DHCP open source, which is integrated with Solaris 8 OE.

RADIUS Server

We choose Funk Software's Steel-Belted RADIUS/SP for FijiNet. Steel-Belted RADIUS can be authenticated via various methods, including directory service. Centralized authentication is the key to manageability for FijiNet in reducing on-going operational costs.

NTP Server

We choose open source Xntp software, which is integrated with Solaris 8 OE.

Choose Software for FijiNet's Operation and Management Services

To support operation and management services, we select software for the following:

- "Backup Servers for FijiNet" on page 218
- "Systems Management Servers for FijiNet" on page 219

Backup Servers for FijiNet

For FijiNet's backup software, we choose Solstice Backup server, which is part of Solaris 8 OE Environment. Solstice Backup software is Sun's branded version of Legato NetWorker software. It is an integrated product that addresses the backup, recovery, and archival needs of heterogeneous computing environments.

Solstice Backup supports a variety of tape drives, automated tape libraries, and tape silos. The software provides manageability, availability, and level of performance required by FijiNet. This solution reduces FijiNet's administrative overhead, improves data reliability and accessibility to users and applications, and reduces the overall cost of ownership.

Systems Management Servers for FijiNet

We choose Sun Management Center (SunMC), which is part of Solaris 8 OE Environment. Other resource management products that are useful for FijiNet are Sun Resource Manger (SRM) and Sun Bandwidth Manager (SBM).

SunMC software is an advanced system management tool. Designed to support Sun systems, SunMC technology provides a platform upon which FijiNet can base its administrative and management operations to help ensure all systems and the services they provide are highly available. A powerful tool for managing the enterprise network, SunMC software enables system administrators to perform remote system management, monitor performance, and isolate hardware and software faults for hundreds of Sun systems, all through an easy-to-use web interface. The following are some features helpful to FijiNet:

- GUI module builder provides a powerful easy-to-use interface for developing custom modules.

- Several enhancements to core applications including alarm manager, discover, console, install, log viewer, scalable tables, and data views.

- Online Hardware Diagnostics provide comprehensive online diagnostics testing and resolution without interrupting customer applications or operations.

- Web interface allows IT managers to view and manage Sun systems from a browser, anywhere on the net.

- Enhanced development including data log interface, device modeling, discovery interfaces, graphics module builder, and more console integration interfaces.

- Support for new UltraSPARC™ III systems which have greatly improved availability features, better detection and isolation features, and better instrumentation.

- New licensing model providing unlimited-node basic functionality package at no charge.

- Advanced systems monitoring add-on licensing including full kernel reader functionality, Solaris health monitoring, processing monitoring, and other advanced features licensed on a per-node basis.

- Premier management applications add-on including group operations, configuration propagation, command line interfaces, and improved data views.

For logical volume management, we choose the Solstice DiskSuite products to provide software-based RAID volume management functionality. We choose this solution because of cost constraints and for the features these products provide. The primary goal of these products is to ease the management of server storage. Disk striping, mirroring, RAID-5, hot spares, and UNIX file system (UFS) logging are the primary features.

Solstice DiskSuite software is a disk and storage management solution designed to meet the demands of both mission-critical enterprise applications and agile dot-com organizations. Solstice DiskSuite meets the need for high data availability and reliability, enhanced system and I/O performance, and large system and disk administration.

All logs should be directed to the management server for archival and analysis. System logs from the infrastructure can be directed to `syslog(1m)` on the management server. When FijiNet scales to a 100,000-user environment or larger, a dedicated log server may be necessary. A log server is a system running `syslog` facility with an appropriate amount of storage for log storage and archival.

Choose Operating Environment for FijiNet

For FijiNet, we choose Solaris 8 OE Environment because it:

- Supports both 32-bit and/or 64-bit operating systems
- Is highly secure, manageable, and available with massive scalability
- Supports dynamic reconfiguration, system domains, live upgrades, IP mutipathing, mobile IP, bandwidth and resource management, clustering, stateful firewall with stealth capability, and so on
- Is bundled with many tools and applications that are essential to ISP environments

Selecting Servers for FijiNet

After selecting software, we select the server components for FijiNet. We choose servers that support the OE and services in such a manner that components integrate to deliver the desired reliability, availability, scalability, and performance.

- "Determine Server Types for FijiNet" on page 221
- "Choose Server Equipment for FijiNet" on page 222
- "Choose Storage Equipment for FijiNet" on page 223

Determine Server Types for FijiNet

To support services, we choose lightweight front-end servers with uniprocessors, which are sufficient for systems at the DMZ and services networks. We choose mid-range servers with limited scalability for content and management networks. TABLE 6-28 lists server types for FijiNet. As FijiNet grows toward a 100,000-user environment, it will need to scale to larger servers.

TABLE 6-28   Server Types for FijiNet

Type	Specification	Associated Tier
Front-end	Uniprocessor (1 CPU, ≤ GB RAM)	DMZ and services networks
Mid-size	Multiprocessor (≤ 4 CPU, ≤ 4 GB RAM)	Content and management networks

Choose Server Equipment for FijiNet

To support services, we choose a Sun Fire™ 280R and two Sun Netra t1 servers (one for firewall, the other for management), as shown in TABLE 6-29.

TABLE 6-29 Enterprise Servers

Name	Vendor
Sun Fire 280R (2x750MHz, 2 GB RAM) ≥ Content server	Sun Microsystems
Sun Netra t1 (1x440MHz, 1GB RAM) ≥ Firewall	Sun Microsystems
Sun Netra t1 (1x440MHz, 1GB RAM) ≥ Management server	Sun Microsystems

Building on the SPARC™ and UltraSPARC II generations of processors, the Sun Fire 280R server uses new the UltraSPARC III processor technology. Sun Fire 280R servers offer many feature enhancements over previous generation products— including the new 150-MHz Sun Coherent Scalable Crossbar (SCSC) interconnect, fibre channel storage, advanced management tools, redundant components, and easy serviceability. The Sun Fire 280R server provides these enterprise-level features in a compact, rack-optimized 4 RU (rack unit) enclosure, giving FijiNet high compute density and the flexibility to scale their processing needs without wasting precious space.

The Sun Fire 280R server is an ideal system for FijiNet, because it offers strong processing power in a small footprint. The Sun Fire 280R server supports up to two 750-MHz UltraSPARC III 64-bit RISC microprocessors with 8 MB of Ecache (L2) each, 8 Gbyte of main memory, two internal 18.2-Gbyte or 36.4-Gbyte hot-swap Fibre Channel disk drives, four PCI slots connected to two high-performance PCI I/O buses that can move over 2.4 Gbytes of data per second, and up to two hot-swap power supplies for N+1 redundancy. The Sun Fire 280R server provides compute density at an affordable price, which is a high priority for FijiNet.

Sun's Netra server products are based on the robust, scalable SPARC architecture running on the Solaris OE, which provides FijiNet with a single environment from development to service deployment on servers from 1- to 64-bit processors. Sun's open systems approach provides the stability, reliability, and outstanding price performance that FijiNet wants. ISP and Telco requirements are converging, creating an even larger market for carrier-grade products. The Netra t1 server is Sun's entry-level server for the service provider server market. The Netra t1 server represents the low end of Sun's carrier-grade Netra products. The Netra product line offers a range of availability options.

The Netra t1 has the following key features:

- Lights out management (LOM) provides optimum availability through remote management.

- Front-accessible drives provide easy access for service and maintenance.

- With the 1 RU form factor, Netra t1 servers can be densely packed into existing racks, lowering operating costs.

Choose Storage Equipment for FijiNet

To support services, we choose equipment for the following:

- "Data Storage" on page 223
- "Tape Library" on page 224

Data Storage

After determining FijiNet's storage specifications, we choose Sun StorEdge D1000. The initial configuration for FijiNet is one Sun StorEdge D1000 with two 36Gbyte disks. As FijiNet grows, more disks can be added to the storage array to handle a larger storage capacity. A fast/wide SCSI (small computer system interface) host adapter is required for the system to connect to the D1000 storage array.

Sun StorEdge D1000 supports 36-Gbyte, 1-inch, low-profile, 10,000-RPM disks. The maximum capacity of the 12-disk Sun StorEdge D1000 array is 436 Gbytes.

The Sun StorEdge D1000 array does not have an embedded hardware RAID controller. Instead, software RAID solutions are achieved by combining the Sun StorEdge D1000 array with the Sun Solstice DiskSuite software or the RAID capabilities that are embedded with the Solaris 8 OE Environment. The Sun StorEdge D1000 array has two UltraSCSI channels (four UltraSCSI connections). The Sun StorEdge D1000 array backplane is split into two 6-drive segments. Two of the UltraSCSI connections can be cascaded (interconnected) to create a single 12-drive segment. The Sun StorEdge D1000 array is a software-RAID solution that offers a host of capabilities and features.

Tape Library

We choose Sun StorEdge L280 as the tape library. The Sun StorEdge L280 autoloader offers 280-Gbyte native capacity in the reliable DLT 7000 format.

Housed in a rackmount chassis, the Sun StorEdge L280 autoloader consists of one DLT 7000 tape drive, eight slots for storing cartridges, and a robotic system to remove cartridges from the slots, load them into the drive, unload them from the drive, and return them to the cartridge slots. FijiNet can use it with Sun Solstice Backup™, Legato Networker, or VERITAS NetBackup products, as well as many other storage management software applications, to easily handle the unattended backup of 150-Gbyte databases in eight hours or less.

The Sun StorEdge L280 autoloader is read/write compatible with the DLT 4000, DLT 2000, and DLT 2000XT formats, enabling tape media written by a DLT 4000 or DLT 2000 drive to be compatible with the same media in the Sun StorEdge L280 autoloader.

Selecting Network Components for FijiNet

After we select software and servers for FijiNet, we select networking equipment.

- "Choose Routers and Switches" on page 226
- "Choose Load Balancers" on page 228
- "Choose Firewalls" on page 228
- "Choose Intrusion Detection Systems" on page 229
- "Choose Console Servers" on page 229
- "Choose Network Access Servers" on page 230

TABLE 6-30 provides a quick reference for the components we choose for FijiNet. The following sections describe our choices.

TABLE 6-30 Network Equipment for FijiNet

Network Devices	Quantity	Description
Core router	1	Cisco 2651
Distribution switch	1	Cisco 3512XL
Premises firewall	1	Cisco PIX 525
Access server	2	Cisco AS5400
Console server	1	Cisco AS2511

Choose Routers and Switches

For routers and switching equipment, we select the following.

Routers

We choose the Cisco 2651 router, a modular router that offers versatility, integration, and power for small to mid-sized ISPs. The modular architecture of the Cisco 2600 series routers easily allows interfaces to be upgraded to accommodate network expansion. With full support of the Cisco IOS® software, Cisco 2651 supports Quality of Service (QoS), security, and network integration features required for service provider networks. FijiNet can use Cisco routers to build a high-performance backbone that provides efficient support for Internet traffic.

The Cisco 2651 provides a cost-effective solution to meet FijiNet's requirements for:

- Internet access
- Multiservice integration
- Analog/digital dial access
- Virtual private network
- Inter-VLAN routing
- Bandwidth management

For FijiNet's 10,000-subscriber environment, a router with two WAN interfaces is needed for Internet connectivity, and at least one LAN port is needed for internal connectivity.

For scalability, two LAN ports will be required when additional routers are added to provide higher availability. Refer to Chapter 5 for capacity planning of WAN/LAN ports for routers.

Note — As an alternative to the Cisco 2651 router, we also considered a NetIron™ (by Foundry) router. However, Foundry stackable router NetIron does not support WAN interfaces slower than an OC-3. Thus, a speed aggregation device, such as Tiara 1400 series, would be required for Internet access.

Switches

For FijiNet's 10,000-subscriber environment, a layer 2 (L2) switch with a sufficient number of LAN (10/100 Mbit/sec) ports is needed. We choose the Cisco 3512-XL switch.

The Cisco 3512-XL switch is a scalable line of stackable 10/100 Mbit/sec and Gigabit Ethernet switches that delivers premium performance, manageability, and flexibility. This line of low-cost, high-performance switching solutions is ideal for small to mid-sized ISPs. The features helpful to FijiNet are the following:

- The 3512-XL switch has 12 10/100-Mbit/sec switched ports and two Gigabit Interface Converter (GBIC) Gigabit Ethernet ports
- 10-Gbit/sec switching fabric and up to 4.8 million packets/sec (pps) forwarding rate, ensuring full wire-speed operation for each 10/100-Mbit/sec and Gigabit Ethernet port
- Full-duplex operation on all ports, delivering up to 200-Mbit/sec on 10/100 Mbit/sec ports or 2-Gbit/sec on Gigabit ports
- GigaStack® GBIC delivers a low-cost, independent stack bus with a 1-Gbit/sec forwarding bandwidth in a daisy-chain configuration, with up to nine 3512-XL or a 2-Gbit/sec forwarding rate in a point-to-point configuration
- Cisco switch clustering technology allows a user to manage up to sixteen interconnected 3512-XL switches through a single IP address
- GBIC-based Gigabit Ethernet ports give customers a choice of 1000BaseSX, 1000BaseLX/LH, or Cisco GigaStack stacking GBICs
- Bandwidth aggregation through fast EtherChannel™ and gigabit EtherChannel technology, enhancing fault tolerance and offering from 400-Mbit/sec up to 4-Gbit/sec of aggregated bandwidth between switches and to routers
- VLAN trunks can be created from any port using either standards 802.1Q tagging or the Cisco ISL VLAN architecture
- Embedded Remote Monitoring (RMON) software agent supports four RMON groups (history, statistics, alarms, and events) for enhanced traffic management, monitoring, and analysis
- IEEE 802.1p L2 prioritization protocol-ready, allowing users to assign data packets to prioritized forwarding queues

To ensure that the number of ports can scale to support up to 100,000 subscribers, more ports must be added on demand for additional network devices and servers. Because of cost constraints, we start with a minimal configuration and recommend that FijiNet scale horizontally when needed. The aggregation of port density can be done by cascading or daisy chaining multiple switches. See Chapter 5 for capacity planning of ports on switches.

Note – As an alternative to Cisco 3512-XL, we could use a Foundry FastIron workgroup switch.

Choose Load Balancers

Due to cost constraints and because there are not enough servers to require balancing loads, we decide that load balancers are not applicable to the FijiNet architecture at the 10,000-subscriber level. However, balancers will be required when FijiNet's subscriber population grows to 100,000 or more and load distribution becomes critical to service availability. Therefore, we believe it is important to plan for future traffic growth and how load balancing fits into the overall architecture, such as scalability, availability, performance, etc.

Choose Firewalls

We choose Cisco PIX 525 as the firewall solution for FijiNet. The Cisco PIX 525 Firewall is for enterprises and service providers. It has a 600-MHz processor and a throughput of 370 Mbit/sec, with the ability to handle as many as 280,000 simultaneous sessions.

The Cisco PIX 525 supports a broad range of network interface cards (NICs). Standard NICs include single-port or four-port 10/100 Fast Ethernet, Gigabit Ethernet, 4/16 Token Ring, and dual-attached multimode FDDI (fiber distributed data interface) cards. Also, the PIX 525 offers multiple power supply options. Users can chose between AC or a 48-DC power supply. You can pair either option with a second PIX for redundancy and high-availability.

Some of the key product features helpful to FijiNet are as follows:

- *End-to-end solution* – Allows businesses to extend a cost-effective, seamless network infrastructure to the branch office
- *Low cost of ownership* – Simple to install and configure, resulting in little network downtime

- *Standards-based virtual private network (VPN)* – Enables administrators to reduce the costs of connecting nomadic users and remote sites to the corporate network over the Internet or other public IP networks
- *Stateful failover/hot standby* – Delivers high availability to maximize network reliability
- *Network address translation (NAT)* – Saves costly public IP addresses, expands network address space (RFC 1918), and obscures IP addresses from the outside world
- *Concurrent connections* – Up to 280,000 simultaneous connections supported
- *Prevention of denial-of-service attacks* – Protects the firewall, as well as the servers and clients behind it, from disruptive or damaging hackers

Choose Intrusion Detection Systems

Because FijiNet's service offering is for residential users with no service level agreement (SLA), an intrusion detection system (IDS) is not required. In addition, intrusion detection system is not cost effective for a 10,000-subscriber environment. However, as FijiNet's subscriber population grows and different types of users and services are added, security will become critical in ensuring privacy. When a higher level of security is required, an IDS will be necessary to prevent unauthorized access to services and data.

Choose Console Servers

We select a Cisco 2511-RJ for the console server. It provides console ports management for FijiNet servers. Multiple console servers can be scaled horizontally to provide more ports as FijiNet's number of servers grow.

The Cisco 2511-RJ provides FijiNet with a low-cost entry console server. This server allows subscribers to connect asynchronous devices, such as dumb terminals, modems, and system/router/switch consoles, into a routed network. The server is a fixed-configuration with 16 asynchronous ports, 1 Ethernet port, and 1 serial port.

Choose Network Access Servers

We choose two Cisco AS5400 servers, where each access server supports one CT3. (To handle a 12.5 percent concurrency of 1,250 users, we need at least two CT3s.) Because the Cisco AS5400 supports only one CT3, we need two servers. With these access servers, FijiNet can scale to 16.7 percent without adding another access server. As FijiNet grows toward 100,000 subscribers, FijiNet can add access servers.

According to Cisco, the AS5400 is the highest-density, carrier-class access server, offering unparalleled capacity in only two rack units (2 RUs) with universal port data, voice, wireless, and fax services on any port at any time. Its high density (up to one CT3), low power consumption, and universal port digital signal processors (DSPs) make it ideal for many network architectures, especially points of presence (POP) for ISPs. Universal port functionality enables the Cisco AS5400 to operate simultaneously as a network access server (NAS) and a voice gateway, delivering universal services on any port at any time. The Cisco AS5400 universal services include dial access, real time voice and fax, and wireless data access. As a carrier-grade universal gateway, the Cisco AS5400 has hot-swap cards and an internal redundant power supply.

The Cisco AS5400 supports three egress (outgoing) interfaces for redundant WAN backhaul methods for moving packets out to the network:

- Two 10/100 Mbit/sec autosensing Fast Ethernet ports
- Two 8-Mbyte serial ports
- Multiple T1, E1, or CT3 trunks

The AS5400 supports two ingress (incoming) interfaces:

- Channelized T3 termination
- Eight-port CT1/CE1/PRI termination

In Cisco's specification on the AS5400, Cisco states that the AS5400 supports the CT3 card for high-density PSTN (public switched telephone network) connectivity. This card provides a maximum of 672 channels via a single CT3 connection. This card is valuable to any customer who wants to reduce the amount of cables required to deliver 672 channels and take advantage of lower tariffs associated with purchasing a single CT3 circuit versus 28 individual T1 circuits. The CT3 card provides a standards-based M13 multiplexer with resources to terminate up to 28 T1s. The CT3 card includes a channel service unit/data service unit (CSU/DSU) for terminating a CT3 trunk directly from the data center network. The CT3 card can be used for both ingress and egress at the same time. This feature allows the Cisco AS5400 to provide a large density of modems in a remote POP environment with only a power cable and a CT3 line running to the server.

Selecting Hardware Rack Equipment for FijiNet

To hold the hardware, we select a Sun rack. It is a telco-grade, universal 19-inch rack that is predominantly used in data centers for service providers.

The rack can have fan trays on top and bottom of the rack to provide air circulation in and out of the rack. Front and back panels allow better air ventilation. The rack has dual circuit breakers for connections to two different power distribution units. The dual breakers ensure that power failure from one power distribution unit does not affect servers on the rack. Sun racks came in different heights. For FijiNet, the shorter 60-inch high rack would work, but for future scalability, we choose the industry-standard 72-inch high rack.

## CHAPTER 7

Implementing a Solution

This chapter offers general practices and recommendations for implementing a design, including recommendations for developing a prototype prior to implementing a solution. Also in this chapter are considerations for adapting to change after an ISP has implemented a solution.

In this chapter, we do not present specialized data for our sample customer FijiNet, because the general information also applies to FijiNet and all ISPs.

Note – Make sure that you address all dependencies before implementing a design. By following the incremental approach presented in this chapter, you should be able to address all implementation dependencies.

This chapter contains the following topics:

Implementing a Prototype

We recommend that you develop and implement a prototype of your design *before* implementing the full-scale design. Develop a prototype so that you can test and validate the solution to ensure that it achieves all the functionality required.

Frequently ISPs fail to implement and thoroughly test a prototype. The biggest issues are performance, scalability, and compatibility. Developing and testing a prototype provides the following benefits:

- Validates that the design works and satisfies all requirements
- Ensures that the solution achieves the desired level of performance
- Establishes profiles for systems and network utilization
- Develops a use-case to test for functionality and usability
- Identifies design flaws
- Allows you to fine-tune the design where needed

The major processes for implementing a prototype are the same as for implementing a full-scale design. Please refer to the other sections in this chapter for information while developing your prototype.

Tip – We recommend that you develop and implement a prototype that matches the design as closely as possible. This practice helps ensure that the result represents the performance of the production environment.

Implementing a Design

The following information provides general guidelines, process, and recommendations for implementing a design efficiently. Operational processes, quality assurance, and the complexity of architectures vary among different environments and may require additional steps.

To implement a design, refer to the following sections:

- "Apply an Incremental Approach" on page 235
- "Test and Optimize Your Implementation" on page 236

Apply an Incremental Approach

Plan the overall implementation process before you start. We recommend that you implement a design in phases. An incremental approach has many benefits, such as:

- Providing a more manageable implementation
- Making it easier to troubleshoot and refine the implementation.
- Ensuring that services which have dependencies are implemented in the correct sequence.

Implement services in the following major phases, based on dependencies:

1. Operating platform

2. Operating system

3. Infrastructure services

4. Basic services

5. Value-added services

Test and Optimize Your Implementation

During each phase, install and configure each component, then test it for functionality. After implementing a phase (infrastructure, basic services, or value-added services), test the overall functionality and performance, then optimize it. This incremental approach streamlines the implementation process and makes troubleshooting easier.

Test your implementation to validate that it performs as expected. Test to determine the baseline performance; then, using this baseline performance data, determine what you should optimize. Typically, the preferred practice of testing is first functionality, then performance.

When performing performance tuning, you need to know the environment and understand how the systems or applications can be tuned to enhance performance. In general, the default settings apply to most configurations. If the tuning is done incorrectly, then systems or applications may negatively affect overall performance.

After each test, optimize the design as necessary until you achieve the desired functionality and performance.

Start with a generic configuration, then fine-tune it. Add complexity and customize one service at a time, testing each new service, then optimizing it until the desired performance is achieved. Concentrate on one service at a time.

When optimizing your implementation, consider the following major characteristics of overall performance:

- *Network characteristics* – Look at the actual level of bandwidth utilization and determine if your network is able to support the traffic load.

- *System utilization* – Review system performance and utilization (CPU, system memory, and storage usage) to determine if resources are sufficient to support subscribers.

- *Application proficiency* – Review the application configuration and determine how it can be tuned for better performance.

Implementing an Operating Platform

We refer to the operating platform as the foundation for an ISP. There are many things involved in preparing to implement the operating platform, such as allocating space at the datacenter for racks, ensuring that there is enough air ventilation, appropriate temperature control, and enough power distribution for the servers, etc. These tasks all deal with the physical aspects of the data center and are beyond the scope of this book. For purposes of implementing an operating platform for an architecture design, we focus on network and system components.

To implement the operating platform, install and configure all the networking components. These components include console servers, routers, switches, load balancers, firewalls, and network access servers.

After the network is in place, install and configure the systems components. These components include all internal hardware components of a system such as the installation of CPU, memory, internal disk, CD-ROM drive, storage, cabling, etc.

In general, implement and configure all hardware before moving to the next phase, installing the operating system and relevant software.

Implementing an Operating System

After you implement the operating platform, install the operating system and all associated software. The operating system must be properly configured and operational before any infrastructure services can be installed and configured.

Implementing Infrastructure Services

Implement your infrastructure services before implementing basic services and value-added services, both of which depend on the infrastructure.

Tip – Start with a generic or basic configuration for the infrastructure services. Do not impose complex policies or sophisticated customizing during the initial implementation process. After you fully test the basic configuration, optimize components one at a time. Note that changes must be done one at a time, and each revision must be fully tested and documented for change management.

▼ To implement infrastructure services:

1. **Install the hardware rack.**

2. **Ensure that the power supply is available from two or more power distribution units (PDUs), and that the environment has adequate air ventilation and temperature control.**

Note – Power, air, and space are part of Internet data center (IDC) design and are beyond the scope of this book. For purposes of implementation, we assume these design issues are already taken care of. Before proceeding with implementation, ensure that these items are in place and meet the specifications required for your design.

---

3. **Gather all your supporting documentation:**

   a. **Use the overall network design diagram (developed in Chapter 5) to identify and implement each design element and network component.**

   b. **Use the IP address schema (developed in Chapter 5) to configure the addresses for network design.**

   c. **Develop or obtain security policies for use later.**

4. Implement network components in the following order:

   a. Implement console servers.

   b. Install and configure routers.

   c. Install and configure switches.

   d. Install and configure network access servers (NASs).

   e. Install and configure load balancers.

   f. Install and configure firewalls.

   g. Install and configure intrusion detection systems (IDSs).

5. Implement domain name system (DNS) servers.

6. Implement lightweight directory access protocol (LDAP) servers.

7. Implement remote access dial-in user service (RADIUS) servers.

8. Implement dynamic host configuration protocol (DHCP) servers.

9. Implement network time protocol (NTP) servers.

10. Install enterprise servers, operating environment, and data storage equipment.

11. Implement backup and management servers.

Implementing Basic Services

After implementing infrastructure services, implement your basic services:

- Mail servers
- Web servers
- News servers
- FTP (file transfer protocol) servers

At a minimum, DNS and LDAP servers must be implemented before you implement basic services. As stated in the previous section, we recommend that you implement all the infrastructure before proceeding to basic services. While implementing basic services, configure them to fit your environment.

Implementing Value-Added Services

After implementing basic services, implement any value-added services.

What constitutes value-added services varies among ISPs and changes quickly as competitors follow industry leaders. Samples of value-added services are calendar, address book, search engine, short messaging service (SMS), IR chat (IRC), and WebMail.

Refer to vendor documentation for any dependencies and implementation recommendations.

Adapting to Changes

After an architecture design is implemented, the ISP becomes responsible for managing the environment. Some common questions that an ISP has after implementation are as follows: Where do we go from here? How do we ensure that the environment can scale to the next level? How can we forecast market trends and respond to market changes?

There are many factors that can directly or indirectly affect an architecture. Everything from tactical business decisions to technological advances in software and hardware can have great impact on an architecture and an ISP's business. Navigating these changes and responding appropriately requires periodic and careful evaluation of many factors, which are beyond the scope of this book.

The following sections provide high-level descriptions and guidelines for addressing the most common factors:

- "Usage Pattern Changes" on page 241
- "Technology Changes" on page 241
- "Business Strategy Changes" on page 241

Usage Pattern Changes

Looking at usage patterns allows an ISP to target new markets, expand existing markets, forecast subscriber interest in new service offerings, and increase scalability. We recommend that an ISP periodically evaluate usage patterns to determine if it needs to anticipate changing the architecture, business plan, services, pricing, and operation and management.

Usage patterns depend upon many factors, but the following are most common:

- Geographic (technology availability based upon location; for example, network traffic may be faster or slower because higher-speed broadband is typically available only in larger cities)
- Demographics (age, gender, income level, etc.)
- Events (cause short-term and long-term increases in traffic)
- User type (residential or business)

Technology Changes

Hardware and software vendors are constantly improving their products and creating new products. Because the ISP application space is rapidly changing and maturing, new solutions frequently become available.

We recommend that ISPs keep up-to-date with changes in technology and new solutions. As new technologies become available, evaluate them for inclusion in future releases. An excellent way to keep up-to-date is to establish and maintain relationships (partnerships) with key vendors.

Business Strategy Changes

ISPs typically need to change their strategies to remain competitive and move ahead of competitors. ISPs must consistently strive to be more efficient and cost effective, reaching new subscribers and adding or enhancing service offerings. ISPs usually redefine their strategies in reaction to the market, positioning themselves for new opportunities. Also, when market conditions change dramatically, such as a market downturn or sudden growth, ISPs usually need to revise or redefine their business plans.

Higher Expectations

Subscribers' expectations increase in response to competitor offerings and new technology. To retain subscribers and win new ones, ISPs must meet these higher expectations.

The following are some of the changes an ISP has to make to gain and maintain a competitive edge over its competitors:

- Offer better customer care
- Offer new value-added services
- Provide higher service level agreements (SLAs)
- Maintain or increase reliability
- Manage operations more efficiently
- Lower costs while increasing profitability

Higher Service Levels

In today's competitive market, business subscribers seek out higher-quality customer service experiences. Typically, they want the best service offerings available combined with the highest level of customer service, for the least amount of money. They certainly don't want to pay any more than they have to, and comparison shopping is now easier than ever over the Internet.

As competition increases among ISPs, those that have better and more reliable service offerings paired with higher-quality customer care are the ones that will fare well in acquiring new business subscribers and retaining current subscribers.

As an ISP moves into offering SLAs or meeting higher service levels, we recommend that it consider the following.

- Infrastructure must be highly reliable to support mission critical business.
- Infrastructure must be scalable to support new service offerings.
- More stringent security policies are required to ensure that subscriber data remains confidential.

For more information about SLAs, refer to:

```
http://www.nextslm.org
```

Questions for Obtaining Design Requirements

This appendix contains common design questions that are provided as a general guideline for obtaining design requirements. Depending upon your customer, some of these questions may not apply, and other questions may not be represented here. Note that related questions are repeated in different sections to provide easy reference for each topic.

This appendix provides questions for the following topics:

- "Internet Relay Chat Questions" on page 253
- "FTP Questions" on page 254
- "Internet News Questions" on page 254
- "Development and Staging Questions" on page 255

General Questions

1. Is this an existing or new ISP?

2. What type of ISP is it (dial-up, broadband, wireless, etc.)?

3. What is its target market (residential, businesses, intranet/extranet, etc.)?

4. What are the services provided (web hosting, messaging, Internet news, etc.)?

5. What is the subscriber profile (residential users, business users, etc.)?

6. What is the service usage profile of the subscribers?

7. What are the expected peak usage hours?

8. What are the training requirements for operations and management staff?

Business-Related Questions

1. What is the marketing strategy?

2. What is the time-to-market?

3. What is the budget?

Support Questions

1. Is there an operations and management team available in-house?

2. What is the skill level of the operations and management team?

3. What are your technical support plans?

Systems and Network Management Questions

1. Is there a system and network management team available in-house?

2. What are the automation requirements for systems and network management?

3. What are the logging requirements for management, business, and customer reporting?

End-User Questions

1. What is the client access method (Netscape™, Microsoft® Internet Explorer, etc.)?

2. Which client platforms will be supported (Solaris, Linux, Windows®, etc.)?

3. Are there any internationalization/multilingual issues (English, French, German, Italian, Spanish, etc.)?

4. What other protocols besides TCP/IP will be supported (NetBEUI, AppleTalk™, etc.)?

Registration Questions

1. What is the registration system?

2. What are the registration channels (web, phone, fax, etc.)?

3. What are the plans for user provisioning?

4. What are the integration requirements with the billing system (directory, database, etc.)?

5. Will your registration system be connected directly to a credit card system?

Customer Care Questions

1. What is the customer care system?

2. What are the integration requirements with the management system?

3. What are the integration requirements with the registration system?

4. What are the integration requirements with the billing system?

5. Are there any internationalization/multilingual issues?

Billing System Questions

1. What is the billing strategy (email, credit card, postal mail, etc.)?

2. What is the billing system (AmdocsHorizon, Portal™, Kenan®, etc.)?

3. Will you use a flat or metered rate?

Service Availability Questions

1. What are the service level agreements (SLAs)?

2. What level of availability is desired (high-availability, fault tolerance, cluster, etc.)?

3. What level of service interruption is tolerable?

4. What are the requirements for service failure versus service degradation?

5. What are the disaster recovery requirements?

6. What are your backup/recovery strategies?

7. What are the performance goals (throughput, response time, etc.)?

Security Questions

1. What are your corporate security policies?

2. What network security is already in place?

3. What level of security is desired?

4. What are the security policies for each service?

5. What is the authentication method (directory, database, NIS/NIS+, etc.)?

6. What are the logging requirements for management, business, and subscriber reporting?

7. Will you allow subscriber's CGIs?

8. Will you allow subscriber's Java servlets?

9. Is there any intention of supporting shell accounts?

10. Do you plan to use VPNs?

11. Will RADIUS be authenticated using LDAP?

12. Will you use NAT (Network Address Translation)?

13. Do you plan to use split-DNS?

14. How are you going to harden each system?

15. How are you going to manage the security posture of each system over time?

16. How will you validate that patches and other software updates do not modify the security posture of a system?

17. Is there a management network to protect and isolate administrative traffic?

18. How are backup tapes protected?

19. When are passwords expired?

20. What is the policy for dealing with employee terminations?

21. What authentication access mechanism is used by administrators?

22. How are terminal servers protected against sniffing and malicious misuse?

23. How often are network scans performed to validate that only appropriate services are offered by the systems?

24. What kind of centralized logging and automated reconciliation infrastructure is in place?

25. What is the process by which security patches are evaluated and decisions made on how quickly they are applied to systems?

26. How often are security assessments to be performed on the environment by internal staff and by a third party?

Demographic Questions

1. What is the total number of subscribers?

2. What is the expected growth in the number of subscribers?

3. What is the average connection time of a user?

4. What is the percentage of concurrent users (10 percent, 12.5 percent, 15 percent, etc.)?

5. What are the scalability requirements of each service?

6. What are the scalability requirements of the architecture? Over what period of time?

Networking Questions

1. What is the current network architecture?

2. What is the current network bandwidth (10 Mbytes/sec, 100 Mbytes/sec, etc.)?

3. Is this a single-site or multiple-site environment?

4. Will there be multiple POPs (point of presence)?

5. Will the data center be the concentrator between POPs and a central site?

6. Any preference for LAN technology (10/100 Mbytes/sec, Fast Ethernet, Gigabit Ethernet, FDDI, ATM, etc.)?

7. Any preference for WAN technology (T1, T3, OC-3, DS-3, ATM, Frame Relay, etc.)?

8. Are there multiple connections to the Internet?

9. Will you use DHCP for dynamic network configuration?

10. Will clients have static or dynamic IP addresses?

11. Will private addresses be used for internal networks?

12. Will you host clients' domain names on your DNS?

13. Will you have a time source for NTP?

Dial-up Questions

1. What is the ratio of modems-to-users (1:10, 1:8, 1:6, etc.)?

2. What is your authentication mechanism (RADIUS, TACACS, etc.)?

3. Which modem speeds are supported (14 Kbytes/sec, 28 Kbytes/sec, 56 Kbytes/sec, etc.)?

Directory Questions

1. What is the method of authentication (directory, database, etc.)?

2. If a directory is used, what are the availability needs?

3. What are the policies or legal issues regarding content?

4. Do you have a DIT (directory information tree) schema?

5. What are the integration requirements for user and service provisioning (registration, customer care, billing, etc.)?

6. Will RADIUS use a directory for authentication?

Email Questions

1. Will you offer email service?

2. What are the methods of email access (POP, IMAP, WebMail, etc.)?

3. Is email forwarding/relaying allowed?

4. Is email accounting required?

5. What is the storage requirement for email queue?

6. What is the average size of an email message (10 Kbytes, 25 Kbytes, etc.)?

7. What is the mailbox maximum size allowed (5 Mbytes, 10 Mbytes, etc.)?

8. Is there a limit on email message size (2 Mbytes, 5 Mbytes, etc.)?

9. What percentage of users will use email (50 percent, 75 percent, etc.)?

10. What is the email backup policy?

11. Will you offer multiple domain services?

12. Will you offer administration delegation for accounts and domains?

13. How many email messages will be sent/received by each user per day?

14. What is your plan for email overflow management for users who exceed storage allocation (bounce, additional charge, etc.)?

15. What are your capacity planning requirements for email storage?

16. What are your requirements for the billing system integration?

17. What are the authentication integration requirements?

18. What are the logging requirements for management, business, and subscriber reporting?

19. What are the policies or legal issues regarding content?

20. Will you provide automated customer care for email aliases?

21. Will you integrate virus scanning and antispam with the email server?

Web Hosting Questions

1. Will you offer web hosting?

2. What percentage of users will be surfing the web? What percentage of their connected time?

3. How many pages will your average user read per hour?

4. What is the average size for user web sites (2 Mbytes, 3 Mbytes, etc.)?

5. What is the maximum storage allowed (5 Mbytes, 10 Mbytes, etc.)?

6. What are the scalability requirements?

7. Will you use dedicated or shared storage?

8. What percentage of users will have a web site (25 percent, 30 percent, etc.)?

9. Will you provide Java services?

10. Will you provide JavaScript services?

11. Will you allow subscriber's CGIs?

12. Will you provide scripting languages?

13. What will be your staging strategy (push, pull, on demand, etc.)?

14. What will be your content management strategies?

15. Will you provide a search engine?

16. Will you provide HTML/links validation services?

17. Will you provide dynamic web hosting?

18. Will you provide professional web hosting (shared, co-located, or dedicated)?

19. What will be your backup policy?

20. What are the integration requirements with the billing system?

21. What are the integration requirements with directory service?

22. Will you use SSL or other secure transaction system?

23. Will you index the pages on the fly as they are published?

24. Will you support individual domains for URLs?

25. What are the policies or legal issues regarding content?

26. What are the logging requirements for management, business, and subscriber reporting?

Search Engine Questions

1. Will you integrate a search engine?

2. Will it be local and/or external?

3. Will you index the pages on the fly as they are published?

4. What are the integration requirements with the billing system?

5. What are the integration requirements with directory?

Caching Proxy Questions

1. Will you provide a caching proxy?

2. Will you provide a multilevel hierarchical caching proxy?

3. Will you use URL pre-loading?

4. Will you use URL filtering?

5. Will you use directory for user authentication?

6. What are the policies or legal issues regarding content access?

7. What are the logging requirements for management, business, and subscriber reporting?

Internet Relay Chat Questions

1. Will you offer chat service?

2. What percentage of users will be chatting?

3. What percentage of users connected time will they be chatting?

4. What are the anticipated traffic and usage patterns?

5. How many channels are to be supported concurrently?

6. Will you host the chat service or will it be outsourced?

7. Will you provide web-based chat service?

8. What are the policies or legal issues regarding content access?

9. What are the logging requirements for management, business, and subscriber reporting?

FTP Questions

1. What percentage of web users will be using the FTP service for web content upload?

2. What is the storage allocated for spooling for content upload?

3. What are the policies or legal issues regarding content access?

4. What are the logging requirements for management, business, and subscriber reporting?

Internet News Questions

1. Will news service be in-house or outsourced?

2. What percentage of users will be using the news service?

3. What percentage of their time will be spent reading news?

4. How are news groups stored, moderated, and filtered?

5. How long do you want to keep news content?

6. What is the average number of news articles that users read per hour?

7. Will you have one or multiple newsfeeds? Upstream or downstream?

8. What are the integration requirements with the email system?

9. What are the integration requirements with the billing system?

10. What are the integration requirements with directory services?

11. Will you implement a multilevel news server hierarchy?

12. What are the policies or legal issues regarding content access?

13. What are the logging requirements for management, business, and subscriber reporting?

Development and Staging Questions

1. Is the production site different from the development/staging site?

2. What are the specifications for the test site?

3. What is the current development infrastructure?

4. What are the tools and processes for source code control and content management?

5. What are the requirements for supporting the development environment?

6. What are the testing and acceptance standards?

.

Sample Network Configurations

The appendix contains sample network configurations for network devices (routers, switches, network access servers, and domain name servers). These configurations are Cisco-specific and correlate to the hardware selected for the design prototype (FijiNet). This appendix provides configurations for the following:

- "Cisco 2651 Router" on page 258
- "Cisco 3512-XL Switch" on page 260
- "Cisco PIX 525 Firewall" on page 262
- "Cisco AS 5400 Access Server" on page 264
- "Cisco AS 2511 Console Server" on page 271

Cisco 2651 Router

The following code example provides a configuration for the Cisco 2651 router.

CODE EXAMPLE B-1 Cisco 2651 Router Sample Configuration

```
!
version 11.3
!
service timestamps debug uptime
service timestamps log uptime
service password-encryption
!
hostname fijinet-router
!
enable secret 5 $1$iQrd$x5J3Up9d/kJ5tH0e7W5UT1
enable password 7 0247135205540B2055
!
ip subnet-zero
ip domain-name fijinet.com
ip name-server 172.20.1.10
ip name-server 172.20.1.11
ip name-server 209.1.1.1
clock timezone pacific -8
!
interface FastEthernet0
 ip address 172.20.1.1 255.255.0.0
 speed 100
 duplex full
!
interface FastEthernet1
 no ip address
 shutdown
!
interface atm 1/0
 ip address 192.168.74.3 255.255.255.0
 atm lbo long
 atm clock internal
 atm ds3-scramble
 atm pvc 1 1 32 aal5snap
 map-group lisCT1
!
map-list lisCT1
```

```
    ip 192.168.1.2 atm-vc 1 broadcast
    ip 192.168.1.3 atm-vc 2 broadcast
 !
router ospf 1
 network 172.20.0.0 0.0.255.255 area 10
 network 192.168.1.0 0.0.0.15 area 10
 default-information originate metric 10 metric-type 1
 !
no ip classless
ip route 0.0.0.0 0.0.0.0 172.20.1.2
 !
line con 0
 session-timeout 2
 exec-timeout 2 0
 password 7 041A1C0F0173484F10
 login
line aux 0
 session-timeout 2
 exec-timeout 2 0
 password 7 0247135205540B2055
 login
 transport input all
line vty 0 4
 session-timeout 2
 exec-timeout 2 0
 password 7 100F1E100B45160A15
 login
 !
end
```

Cisco 3512-XL Switch

The following code example provides a configuration for the Cisco 3512-XL switch.

CODE EXAMPLE B-2   Cisco 3512-XL Switch Sample Configuration

```
!
version 12.0
no service pad
service timestamps debug uptime
service timestamps log uptime
no service password-encryption
!
hostname fijinet-switch
!
no spanning-tree vlan 1
no spanning-tree vlan 2
!
ip subnet-zero
!
interface FastEthernet0/1
 description VLAN2
 switchport access vlan 2
!
interface FastEthernet0/2
 description VLAN2
 switchport access vlan 2
!
interface FastEthernet0/3
 description VLAN2
 switchport access vlan 2
!
interface FastEthernet0/4
 description VLAN2
 switchport access vlan 2
!
interface FastEthernet0/5
 description VLAN2
 switchport access vlan 2
!
interface FastEthernet0/6
description VLAN2
 switchport access vlan 2
```

```
!
interface FastEthernet0/7
 description VLAN3
 switchport access vlan 3
!
interface FastEthernet0/8
 description VLAN3
 switchport access vlan 3
!
interface FastEthernet0/9
  description VLAN3
switchport access vlan 3
!
interface FastEthernet0/10
 description VLAN3
switchport access vlan 3
!
interface FastEthernet0/11
 description VLAN3
switchport access vlan 3
!
interface FastEthernet0/12
 description VLAN3
switchport access vlan 3
!
interface GigabitEthernet0/0
!
interface GigabitEthernet0/1
!
interface VLAN1
 description *** Private Interface ***
 ip address 10.1.1.1 255.255.255
 no ip directed-broadcast
 no ip route-cache
!
line con 0
 transport input none
 stopbits 1
line vty 0 4
 login
line vty 5 15
 login
!
end
```

Cisco PIX 525 Firewall

The following code example provides a configuration for the Cisco PIX 525 firewall.

CODE EXAMPLE B-3   Cisco PIX 525 Firewall Sample Configuration

```
!
nameif ethernet0 outside security0
nameif ethernet1 inside security100
interface ethernet0 100baset
interface ethernet1 100baset
!
ip address inside 10.1.1.1 255.255.255.0
ip address outside 209.165.201.1 255.255.255.224
!
logging on
logging host 10.1.1.11
logging trap 7
logging facility 20
no logging console
arp timeout 600
!
nat (inside) 1 0.0.0.0 0.0.0.0
nat (inside) 2 192.168.3.0 255.255.255.0
!
global (outside) 1 209.165.201.6-209.165.201.8 netmask
255.255.255.224
global (outside) 1 209.165.201.10 netmask 255.255.255.224
global (outside) 2 209.165.200.225-209.165.200.254 netmask
255.255.255.224
!
access-list acl_in permit icmp any any
access-list acl_out permit icmp any any
!
access-list acl_in deny tcp host 192.168.3.3 any eq 1720
access-list acl_in deny tcp any any eq 80
access-list acl_in permit host 192.168.3.3 any eq 80
access-list acl_in permit host 10.1.1.11 any eq 80
!
no rip outside passive
no rip outside default
rip inside passive
rip inside default
```

```
!
route outside 0 0 209.165.201.4 1
!
static (inside, outside) 209.165.201.16 192.168.3.16 netmask
255.255.255.240
access-list acl_out permit tcp any host 209.165.201.16 eq h323
!
static (inside, outside) 209.165.201.11 10.1.1.11
access-list acl_out permit tcp any host 209.165.201.11 eq 80
!
access-list acl_out permit udp host 209.165.201.2 host
209.165.201.11 eq rpc
!
rpcinfo -u 209.165.201.11 150001
!
access-list acl_out permit udp host 209.165.201.2 host
209.165.201.11 eq 2049
!
static (inside, outside) 209.165.201.12 10.1.1.3 netmask
255.255.255.255 0 0
access-list acl_out permit tcp any host 209.165.201.12 eq smtp
!
fixup protocol smtp 25
!
access-list acl_out permit tcp any host 209.165.201.12 eq 113
access-group acl_out in interface outside
!
snmp-server host 192.168.3.2
snmp-server location building 42
snmp-server contact polly hedra
snmp-server community ohwhatakeyisthee
!
telnet 10.1.1.11 255.255.255.255
telnet 192.168.3.0 255.255.255.0
```

Cisco AS 5400 Access Server

The following code example provides a configuration for the Cisco AS 5400 access server.

CODE EXAMPLE B-4 Cisco AS 5400 Access Server Sample Configuration

```
!
version 12.2
!
no service single-slot-reload-enable
no service pad
service timestamps debug datetime msec show-timezone
service timestamps log datetime msec show-timezone
service password-encryption
service internal
!
hostname fijinet-access1
!
no boot startup-test
logging buffered 1000000 debugging
logging rate-limit 10 except errors
no logging console guaranteed
no logging console
logging trap debugging
logging facility local4
logging source-interface FastEthernet0/1
logging 161.1.0.109
aaa new-model
aaa group server tacacs+ LAB
 server 161.1.0.109
!
aaa group server radius Proxy
 server 151.1.0.97 auth-port 1645 acct-port 1646
!
aaa authentication login default local group Proxy
aaa authentication login ADMIN group LAB local
aaa authentication login h323 group Proxy
aaa authentication ppp default if-needed local group Proxy
aaa authorization exec default group Proxy if-authenticated
aaa authorization exec ADMIN group LAB if-authenticated
aaa authorization exec h323 group Proxy
aaa authorization network default group Proxy if-authenticated
```

```
aaa accounting suppress null-username
aaa accounting delay-start
aaa accounting exec default start-stop group Proxy
aaa accounting exec ADMIN wait-start group LAB
aaa accounting network default start-stop group Proxy
aaa accounting connection ADMIN wait-start group LAB
aaa accounting connection h323 start-stop group Proxy
aaa accounting system default wait-start group LAB
aaa nas port extended
aaa processes 5
enable secret 5 $1$btpD$fe2deMBG3enR79mJflRQ00
!
username dialtme password 7 104A001809031F0E
!
dial-tdm-clock  priority 1 freerun
!
voice-fastpath enable
ip subnet-zero
no ip source-route
no ip gratuitous-arps
ip tftp source-interface FastEthernet0/1
no ip domain-lookup
ip host fijinet-access1 172.19.49.14
!
ip cef
no ip dhcp-client network-discovery
isdn switch-type primary-5ess
!
fax interface-type modem
mta receive maximum-recipients 0
!
controller T3 1/0
 framing m23
 cablelength 20
 t1 1-13 controller
!
controller T1 1/01
 framing esf
 pri-group timeslots 1-24
!
controller T1 1/02
 framing esf
 pri-group timeslots 1-24
!
controller T1 1/03
 framing esf
```

```
 pri-group timeslots 1-24
!
controller T1 1/04
 framing esf
 pri-group timeslots 1-24
!
controller T1 1/05
 framing esf
!
controller T1 1/06
 framing esf
!
controller T1 1/07
 framing esf
!
controller T1 1/08
 framing esf
!
controller T1 1/09
 framing esf
!
controller T1 1/010
 framing esf
!
controller T1 1/011
 framing esf
!
controller T1 1/012
 framing esf
!
controller T1 1/013
 framing esf
!
gw-accounting h323
gw-accounting h323 vsa
gw-accounting voip
translation-rule 1
!
interface Loopback0
 ip address 191.0.0.1 255.255.255.255
 no ip mroute-cache
 no keepalive
!
interface FastEthernet0/0
 description POP Data Network
 mac-address 0015.0000.0001
```

```
 ip address 151.0.0.1 255.255.255.0
 no ip mroute-cache
 load-interval 60
 duplex full
 speed 100
 no cdp enable
 h323-gateway voip interface
!
interface FastEthernet0/1
 description POP Control Network
 ip address 172.19.50.45 255.255.255.128
 no ip mroute-cache
 load-interval 60
 duplex full
 speed 100
 no cdp enable
!
interface Serial0/0
 no ip address
 shutdown
 clockrate 2000000
 no cdp enable
!
interface Serial0/1
 no ip address
 shutdown
 clockrate 2000000
 no cdp enable
!
interface Serial1/0123
 no ip address
 no ip proxy-arp
 encapsulation ppp
 no logging event link-status
 no keepalive
 dialer rotary-group 1
 no snmp trap link-status
 isdn switch-type primary-5ess
 isdn incoming-voice modem
 no fair-queue
 no cdp enable
!
interface Serial1/0223
 no ip address
 no ip proxy-arp
 encapsulation ppp
```

```
 no logging event link-status
 no keepalive
 dialer rotary-group 1
 no snmp trap link-status
 isdn switch-type primary-5ess
 isdn incoming-voice modem
 no fair-queue
 no cdp enable
!
interface Serial1/0323
 no ip address
 no ip proxy-arp
 encapsulation ppp
 no logging event link-status
 no keepalive
 dialer rotary-group 1
 no snmp trap link-status
 isdn switch-type primary-5ess
 isdn incoming-voice modem
 no fair-queue
 no cdp enable
!
interface Serial1/0423
 no ip address
 no ip proxy-arp
 encapsulation ppp
 no logging event link-status
 no keepalive
 dialer rotary-group 1
 no snmp trap link-status
 isdn switch-type primary-5ess
 isdn incoming-voice modem
 no fair-queue
 no cdp enable
!
interface Group-Async0
 ip unnumbered Loopback0
 encapsulation ppp
 no ip mroute-cache
 load-interval 60
 dialer in-band
 dialer idle-timeout 2147483
 async mode interactive
 no snmp trap link-status
 no peer default ip address
 ppp authentication chap callin
```

```
 group-range 2/00 7/107
 hold-queue 100 in
!
interface Dialer1
 ip address negotiated
 encapsulation ppp
 no ip route-cache cef
 no ip mroute-cache
 load-interval 60
 dialer in-band
 dialer idle-timeout 28800
 dialer-group 1
 autodetect encapsulation ppp
 no peer default ip address
 no fair-queue
 no cdp enable
 ppp authentication chap callin
!
ip classless
ip route 151.1.0.0 255.255.0.0 15.0.0.254
ip route 161.1.0.0 255.255.0.0 16.0.0.254
ip route 161.1.0.0 255.255.0.0 15.0.0.254
ip route 171.0.0.0 255.0.0.0 15.0.0.254
ip route 172.0.0.0 255.0.0.0 172.19.50.1
ip route 172.0.0.0 255.0.0.0 15.0.0.254
ip tacacs source-interface FastEthernet0/1
no ip http server
!
ip radius source-interface FastEthernet0/0
no cdp run
!
async-bootp dns-server 172.16.224.100 172.16.154.101
async-bootp nbns-server 172.16.224.10 172.16.4.2
ip dhcp-server 172.16.162.10
!
tftp-server flashc5400-js-mz.121-5.XM2
tftp-server flashc5400-js-mz.xa.Apr20
tacacs-server host 161.1.0.109 key pop-tac-key
tacacs-server host 172.22.44.36 key tmelab
tacacs-server administration
snmp-server engineID local 80000009030000014280B352
snmp-server community public RO
!
radius-server host 151.1.0.97 auth-port 1645 acct-port 1646 non-
standard key 7 19
radius-server retransmit 2
```

```
radius-server timeout 1
radius-server deadtime 1
radius-server attribute 6 on-for-login-auth
radius-server attribute 44 include-in-access-req
radius-server attribute 25 nas-port format c
radius-server attribute nas-port format c
radius-server unique-ident 8
radius-server vsa send accounting
radius-server vsa send authentication
call rsvp-sync
!
call application voice remote-auth tftp//sleepy/tcl/2.0/
app_remote_ip_authentil
!
line con 0
 exec-timeout 60 0
 password 7 0300520A0A1B2C49
 authorization exec ADMIN
 accounting commands 0 ADMIN
 accounting commands 15 ADMIN
 accounting exec ADMIN
 logging synchronous
 login authentication ADMIN
line aux 0
 no exec
 logging synchronous
line vty 0 4
 exec-timeout 60 0
 authorization commands 0 ADMIN
 authorization commands 15 ADMIN
 accounting commands 15 ADMIN
 accounting exec ADMIN
 login authentication ADMIN
line 2/00 7/107
 exec-timeout 5 0
 no flush-at-activation
 modem Dialin
 transport input all
 autoselect during-login
 autoselect ppp
!
scheduler allocate 10000 400
ntp clock-period 17179773
ntp server 15.1.0.97
ntp server 16.1.0.109 prefer
end
```

Cisco AS 2511 Console Server

The following code example provides a configuration for the Cisco AS 2511 console server.

CODE EXAMPLE B-5   Cisco AS 2511 Console Server Sample Configuration

```
!
version 12.0
!
service timestamps debug datetime msec localtime show-timezone
service timestamps log datetime msec localtime show-timezone
service password-encryption
!
hostname fijinet-console
!
enable secret 5 $1$Q/MX$ki9h6Ym6m9ItVrhvPBMnv0
!
username fijiadmin password KpcOfgs8
!
ip subnet-zero
ip domain-list fijinet.com
no ip domain-lookup
!
ip host fijinet-router 2001 172.21.1.1
ip host fijinet-switch 2002 172.21.1.1
ip host fijinet-firewall 2003 172.21.1.1
ip host fijinet-console 2004 172.21.1.1
ip host fijinet-access1 2005 172.21.1.1
ip host fijinet-access2 2006 172.21.1.1
ip host fijinet-web1 2007 172.21.1.1
ip host fijinet-content1 2008 172.21.1.1
ip host fijinet-management 2009 172.21.1.1
ip host fijinet-reserve1 2010 172.21.1.1
ip host fijinet-reserve2 2011 172.21.1.1
ip host fijinet-reserve3 2012 172.21.1.1
ip host fijinet-reserve4 2013 172.21.1.1
ip host fijinet-reserve5 2014 172.21.1.1
ip host fijinet-reserve6 2015 172.21.1.1
ip host fijinet-reserve7 2016 172.21.1.1
!
process-max-time 200
!
```

```
interface Loopback1
ip address 172.21.1.1 255.0.0.0
no ip directed-broadcast
!
interface Ethernet0
ip address 171.55.31.5 255.255.255.192
no ip directed-broadcast
no ip mroute-cache
!
interface Serial0
no ip address
no ip directed-broadcast
no ip mroute-cache
shutdown
!
ip default-gateway 171.55.31.1
ip classless
ip route 0.0.0.0 0.0.0.0 171.55.31.1
no ip http server
!
line con 0
transport input all
line 1 16
session-timeout 20
No exec
exec-timeout 0 0
transport input all
line aux 0
modem InOut
transport preferred telnet
transport input all
speed 38400
flowcontrol hardware
line vty 0 4
exec-timeout 60 0
password KpcOfgs8
login
!
end
```

Sample DNS Configurations

This appendix provides sample configurations for domain name service (DNS) servers. This configuration is for the design prototype (FijiNet), which uses a split-DNS configuration. This DNS configuration is compatible for BIND v8.x or higher. This appendix contains the following topics:

External DNS Configurations

This section provides sample configurations for DNS external servers.

Note – We recommend that you do not run DNS on an external firewall. However, if you must, then secure DNS completely. Additionally, DNS must be run in `chroot` environment with changed UID/GID.

Primary External Server

This section provides sample configurations for the following:

- "named.conf Primary External Sample Configuration" on page 274
- "fijinet.local Primary External Sample Configuration" on page 276
- "fijinet.cache Primary External Sample Configuration" on page 276
- "fijinet.com Primary External Sample Configuration" on page 277
- "fijinet.129.153.47 Primary External Sample Configuration" on page 278

`named.conf` Primary External Sample Configuration

CODE EXAMPLE C-1   Configuration for Primary External `named.conf`

```
options {
    directory           "/var/named";
    pid-file            "/var/named/named.pid";
    dump-file           "/var/named/named.dump";
    statistics-file     "/var/named/named.stats";
    named-xfer          "/usr/sbin/named-xfer";
    listen-on           { 129.153.47.101; };
};

logging {
    channel fijinet_syslog {
            syslog daemon;
            severity info;
    };
```

```
    channel fijinet_debug {
            file "/var/named/named.debug";
            severity dynamic;
    };
    category statistics {
            fijinet_syslog;
            fijinet_debug;
    };
    category queries {
            fijinet_debug;
    };
    category default {
            null;
    };
};

zone "." in {
    type hint;
    file "fijinet.cache";
};

zone "0.0.127.in-addr.arpa" in {
    type master;
    file "fijinet.local";
};

zone "47.153.129.in-addr.arpa" in {
    type master;
    file "fijinet.129.153.47";
    check-names warn;
    allow-update { 129.153.47.102; };
    allow-transfer { 129.153.47.102; };
    allow-query { any; };
    also-notify { };

};

zone "fijinet.com" in {
    type master;
    file "fijinet.com";
    check-names warn;
    allow-update { 129.153.47.102; };
    allow-transfer { 129.153.47.102; };
    allow-query { any; };
    also-notify { };
};
```

fijinet.local Primary External Sample Configuration

CODE EXAMPLE C-2 Configuration for Primary External `fijinet.local`

```
@ IN SOA dns1.fijinet.com. root.dns1.fijinet.com. (
    20010321    ; serial
    5M          ; Refresh after 5 minutes
    10M         ; Retry after 10 minutes
    5D          ; Expire after 5 days
    1D )        ; Minimum TTL of 1 day
;
; Name servers for fijinet.com. domain
;
    IN NS   dns1.fijinet.com.
    IN A    129.153.47.101
    IN NS   dns2.fijinet.com.
    IN A    129.153.47.102
;
; Loopback
;
1   IN PTR localhost.
```

fijinet.cache Primary External Sample Configuration

You can retrieve the list of root name servers via anonymous FTP from:

```
http//ftp.rs.internic.net
```

CODE EXAMPLE C-3 Configuration for Primary External `fijinet.cache`

```
.                       3600000    IN   NS   A.ROOT-SERVERS.NET.
A.ROOT-SERVERS.NET.     3600000         A    198.41.0.4
.                       3600000    IN   NS   B.ROOT-SERVERS.NET.
B.ROOT-SERVERS.NET.     3600000         A    128.9.0.107
.                       3600000    IN   NS   C.ROOT-SERVERS.NET.
C.ROOT-SERVERS.NET.     3600000         A    192.33.4.12
.                       3600000    IN   NS   D.ROOT-SERVERS.NET.
D.ROOT-SERVERS.NET.     3600000         A    128.8.10.90
.                       3600000    IN   NS   E.ROOT-SERVERS.NET.
E.ROOT-SERVERS.NET.     3600000         A    192.203.230.10
.                       3600000    IN   NS   F.ROOT-SERVERS.NET.
F.ROOT-SERVERS.NET.     3600000         A    192.5.5.241
```

CODE EXAMPLE C-3 Configuration for Primary External `fijinet.cache` *(Continued)*

```
.                              3600000     IN    NS    G.ROOT-SERVERS.NET.
G.ROOT-SERVERS.NET.            3600000           A     192.112.36.4
.                              3600000     IN    NS    H.ROOT-SERVERS.NET.
H.ROOT-SERVERS.NET.            3600000           A     128.63.2.53
.                              3600000     IN    NS    I.ROOT-SERVERS.NET.
I.ROOT-SERVERS.NET.            3600000           A     192.36.148.17
.                              3600000     IN    NS    J.ROOT-SERVERS.NET.
J.ROOT-SERVERS.NET.            3600000           A     198.41.0.10
.                              3600000     IN    NS    K.ROOT-SERVERS.NET.
K.ROOT-SERVERS.NET.            3600000           A     193.0.14.129
.                              3600000     IN    NS    L.ROOT-SERVERS.NET.
L.ROOT-SERVERS.NET.            3600000           A     198.32.64.12
.                              3600000     IN    NS    M.ROOT-SERVERS.NET.
M.ROOT-SERVERS.NET.            3600000           A     202.12.27.33
```

`fijinet.com` Primary External Sample Configuration

CODE EXAMPLE C-4 Configuration for Primary External `fijinet.com`

```
@ IN SOA dns1.fijinet.com. root.dns1.fijinet.com. (
    20010321          ; serial
    5M                ; Refresh after 5 minutes
    10M               ; Retry after 10 minutes
    5D                ; Expire after 5 days
    1D )              ; Minimum TTL of 1 day
;
; Name servers for fijinet.com. domain
;
            IN NS  dns1.fijinet.com.
            IN A   129.153.47.101
            IN MX  10 relay1.fijinet.com.
            IN NS  dns2.fijinet.com.
            IN A   129.153.47.102
            IN MX  20 relay2.fijinet.com.
;
; Hosts for fijinet.com. domain
;
localhost   IN A   127.0.0.1
firewall    IN A   129.153.47.1
firewall    IN A   129.153.47.1
dns1        IN A   129.153.47.101
dns2        IN A   129.153.47.102
```

```
relay1        IN A    129.153.47.151
relay2        IN A    129.153.47.152
proxy1        IN A    129.153.47.161
proxy2        IN A    129.153.47.162
web1          IN A    129.153.47.171
web2          IN A    129.153.47.172
;
; Aliases for fijinet.com. domain
;
gateway       IN CNAME firewall
```

`fijinet.129.153.47` Primary External Sample Configuration

CODE EXAMPLE C-5   Configuration for Primary External `fijinet.129.153.47`

```
@ IN SOA dns1.fijinet.com. root.dns1.fijinet.com. (
    20010321        ; serial
    5M              ; Refresh after 5 minutes
    10M             ; Retry after 10 minutes
    5D              ; Expire after 5 days
    1D )            ; Minimum TTL of 1 day
;
; Name servers for fijinet.com. domain
;
      IN NS   dns1.fijinet.com.
      IN A    129.153.47.101
      IN NS   dns2.fijinet.com.
      IN A    129.153.47.102
;
; Hosts for fijinet.com. domain
;
1     IN PTR     firewall.fijinet.com.
101   IN PTR     dns1.fijinet.com.
102   IN PTR     dns2.fijinet.com.
151   IN PTR     relay1.fijinet.com.
152   IN PTR     relay2.fijinet.com.
161   IN PTR     proxy1.fijinet.com.
162   IN PTR     proxy2.fijinet.com.
171   IN PTR     web1.fijinet.com.
172   IN PTR     web2.fijinet.com.
```

Secondary External Servers

This section provides sample configurations for the following:

- "named.conf Secondary External Sample Configuration" on page 279
- "fijinet.local Secondary External Sample Configuration" on page 281
- "fijinet.cache Secondary External Sample Configuration" on page 281

`named.conf` Secondary External Sample Configuration

CODE EXAMPLE C-6   Configuration for Secondary External `named.conf`

```
options {
    directory       "/var/named";
    pid-file        "/var/named/named.pid";
    dump-file       "/var/named/named.dump";
    statistics-file "/var/named/named.stats";
    named-xfer      "/usr/sbin/named-xfer";
    listen-on       { 129.153.47.102; };
};

logging {
    channel fijinet_syslog {
            syslog daemon;
            severity info;
    };
    channel fijinet_debug {
            file "/var/named/named.debug";
            severity dynamic;
    };
    category statistics {
            fijinet_syslog;
            fijinet_debug;
    };
    category queries {
            fijinet_debug;
    };
    category default {
            null;
    };
};
zone "." in {
    type hint;
```

```
        file "fijinet.cache";
};

zone "0.0.127.in-addr.arpa" in {
    type master;
    file "fijinet.local";
};
zone "47.153.129.in-addr.arpa" in {
    type slave;
    file "fijinet.129.153.47";
    masters { 129.153.47.101; };
    check-names warn;
    allow-update { none; };
    allow-transfer { none; };
    allow-query { any; };
    also-notify { };
};
zone "fijinet.com" in {
    type slave;
    file "fijinet.com";
    masters { 129.153.47.101; };
    check-names warn;
    allow-update { none; };
    allow-transfer { none; };
    allow-query { any; };
    also-notify { };
};
```

`fijinet.local` Secondary External Sample Configuration

CODE EXAMPLE C-7   Configuration for Secondary External `fijinet.local`

```
@ IN SOA dns2.fijinet.com. root.dns2.fijinet.com. (
    20010321        ; serial
    5M              ; Refresh after 5 minutes
    10M             ; Retry after 10 minutes
    5D              ; Expire after 5 days
    1D )            ; Minimum TTL of 1 day
;
; Name servers for fijinet.com. domain
;
    IN NS   dns1.fijinet.com.
    IN A    129.153.47.101
    IN NS   dns2.fijinet.com.
    IN A    129.153.47.102
;
; Loopback
;
1    IN PTR localhost.
```

`fijinet.cache` Secondary External Sample Configuration

You can retrieve the list of `root` name servers (`/domain/named.root`) via anonymous FTP from:

```
ftp.rs.internic.net
```

CODE EXAMPLE C-8   Configuration for Secondary External `fijinet.cache`

```
.                       3600000     IN  NS  A.ROOT-SERVERS.NET.
A.ROOT-SERVERS.NET.     3600000         A   198.41.0.4
.                       3600000     IN  NS  B.ROOT-SERVERS.NET.
B.ROOT-SERVERS.NET.     3600000         A   128.9.0.107
.                       3600000     IN  NS  C.ROOT-SERVERS.NET.
C.ROOT-SERVERS.NET.     3600000         A   192.33.4.12
.                       3600000     IN  NS  D.ROOT-SERVERS.NET.
D.ROOT-SERVERS.NET.     3600000         A   128.8.10.90
.                       3600000     IN  NS  E.ROOT-SERVERS.NET.
E.ROOT-SERVERS.NET.     3600000         A   192.203.230.10
```

```
.                          3600000      IN    NS    F.ROOT-SERVERS.NET.
F.ROOT-SERVERS.NET.        3600000            A     192.5.5.241
.                          3600000      IN    NS    G.ROOT-SERVERS.NET.
G.ROOT-SERVERS.NET.        3600000            A     192.112.36.4
.                          3600000      IN    NS    H.ROOT-SERVERS.NET.
H.ROOT-SERVERS.NET.        3600000            A     128.63.2.53
.                          3600000      IN    NS    I.ROOT-SERVERS.NET.
I.ROOT-SERVERS.NET.        3600000            A     192.36.148.17
.                          3600000      IN    NS    J.ROOT-SERVERS.NET.
J.ROOT-SERVERS.NET.        3600000            A     198.41.0.10
.                          3600000      IN    NS    K.ROOT-SERVERS.NET.
K.ROOT-SERVERS.NET.        3600000            A     193.0.14.129
.                          3600000      IN    NS    L.ROOT-SERVERS.NET.
L.ROOT-SERVERS.NET.        3600000            A     198.32.64.12
.                          3600000      IN    NS    M.ROOT-SERVERS.NET.
M.ROOT-SERVERS.NET.        3600000            A     202.12.27.33
```

Internal DNS Configurations

This section provides sample configurations for DNS internal servers.

Primary Internal Server

This section provides sample configurations for the following:

- "named.conf Primary Internal Sample Configuration" on page 283
- "fijinet.local Primary Internal Sample Configuration" on page 284
- "fijinet.cache Primary Internal Sample Configuration" on page 285
- "fijinet.com Primary Internal Sample Configuration" on page 285
- "fijinet.10.153.47 Primary Internal Sample Configuration" on page 286
- "fijinet 10.153.48 Primary Internal Sample Configuration" on page 287

named.conf Primary Internal Sample Configuration

CODE EXAMPLE C-9   Configuration for Primary Internal named.conf

```
options {
    directory        "/var/named";
    pid-file         "/var/named/named.pid";
    dump-file        "/var/named/named.dump";
    statistics-file "/var/named/named.stats";
    named-xfer       "/usr/sbin/named-xfer";
    listen-on        { 10.153.47.101; };
    forward          only;
    forwarders       { 129.153.47.101; 129.153.47.102; };
};
logging {
    channel fijinet_syslog {
            syslog daemon;
            severity info;
    };
    channel fijinet_debug {
            file "/var/named/named.debug";
            severity dynamic;
    };
    category statistics {
            fijinet_syslog;
            fijinet_debug;
    };
    category queries {
            fijinet_debug;
    };
    category default {
            null;
    };
};
zone "." in {
    type hint;
    file "fijinet.cache";
};
zone "0.0.127.in-addr.arpa" in {
    type master;
    file "fijinet.local";
};
zone "47.153.10.in-addr.arpa" in {
    type master;
    file "fijinet.10.153.47";
    check-names warn;
    allow-update { 10.153.47.102; };
```

```
        allow-transfer { 10.153.47.102; };
        allow-query { 10/8; };
        also-notify { };
};
zone "48.153.10.in-addr.arpa" in {
    type master;
    file "fijinet.10.153.48";
    check-names warn;
    allow-update { 10.153.47.102; };
    allow-transfer { 10.153.47.102; };
    allow-query { 10/8; };
    also-notify { };
};
zone "fijinet.com" in {
    type master;
    file "fijinet.com";
    check-names warn;
    allow-update { 10.153.47.102; };
    allow-transfer { 10.153.47.102; };
    allow-query { 10/8 };
    also-notify { };
};
```

fijinet.local Primary Internal Sample Configuration

CODE EXAMPLE C-10 Configuration for Primary Internal `fijinet.local`

```
@ IN SOA dns1.fijinet.com. root.dns1.fijinet.com. (
        20010321      ; serial
        5M            ; Refresh after 5 minutes
        10M           ; Retry after 10 minutes
        5D            ; Expire after 5 days
        1D )          ; Minimum TTL of 1 day
;
; Name servers for fijinet.com. domain
;
    IN NS  dns1.fijinet.com.
    IN A   10.153.47.101
    IN NS  dns2.fijinet.com.
    IN A   10.153.47.102
;
```

```
; Loopback
;
1   IN PTR localhost.
```

`fijinet.cache` Primary Internal Sample Configuration

CODE EXAMPLE C-11 Configuration for Primary Internal `fijinet.cache`

```
.                       3600000 IN NS    DNS1.FIJINET.COM.
DNS1.FIJINET.COM.       3600000    A     129.153.47.101

.                       3600000 IN NS    DNS2.FIJINET.COM.
DNS2.FIJINET.COM.       3600000    A     129.153.47.102
```

`fijinet.com` Primary Internal Sample Configuration

CODE EXAMPLE C-12 Configuration for Primary Internal `fijinet.com`

```
@ IN SOA dns1.fijinet.com. root.dns1.fijinet.com. (
      20010321       ; serial
      5M             ; Refresh after 5 minutes
      10M            ; Retry after 10 minutes
      5D             ; Expire after 5 days
      1D )           ; Minimum TTL of 1 day
;
; Name servers for fijinet.com. domain
;
              IN NS  dns1.fijinet.com.
              IN A   10.153.47.101
              IN MX  10 relay1.fijinet.com.
              IN NS  dns2.fijinet.com.
              IN A   10.153.47.102
              IN MX  20 relay2.fijinet.com.
;
; Hosts for fijinet.com. domain
;
localhost        IN A     127.0.0.1
```

```
firewall       IN A     10.153.47.1
dhcp1          IN A     10.153.47.11
dhcp2          IN A     10.153.47.12
ldap1          IN A     10.153.47.21
ldap2          IN A     10.153.47.22
ntp1           IN A     10.153.47.31
ntp2           IN A     10.153.47.32
dns1           IN A     10.153.47.101
dns2           IN A     10.153.47.102
app1           IN A     10.153.47.181
app2           IN A     10.153.47.182
content1       IN A     10.153.47.191
content2       IN A     10.153.47.192
console        IN A     10.153.48.101
management     IN A     10.153.48.102
backup         IN A     10.153.48.103
;
; Aliases for fijinet.com. domain
;
gateway        IN CNAME firewall
```

fijinet.10.153.47 Primary Internal Sample Configuration

CODE EXAMPLE C-13 Configuration for Primary Internal fijinet.10.153.47

```
@ IN SOA dns1.fijinet.com. root.dns1.fijinet.com. (
      20010321      ; serial
      5M            ; Refresh after 5 minutes
      10M           ; Retry after 10 minutes
      5D            ; Expire after 5 days
      1D )          ; Minimum TTL of 1 day
;
; Name servers for fijinet.com. domain
;
      IN NS  dns1.fijinet.com.
      IN A   10.153.47.101
      IN NS  dns2.fijinet.com.
      IN A   10.153.47.102
;
; Hosts for 10.153.47/24 subnet
```

CODE EXAMPLE C-13 Configuration for Primary Internal `fijinet.10.153.47` *(Continued)*

```
;
1       IN  PTR         firewall.fijinet.com.
11      IN  PTR         dhcp1.fijinet.com.
12      IN  PTR         dhcp2.fijinet.com.
21      IN  PTR         ldap1.fijinet.com.
22      IN  PTR         ldap2.fijinet.com.
31      IN  PTR         ntp1.fijinet.com.
32      IN  PTR         ntp2.fijinet.com.
101     IN  PTR         dns1.fijinet.com.
102     IN  PTR         dns2.fijinet.com.
151     IN  PTR         relay1.fijinet.com.
152     IN  PTR         relay2.fijinet.com.
161     IN  PTR         proxy1.fijinet.com.
162     IN  PTR         proxy2.fijinet.com.
171     IN  PTR         web1.fijinet.com.
172     IN  PTR         web2.fijinet.com.
181     IN  PTR         app1.fijinet.com.
182     IN  PTR         app2.fijinet.com.
191     IN  PTR         content1.fijinet.com.
192     IN  PTR         content2.fijinet.com.
```

`fijinet 10.153.48` Primary Internal Sample Configuration

CODE EXAMPLE C-14 Configuration for Primary Internal `fijinet.10.153.48`

```
@ IN SOA dns1.fijinet.com. root.dns1.fijinet.com. (
    20010321; serial
    5M              ; Refresh after 5 minutes
    10M             ; Retry after 10 minutes
    5D              ; Expire after 5 days
    1D )            ; Minimum TTL of 1 day
;
; Name servers for fijinet.com. domain
;
    IN NS   dns1.fijinet.com.
    IN A    10.153.47.101
    IN NS   dns2.fijinet.com.
    IN A    10.153.47.102
;
; Hosts for 10.153.48/24 subnet
```

```
;
101 IN PTR   console.fijinet.com.
102 IN PTR   management.fijinet.com.
103 IN PTR   backup.fijinet.com.
```

Secondary Internal Servers

This section provides sample configurations for the following:

- "named.conf Secondary Internal Sample Configuration" on page 288
- "fijinet.local Secondary Internal Sample Configuration" on page 290
- "fijinet.cache Secondary Internal Sample Configuration" on page 290

`named.conf` Secondary Internal Sample Configuration

CODE EXAMPLE C-15 Configuration for Secondary Internal `named.conf`

```
options {
    directory       "/var/named";
    pid-file        "/var/named/named.pid";
    dump-file       "/var/named/named.dump";
    statistics-file "/var/named/named.stats";
    named-xfer      "/usr/sbin/named-xfer";
    listen-on       { 10.153.47.101; };
    forward         only;
    forwarders      { 129.153.47.101; 129.153.47.102; };
};
logging {
    channel fijinet_syslog {
            syslog daemon;
            severity info;
    };
    channel fijinet_debug {
            file "/var/named/named.debug";
            severity dynamic;
    };
    category statistics {
            fijinet_syslog;
            fijinet_debug;
```

```
    };
    category queries {
            fijinet_debug;
    };
    category default {
            null;
    };
};
zone "." in {
    type hint;
    file "fijinet.cache";
};
zone "0.0.127.in-addr.arpa" in {
    type master;
    file "fijinet.local";
};
zone "47.153.10.in-addr.arpa" in {
    type slave;
    type forward;
    file "fijinet.10.153.47";
    masters { 10.153.47.101; };
    check-names warn;
    allow-update { none; };
    allow-transfer { none; };
    allow-query { 10/8; };
    also-notify { };
};
zone "48.153.10.in-addr.arpa" in {
    type slave;
    type forward;
    file "fijinet.10.153.48";
    masters { 10.153.47.101; };
    check-names warn;
    allow-update { none; };
    allow-transfer { none; };
    allow-query { 10/8; };
    also-notify { };
};
zone "fijinet.com" in {
    type slave;
    type forward;
    file "fijinet.com";
    masters { 10.153.47.101; };
    check-names warn;
    allow-update { none; };
    allow-transfer { none; };
```

Configuration for Secondary Internal `named.conf` *(Continued)*

```
    allow-query { 10/8 };
    also-notify { };
};
```

`fijinet.local` Secondary Internal Sample Configuration

CODE EXAMPLE C-16 Configuration for Secondary Internal `fijinet.local`

```
@ IN SOA dns2.fijinet.com. root.dns2.fijinet.com. (
     20010321      ; serial
     5M            ; Refresh after 5 minutes
     10M           ; Retry after 10 minutes
     5D            ; Expire after 5 days
     1D )          ; Minimum TTL of 1 day
;
; Name servers for fijinet.com. domain
;
    IN NS  dns1.fijinet.com.
    IN A   10.153.47.101
    IN NS  dns2.fijinet.com.
    IN A   10.153.47.102
;
; Loopback
;
1   IN PTR localhost.
```

`fijinet.cache` Secondary Internal Sample Configuration

CODE EXAMPLE C-17 Configuration for Secondary Internal `fijinet.cache`

```
.                       3600000 IN NS   DNS1.FIJINET.COM.
DNS1.FIJINET.COM.       3600000    A    129.153.47.101

.                       3600000 IN NS   DNS2.FIJINET.COM.
DNS2.FIJINET.COM.       3600000    A    129.153.47.102
```

DHCP Server Configuration

This appendix contains a sample configuration (`dhcp.conf`) for the DHCP server. This configuration is Solaris-specific and correlates to the design prototype (FijiNet).

CODE EXAMPLE D-1   Sample Configuration for DHCP Server

```
# option definitions common to all supported networks

option domain-name "fijinet.com";
option domain-name-servers dns1.fijinet.com, dns2.fijinet.com;

default-lease-time 600;
max-lease-time 7200;

# If this DHCP server is the official DHCP server for the local
# network, the authoritative directive should be uncommented

#authoritative;

# Use this to send dhcp log messages to a different log file
# (you also have to hack syslog.conf to complete the redirection)

log-facility local7;

# No service will be given on this subnet, but declaring it
# helps the  DHCP server to understand the network topology

subnet 10.153.48.0 netmask 255.255.255.0 {
}

# This is a very basic subnet declaration

subnet 10.153.49.0 netmask 255.255.255.0 {
```

```
   range 10.153.49.2 10.153.49.253;
   option routers fijinet-router.fijinet.com;
}

subnet 10.153.50.0 netmask 255.255.255.0 {
   range 10.153.50.2 10.153.50.253;
   option routers fijinet-router.fijinet.com;
}

# This declaration allows BOOTP clients to get dynamic addresses,
# which we don't really recommend

#subnet 10.153.48.0 netmask 255.255.255.0 {
#   range dynamic-bootp 10.153.48.100 10.153.48.200;
#   option broadcast-address 10.153.48.255;
#   option routers fijinet-router.fijinet.com;
#}

# A slightly different configuration for an internal subnet

#subnet 10.153.48.0 netmask 255.255.255.0 {
#   range 10.153.48.100 10.153.48.200;
#   option domain-name-servers dns1.fijinet.com;
#   option domain-name "fijinet.com";
#   option routers fijinet-router.fijinet.com;
#   option broadcast-address 10.153.48.255;
#   default-lease-time 600;
#   max-lease-time 7200;
#}

# Hosts which require special configuration options can be
# listed in host statements. If no address is specified, the
# address will be allocated dynamically (if possible), but
# the host-specific information will still come from the host
# declaration.

# host passacaglia {
# hardware ethernet 0:0:c0:5d:bd:95;
# filename "vmunix.passacaglia";
# server-name "toccata.fugue.com";
#}

# Fixed IP addresses can also be specified for hosts. These
# addresses should not also be listed as being available for
# dynamic assignment. Hosts for which fixed IP addresses have
# been specified can boot using BOOTP or DHCP. Hosts for
```

```
# which no fixed address is specified can only be booted with
# DHCP, unless there is an address range on the subnet to
# which a BOOTP client is connected which has the dynamic-bootp
# flag set

host fijinet-dns1 {
  hardware ethernet 08:00:20:fd:d5:94;
  fixed-address fijinet-dns1.fijinet.com;
}

host fijinet-dns2 {
  hardware ethernet 08:00:20:fd:ab:2c;
  fixed-address fijinet-dns1.fijinet.com;
}

host fijinet-nas1 {
  hardware ethernet 08:00:20:fe:91:29;
  fixed-address fijinet-dns1.fijinet.com;
}

host fijinet-nas2 {
  hardware ethernet 08:00:20:f8:1e:14;
  fixed-address fijinet-dns1.fijinet.com;
}

host fijinet-ntp1 {
  hardware ethernet 08:00:20:fe:7a:28;
  fixed-address fijinet-dns1.fijinet.com;
}

host fijinet-dhcp1 {
  hardware ethernet 08:00:20:f8:47:ae;
  fixed-address fijinet-dns1.fijinet.com;
}

# You can declare a class of clients and then do address
# allocation based on that. The example below shows a case
# where all clients in a certain class get addresses on
# the 10.17.224/24 subnet, and all other clients get
# addresses on the 10.0.29/24 subnet.

#class "foo" {
#  match if substring (option vendor-class-identifier, 0, 4) =
"SUNW";
#}
#
```

```
#shared-network 224-29 {
#  subnet 10.17.224.0 netmask 255.255.255.0 {
#    option routers rtr-224.example.org;
#  }
#  subnet 10.0.29.0 netmask 255.255.255.0 {
#    option routers rtr-29.example.org;
#  }
#  pool {
#    allow members of "foo";
#    range 10.17.224.10 10.17.224.250;
#  }
#  pool {
#    deny members of "foo";
#    range 10.0.29.10 10.0.29.230;
#  }
#}
```

NTP Server Configuration

This appendix provides a sample configuration (`ntp.conf`) for the NTP server. This configuration is Solaris-specific and correlates to the design prototype (FijiNet).

CODE EXAMPLE E-1   Sample Configuration for NTP Server

```
#
# Default server NTP configuration is to listen for NTP
# broadcast & multicast
#
#
# stratum 3 servers
#
server domainclock01.fijinet.com
server domainclock02.fijinet.com
peer   domainclock03.fijinet.com
#
# stratum 4 servers
#
peer timetone01.fijinet.com
peer timetone02.fijinet.com
#
# set up for local network broadcast
#
broadcast 129.153.85.0
#
# set up for site-wide multicast
#
broadcast 224.0.1.1 ttl 1
enable monitor
driftfile /var/ntp/ntp.drift
statsdir /var/ntp/ntpstats/
```

```
filegen peerstats file peerstats type day enable
filegen loopstats file loopstats type day enable
filegen clockstats file clockstats type day enable
```

DNS Benchmark Data for Sun Enterprise Servers

This appendix contains benchmark results from a DNS benchmark running Berkeley Internet name domain (BIND) v8.1.2 and v9.1.0 on Solaris 8 and Sun Enterprise servers. (For more information, refer to the *Sun DNS/BIND Benchmarking and Sizing Guide*.) We use this data for making assumptions about performance when using the BIND for domain name services. This software is freely available from the Internet Software Consortium (ISC).

When designing an architecture, obtain benchmark performance results for the equipment you select, and use the data to predict performance and load.

This appendix contains the following topics:

The tables in this appendix are organized by version of BIND. The columns of the tables are defined TABLE F-1.

TABLE F-1 Key to BIND Benchmark Tables

Column	Description
Server	Sun server platform
Number of CPUs	CPUs per DNS server
NIC Speed	Network interface speed
CPU Speed	CPU speed in MHz
System Memory	Amount of RAM in the system
Peak %user	Peak CPU utilization of DNS processes in user mode
Peak %sys	Peak CPU utilization of DNS processes in system mode
Peak %wio	Peak CPU utilization of DNS processes in waiting for block I/O
Peak rss	Peak resident set size of memory of DNS processes in Kbytes
Peak rps	Peak requests per second processed by the DNS server
Peak ipps	Peak inbound packets per second processed by DNS server
Peak opps	Peak outbound packets per second processed by DNS server
Peak imbps	Peak inbound data (mbps) processed by DNS server
Peak ombps	Peak outbound data (mbps) processed by DNS server

Benchmark Data for BIND v8.1.2

The following tables (TABLE F-2 and TABLE F-3) provide benchmark data for CPU, memory utilization, and network utilization for BIND version 8.1.2.

TABLE F-2   CPU and Memory Utilization

Server	Number of CPUs	CPU Speed	System Memory	Peak %user	Peak %sys	Peak %wio	Peak rss
Netra t1	1	440 MHz	1 GB	56.70	45.70	3.30	1,744.00
Netra 1125	2	300 MHz	256 MB	50.50	48.50	2.00	1,720.00
Ultra 220R	2	450 MHz	256 MB	49.70	49.40	1.00	1,712.00
Ultra 250	2	296 MHz	1 GB	54.80	45.80	0.80	1,720.00
Ultra 420R	4	450 MHz	4 GB	53.70	46.40	0.00	1,712.00
Ultra 450	4	296 MHz	1 GB	54.20	45.80	0.10	1,728.00
Ultra 4500	12	400 MHz	12 GB	45.80	54.30	0.00	1,688.00

TABLE F-3   Network Utilization

Server	NIC speed	Peak rps	Peak ipps	Peak opps	Peak imbps	Peak ombps
Netra t1	hme (100 Mbps)	5,156.50	5,075.00	5,075.00	3.29	6.21
Netra 1125	qfe (100 Mbps)	4,028.10	4,018.00	4,018.00	2.60	4.91
Ultra 220R	hme (100 Mbps)	5,726.10	5,681.00	5,681.00	3.68	6.95
Ultra 250	hme (100 Mbps)	4,507.60	4,513.00	4,513.00	2.93	5.52
Ultra 420R	qfe (100 Mbps)	7,091.50	7,105.00	7,105.00	4.61	8.69
Ultra 450	qfe (100 Mbps)	4,680.40	4,683.00	4,683.00	3.04	5.73
Ultra 4500	hme (100 Mbps)	5.117.30	0.00	0.00	0.00	0.00

Benchmark Data for BIND v8.2.2-P7

The following tables (TABLE F-4 and TABLE F-5) provide benchmark data for CPU, memory utilization, and network utilization for BIND version 8.2.2-P7.

TABLE F-4   CPU and Memory Utilization

Server	Number of CPUs	CPU Speed	System Memory	Peak %user	Peak %sys	Peak %wio	Peak rss
Netra t1	1	440 MHz	1 GB	55.10	43.60	3.70	1,808.00
Netra 1125	2	300 MHz	256 MB	48.40	48.30	1.30	1,752.00
Ultra 220R	2	450 MHz	256 MB	47.30	51.10	0.40	1,792.00
Ultra 250	2	296 MHz	1 GB	56.50	43.60	0.70	1,752.00
Ultra 420R	4	450 MHz	4 GB	56.40	43.90	0.00	1,776.00
Ultra 450	4	296 MHz	1 GB	54.70	45.40	0.10	1,784.00
Ultra 4500	12	400 MHz	12 GB	45.30	54.70	0.00	1,888.00

TABLE F-5   Network Utilization

Server	NIC speed	Peak rps	Peak ipps	Peak opps	Peak imbps	Peak ombps
Netra t1	hme (100 Mbps)	5,814.00	5,686.00	5,686.00	3.69	6.96
Netra 1125	qfe (100 Mbps)	5,312.10	4,500.00	4,500.00	2.92	5.50
Ultra 220R	hme (100 Mbps)	6,857.30	6,870.00	6,870.00	4.45	8.40
Ultra 250	hme (100 Mbps)	5,617.50	5,417.00	5,418.00	3.51	6.63
Ultra 420R	qfe (100 Mbps)	8,351.10	8,384.00	8,384.00	5.44	10.25
Ultra 450	qfe (100 Mbps)	5,429.60	5,251.00	5,251.00	3.40	6.42
Ultra 4500	hme (100 Mbps)	4,609.60	0.00	0.00	0.00	0.00

Benchmark Data for BIND v9.1.0

The following tables (TABLE F-6 and TABLE F-7) provide benchmark data for CPU, memory utilization, and network utilization for BIND version 9.1.0.

TABLE F-6 CPU and Memory Utilization

Server	Number of CPUs	CPU Speed	System Memory	Peak %user	Peak %sys	Peak %wio	Peak rss
Netra t1	1	440 MHz	1 GB	71.10	25.90	21.90	4,800.00
Netra 1125	2	300 MHz	256 MB	89.00	42.60	187.30	5,024.00
Ultra 220R	2	450 MHz	256 MB	99.10	54.40	187.20	5,344.00
Ultra 250	2	296 MHz	1 GB	100.40	31.20	186.10	4,928.00
Ultra 420R	4	450 MHz	4 GB	193.20	70.10	208.60	4,936.00
Ultra 450	4	296 MHz	1 GB	192.20	66.40	213.90	5,024.00
Ultra 4500	12	400 MHz	12 GB	168.50	197.20	274.30	9,224.00

TABLE F-7 Network Utilization

Server	NIC speed	Peak rps	Peak ipps	Peak opps	Peak imbps	Peak ombps
Netra t1	hme (100 Mbps)	2,104.70	2,079.00	2,079.00	1.35	2.33
Netra 1125	qfe (100 Mbps)	2,081.20	2,064.00	2,064.00	1.34	2.31
Ultra 220R	hme (100 Mbps)	3,046.30	2,994.00	2,994.00	1.94	3.35
Ultra 250	hme (100 Mbps)	2,138.50	2,150.00	2,150.00	1.39	2.41
Ultra 420R	qfe (100 Mbps)	5,211.10	5,239.00	5,239.00	3.40	5.87
Ultra 450	qfe (100 Mbps)	3,769.70	3,713.00	3,713.00	2.41	4.16
Ultra 4500	hme (100 Mbps)	2,866.30	0.00	0.00	0.00	0.00

Network Capacity

This appendix lists signaling types and associated bandwidths for network capacity. It contains the following:

- "North American Digital Hierarchy" on page 304
- "Committee of European Postal and Telephone Hierarchy" on page 304
- "Synchronous Digital Hierarchy" on page 305

North American Digital Hierarchy

TABLE G-1 provides network capacity specifications for the North American digital hierarchy.

TABLE G-1   North America Digital Hierarchy

Signal	Capacity	Number of DS-0
DS-0	64 Kbps	1
DS-1 (T1)	1.544 Mbps	24
DS-2 (T2)	6.312 Mbps	96
DS-3 (T3)	44.736 Mbps	672

Committee of European Postal and Telephone Hierarchy

TABLE G-2 provides network capacity specifications for the Committee of European Postal and Telephone hierarchy.

TABLE G-2   Committee of European Postal and Telephone (CEPT) Hierarchy

Signal	Capacity	Number of E1
E0	64 Kbps	n/a
E1	2.048 Mbps	1
E2	8.448 Mbps	4
E3	34.368 Mbps	16

Synchronous Digital Hierarchy

TABLE G-3 provides network capacity specifications for synchronous digital hierarchy.

TABLE G-3   Synchronous Digital Hierarchy (SDH)

STS Rate	Capacity	OC Level
STS-1	51.84 Mbps	OC-1
STS-3	155.52 Mbps	OC-3
STS-12	622.08 Mbps	OC-12
STS-24	1.244 Gbps	OC-24
STS-48	2.488 Gbps	OC-48
STS-96	4.976 Gbps	OC-96
STS-192	9.952 Gbps	OC-192

HTTP Throughput

This appendix provides a table of HTTP performance by signaling types.

TABLE H-1 HTTP Throughput

Signal	Capacity	Peak HTTP operations/second
28.8K modem	28.8 Kbps	0.25
56K modem	56 Kbps	0.4
ISDN (BRI)	64 Kbps	0.5
T1	1.544 Mbps	10
10BaseT	10 Mbps	60
T3	44.736 Mbps	300
Fast Ethernet	100 Mbps	500
FDDI	100 Mbps	600
OC-3	155.52 Mbps	900
OC-12	622.08 Mbps	3500
Gigabit Ethernet	1000 Mbps	5000

Port and Protocol List

This appendix provides a *partial* list of protocols and ports helpful in identifying services and associated protocols/ports for firewall rules. For a complete list of ports, see Internet Assigned Numbers Authority's (IANA) website at:

```
http://www.iana.org/assignments/port-numbers
```

Port numbers are divided into three ranges: well-known ports, registered ports, and dynamic and/or private ports.

- Well-known ports range from 0 through 1023.
- Registered ports range from 1024 through 49151.
- Dynamic and/or private ports range from 49152 through 65535.

TABLE I-1 provides service, port/protocol, and description for well-known ports.

TABLE I-1   Well-Known Ports

Service	Port/Protocol	Description
tcpmux	1/tcp/udp	TCP port service multiplexer
compressnet	2/tcp/udp	Management utility
compressnet	3/tcp/udp	Compression process
	4/tcp/udp	(Unassigned)
rje	5/tcp/udp	Remote job entry
	6/tcp/udp	(Unassigned)
echo	7/tcp/udp	Echo
	8/tcp/udp	(Unassigned)
discard	9/tcp/udp	Discard

TABLE I-1 Well-Known Ports *(Continued)*

Service	Port/Protocol	Description
	10/tcp/udp	(Unassigned)
systat	11/tcp/udp	Active users
	12/tcp/udp	(Unassigned)
daytime	13/tcp/udp	Daytime
	14/tcp/udp	(Unassigned)
	15/tcp/udp	(Unassigned)
	16/tcp/udp	(Unassigned)
qotd	17/tcp/udp	Quote of the day
msp	18/tcp/udp	Message send protocol
chargen	19/tcp/udp	Character generator
ftp-data	20/tcp/udp	File transfer (data)
ftp	21/tcp/udp	File transfer (control)
ssh	22/tcp/udp	SSH remote login protocol
telnet	23/tcp/udp	Telnet
	24/tcp/udp	Any private mail system
smtp	25/tcp/udp	Simple mail transfer protocol (SMTP)
	26/tcp/udp	(Unassigned)
nsw-fe	27/tcp/udp	NSW user system Fast Ethernet
	28/tcp/udp	(Unassigned)
msg-icp	29/tcp/udp	MSG ICP
	30/tcp/udp	(Unassigned)
msg-auth	31/tcp/udp	MSG authentication
	32/tcp/udp	(Unassigned)
dsp	33/tcp/udp	Display support protocol
	34/tcp/udp	(Unassigned)
	35/tcp/udp	Any private printer server
	36/tcp/udp	(Unassigned)
time	37/tcp/udp	Time
rap	38/tcp/udp	Route access protocol
rlp	39/tcp/udp	Resource location protocol

TABLE I-1 Well-Known Ports (*Continued*)

Service	Port/Protocol	Description
	40/tcp/udp	(Unassigned)
graphics	41/tcp/udp	Graphics
name	42/tcp/udp	Host name server
nicname	43/tcp/udp	Who is
mpm-flags	44/tcp/udp	MPM FLAGS protocol
mpm	45/tcp/udp	Message processing module
mpm-snd	46/tcp/udp	MPM (default send)
ni-ftp	47/tcp/udp	NI FTP
auditd	48/tcp/udp	Digital audit daemon
tacacs	49/tcp/udp	Login host protocol, terminal access controller access control system (TACACS)
re-mail-ck	50/tcp/udp	Remote mail checking protocol
la-maint	51/tcp/udp	IMP logical address maintenance
xns-time	52/tcp/udp	XNS time protocol
domain	53/tcp/udp	Domain name server
xns-ch	54/tcp/udp	XNS clearinghouse
isi-gl	55/tcp/udp	ISI graphics language
xns-auth	56/tcp/udp	XNS authentication
	57/tcp/udp	Any private terminal access
xns-mail	58/tcp/udp	XNS mail
	59/tcp/udp	Any private file service
	60/tcp/udp	(Unassigned)
ni-mail	61/tcp/udp	NI mail
acas	62/tcp/udp	ACA services
whois++	63/tcp/udp	Whois++
covia	64/tcp/udp	Communications integrator (CI)
tacacs-ds	65/tcp/udp	TACACS-database service
sql*net	66/tcp/udp	Oracle® SQL*NET®
bootps	67/tcp/udp	Bootstrap protocol server
bootpc	68/tcp/udp	Bootstrap protocol client
tftp	69/tcp/udp	Trivial file transfer

TABLE I-1   Well-Known Ports *(Continued)*

Service	Port/Protocol	Description
gopher	70/tcp/udp	Gopher
netrjs-1	71/tcp/udp	Remote job service
netrjs-2	72/tcp/udp	Remote job service
netrjs-3	73/tcp/udp	Remote job service
netrjs-4	74/tcp/udp	Remote job service
	75/tcp/udp	Any private dial out service
deos	76/tcp/udp	Distributed external object store
	77/tcp/udp	Any private RJE service
vettcp	78/tcp/udp	Vettcp
finger	79/tcp/udp	Finger
http	80/tcp/udp	World Wide Web HTTP
hosts2-ns	81/tcp/udp	HOSTS2 name server
xfer	82/tcp/udp	XFER utility
mit-ml-dev	83/tcp/udp	MIT ML device
ctf	84/tcp/udp	Common trace facility
mit-ml-dev	85/tcp/udp	MIT ML device
mfcobol	86/tcp/udp	Micro Focus COBOL™
	87/tcp/udp	Any private terminal link
kerberos	88/tcp/udp	Kerberos
su-mit-tg	89/tcp/udp	SU/MIT telnet gateway
dnsix	90/tcp/udp	DNSIX securit attribute token map
mit-dov	91/tcp/udp	MIT® Dover spooler
npp	92/tcp/udp	Network printing protocol
dcp	93/tcp/udp	Device control protocol
objcall	94/tcp/udp	Tivoli Object Dispatcher
supdup	95/tcp/udp	SUPDUP
dixie	96/tcp/udp	DIXIE protocol specification
swift-rvf	97/tcp/udp	Swift remote virtural file protocol
tacnews	98/tcp/udp	TAC news
metagram	99/tcp/udp	Metagram relay

TABLE I-1   Well-Known Ports *(Continued)*

Service	Port/Protocol	Description
newacct	100/tcp/udp	(Unauthorized use)
hostname	101/tcp/udp	NIC host name server
iso-tsap	102/tcp/udp	ISO-TSAP class 0
gppitnp	103/tcp/udp	Genesis point-to-point trans net
acr-nema	104/tcp/udp	ACR-NEMA Digital Imag. & Comm. 300
cso	105/tcp/udp	CCSO name server protocol
3com-tsmux	106/tcp/udp	3COM-TSMUX
rtelnet	107/tcp/udp	Remote telnet service
snagas	108/tcp/udp	SNA gateway access server
pop2	109/tcp/udp	Post office protocol - version 2
pop3	110/tcp/udp	Post office protocol - version 3
sunrpc	111/tcp/udp	Sun remote procedure call
mcidas	112/tcp/udp	McIDAS data transmission protocol
auth	113/tcp/udp	Authentication service
audionews	114/tcp/udp	Audio news multicast
sftp	115/tcp/udp	Simple file transfer protocol
ansanotify	116/tcp/udp	ANSA REX notify
uucp-path	117/tcp/udp	UUCP path service
sqlserv	118/tcp/udp	SQL services
nntp	119/tcp/udp	Network news transfer protocol
cfdptkt	120/tcp/udp	CFDPTKT
erpc	121/tcp/udp	Encore expedited remote pro.call
smakynet	122/tcp/udp	SMAKYNET
ntp	123/tcp/udp	Network time protocol
ansatrader	124/tcp/udp	ANSA REX trader
locus-map	125/tcp/udp	Locus™ PC-Interface net map ser
nxedit	126/tcp/udp	NXEdit
locus-con	127/tcp/udp	Locus PC-interface conn server
gss-xlicen	128/tcp/udp	GSS X license verification
pwdgen	129/tcp/udp	Password generator protocol

TABLE I-1   Well-Known Ports *(Continued)*

Service	Port/Protocol	Description
cisco-fna	130/tcp/udp	Cisco FNATIVE
cisco-tna	131/tcp/udp	Cisco TNATIVE
cisco-sys	132/tcp/udp	Cisco SYSMAINT
statsrv	133/tcp/udp	Statistics service
ingres-net	134/tcp/udp	INGRES-NET service
epmap	135/tcp/udp	DCE endpoint resolution
profile	136/tcp/udp	PROFILE naming system
netbios-ns	137/tcp/udp	NETBIOS/IXQ™ name service
netbios-dgm	138/tcp/udp	NETBIOS datagram service
netbios-ssn	139/tcp/udp	NETBIOS session service
emfis-data	140/tcp/udp	EMFIS data service
emfis-cntl	141/tcp/udp	EMFIS control service
bl-idm	142/tcp/udp	Britton-Lee IDM
imap	143/tcp/udp	Internet message access protocol
uma	144/tcp/udp	Universal management architecture
uaac	145/tcp/udp	UAAC protocol
iso-tp0	146/tcp/udp	ISO-IP0
iso-ip	147/tcp/udp	ISO-IP
jargon	148/tcp/udp	Jargon
aed-512	149/tcp/udp	AED 512 emulation service
sql-net	150/tcp/udp	SQL-NET
hems	151/tcp/udp	HEMS
bftp	152/tcp/udp	Background file transfer program
sgmp	153/tcp/udp	SGMP
netsc-prod	154/tcp/udp	NETSC
netsc-dev	155/tcp/udp	NETSC
sqlsrv	156/tcp/udp	SQL Service
knet-cmp	157/tcp/udp	KNET/VM command/message protocol
pcmail-srv	158/tcp/udp	PCMail server
nss-routing	159/tcp/udp	NSS-routing

TABLE I-1   Well-Known Ports *(Continued)*

Service	Port/Protocol	Description
sgmp-traps	160/tcp/udp	SGMP-TRAPS
snmp	161/tcp/udp	SNMP
snmptrap	162/tcp/udp	SNMPTRAP
cmip-man	163/tcp/udp	CMIP/tcp/udp manager
cmip-agent	164/tcp/udp	CMIP/tcp/udp agent
xns-courier	165/tcp/udp	Xerox®
s-net	166/tcp/udp	Sirius™ systems (LightWork Design)
namp	167/tcp/udp	NAMP
rsvd	168/tcp/udp	RSVD
send	169/tcp/udp	SEND
print-srv	170/tcp/udp	Network postscript
multiplex	171/tcp/udp	Network Innovations multiplex
cl/1	172/tcp/udp	Network Innovations CL/1
xyplex-mux	173/tcp/udp	Xyplex™
mailq	174/tcp/udp	MAILQ
vmnet	175/tcp/udp	VMNET
genrad-mux	176/tcp/udp	GENRAD-MUX
xdmcp	177/tcp/udp	X display manager control protocol
nextstep	178/tcp/udp	NextStep window server
bgp	179/tcp/udp	Border gateway protocol
ris	180/tcp/udp	Intergraph
unify	181/tcp/udp	Unify®
audit	182/tcp/udp	Unisys® audit SITP
ocbinder	183/tcp/udp	OCBinder
ocserver	184/tcp/udp	OCServer
remote-kis	185/tcp/udp	Remote KIS®
kis	186/tcp/udp	KIS protocol
aci	187/tcp/udp	Application communication interface
mumps	188/tcp/udp	Plus Five's MUMPS
qft	189/tcp/udp	Queued file transport

TABLE I-1   Well-Known Ports (*Continued*)

Service	Port/Protocol	Description
gacp	190/tcp/udp	Gateway™ access control protocol
prospero	191/tcp/udp	Prospero® directory service
osu-nms	192/tcp/udp	OSU™ network monitoring system
srmp	193/tcp/udp	Spider remote monitoring protocol
irc	194/tcp/udp	Internet relay chat protocol
dn6-nlm-aud	195/tcp/udp	DNSIX network level module audit
dn6-smm-red	196/tcp/udp	DNSIX session mgt module audit redir
dls	197/tcp/udp	Directory location service
dls-mon	198/tcp/udp	Directory location service monitor
smux	199/tcp/udp	SMUX
src	200/tcp/udp	IBM system resource controller
at-rtmp	201/tcp/udp	AppleTalk routing maintenance
at-nbp	202/tcp/udp	AppleTalk name binding
at-3	203/tcp/udp	AppleTalk unused
at-echo	204/tcp/udp	AppleTalk echo
at-5	205/tcp/udp	AppleTalk unused
at-zis	206/tcp/udp	AppleTalk zone information
at-7	207/tcp/udp	AppleTalk unused
at-8	208/tcp/udp	AppleTalk unused
qmtp	209/tcp/udp	Quick mail transfer protocol
z39.50	210/tcp/udp	ANSI Z39.50
914c/g	211/tcp/udp	Texas Instruments™ 914C/G terminal
anet	212/tcp/udp	ATEXSSTR
ipx	213/tcp/udp	IPX
vmpwscs	214/tcp/udp	VM PWSCS
softpc	215/tcp/udp	Insignia Solutions®
CAIlic	216/tcp/udp	Computer Associates International, Inc.® License Server
dbase	217/tcp/udp	dBASE Unix
mpp	218/tcp/udp	Netix message posting protocol
uarps	219/tcp/udp	Unisys ARPs

TABLE I-1 Well-Known Ports *(Continued)*

Service	Port/Protocol	Description
imap3	220/tcp/udp	Interactive mail access protocol v3
fln-spx	221/tcp/udp	Berkeley rlogind with SPX auth
rsh-spx	222/tcp/udp	Berkeley rshd with SPX auth
cdc	223/tcp/udp	Certificate distribution center
masqdialer	224/tcp/udp	Masqdialer
	225-241	(reserved)
direct	242/tcp/udp	Direct
sur-meas	243/tcp/udp	Survey measurement
inbusiness	244/tcp/udp	Inbusiness™
link	245/tcp/udp	LINK
dsp3270	246/tcp/udp	Display systems protocol
subntbcst_tftp	247/tcp/udp	SUBNTBCST_TFTP
bhfhs	248/tcp/udp	Bhfhs
	249-255	(Reserved)
rap	256/tcp/udp	RAP
set	257/tcp/udp	Secure electronic transaction
yak-chat	258/tcp/udp	Yak[SM] Winsock personal chat
esro-gen	259/tcp/udp	Efficient short remote operations
openport	260/tcp/udp	Openport
nsiiops	261/tcp/udp	IIOP™ name service over TLS/SSL
arcisdms	262/tcp/udp	Arcisdms
hdap	263/tcp/udp	HDAP
bgmp	264/tcp/udp	BGMP
x-bone-ctl	265/tcp/udp	X-Bone CTL
sst	266/tcp/udp	SCSI on ST
td-service	267/tcp/udp	Tobit David service layer
td-replica	268/tcp/udp	Tobit David replica
	269-279	(Unassigned)
http-mgmt	280/tcp/udp	Http-mgmt
personal-link	281/tcp/udp	Personal link

TABLE I-1   Well-Known Ports *(Continued)*

Service	Port/Protocol	Description
cableport-ax	282/tcp/udp	Cable port A/X
rescap	283/tcp/udp	Rescap
corerjd	284/tcp/udp	Corerjd
	285	(Unassigned)
fxp-1	286/tcp/udp	FXP-1
k-block	287/tcp/udp	K-BLOCK
	288-307	(Unassigned)
novastorbakcup	308/tcp/udp	Novastor backup
entrusttime	309/tcp/udp	EntrustTime
bhmds	310/tcp/udp	Bhmds
asip-webadmin	311/tcp/udp	AppleShare® IP WebAdmin
vslmp	312/tcp/udp	VSLMP
magenta-logic	313/tcp/udp	Magenta Logic
opalis-robot	314/tcp/udp	Opalis Robot
dpsi	315/tcp/udp	DPSI™
decauth	316/tcp/udp	decAuth
zannet	317/tcp/udp	Zannet
pkix-timestamp	318/tcp/udp	PKIX TimeStamp
ptp-even	319/tcp/udp	PTP event
ptp-general	320/tcp/udp	PTP general
pip	321/tcp/udp	PIP
rtsps	322/tcp/udp	RTSPS
	323-332	(Unassigned)
texar	333/tcp/udp	Texar™ security port
	334-343	(Unassigned)
pdap	344/tcp/udp	Prospero data access protocol
pawserv	345/tcp/udp	Perf analysis workbench
zserv	346/tcp/udp	Zebra® server
fatserv	347/tcp/udp	Fatmen server
csi-sgwp	348/tcp/udp	Cabletron^{SM} management protocol

TABLE I-1   Well-Known Ports *(Continued)*

Service	Port/Protocol	Description
mftp	349/tcp/udp	Mftp
matip-type-a	350/tcp/udp	MATIP Type A
matip-type-b	351/tcp/udp	MATIP Type B
dtag-ste-sb	352/tcp/udp	DTAG
ndsauth	353/tcp/udp	NDSAUTH
bh611	354/tcp/udp	bh611
datex-asn	355/tcp/udp	DATEX-ASN
cloanto-net-1	356/tcp/udp	Cloanto® Net 1
bhevent	357/tcp/udp	Bhevent
shrinkwrap	358/tcp/udp	Shrinkwrap™
nsrmp	359/tcp/udp	Network security risk mgt protocol
scoi2odialog	360/tcp/udp	Scoi2odialog
semantix	361/tcp/udp	Semantix
srssend	362/tcp/udp	SRS Send
rsvp_tunnel	363/tcp/udp	RSVP Tunnel
aurora-cmgr	364/tcp/udp	Aurora CMGR
dtk	365/tcp/udp	DTK
odmr	366/tcp/udp	ODMR
mortgageware	367/tcp/udp	MortgageWare™
qbikgdp	368/tcp/udp	QbikGDP
rpc2portmap	369/tcp/udp	Rpc2portmap
codaauth2	370/tcp/udp	Codaauth2
clearcase	371/tcp/udp	Clearcase®
ulistproc	372/tcp/udp	ListProcessor
legent-1	373/tcp/udp	Legent Corporation, now owned by Computer Associates International, Inc.
legent-2	374/tcp/udp	Legent Corporation, now owned by Computer Associates International, Inc.
hassle	375/tcp/udp	Hassle
nip	376/tcp/udp	Amiga™ Envoy Network Inquiry Proto
tnETOS	377/tcp/udp	NEC Corporation™

TABLE I-1   Well-Known Ports *(Continued)*

Service	Port/Protocol	Description
dsETOS	378/tcp/udp	NEC Corporation
is99c	379/tcp/udp	TIA/EIA/IS-99 modem client
is99s	380/tcp/udp	TIA/EIA/IS-99 modem server
hp-collector	381/tcp/udp	HP[SM] performance data collector
hp-managed-node	382/tcp/udp	HP performance data managed node
hp-alarm-mgr	383/tcp/udp	HP performance data alarm manager
arns	384/tcp/udp	A remote network server system
ibm-app	385/tcp/udp	IBM application
asa	386/tcp/udp	ASA message router object def.
aurp	387/tcp/udp	AppleTalk® Update-Based Routing Pro.
unidata-ldm	388/tcp/udp	Unidata LDM
ldap	389/tcp/udp	Lightweight directory access protocol
uis	390/tcp/udp	UIS
synotics-relay	391/tcp/udp	SynOptics SNMP relay port
synotics-broker	392/tcp/udp	SynOptics port broker port
meta5	393/tcp/udp	Meta5
embl-ndt	394/tcp/udp	EMBL Nucleic data transfer
netcp	395/tcp/udp	Netscout™ control protocol
netware-ip	396/tcp/udp	Novell® Netware® over IP
mptn	397/tcp/udp	Multi protocol trans. net.
kryptolan	398/tcp/udp	Kryptolan
iso-tsap-c2	399/tcp/udp	ISO Transport class 2 non-control over TCP
work-sol	400/tcp/udp	Workstation Solutions™
ups	401/tcp/udp	Uninterruptible power supply
genie	402/tcp/udp	Genie protocol
decap	403/tcp/udp	Decap
nced	404/tcp/udp	Nced
ncld	405/tcp/udp	Ncld
imsp	406/tcp/udp	Interactive mail support protocol
timbuktu	407/tcp/udp	Timbuktu®

TABLE I-1   Well-Known Ports *(Continued)*

Service	Port/Protocol	Description
prm-sm	408/tcp/udp	Prospero Resource Manager Sys. Man.
prm-nm	409/tcp/udp	Prospero Resource Manager Node Man.
decladebug	410/tcp/udp	DECLadebug remote debug protocol
rmt	411/tcp/udp	Remote MT protocol
synoptics-trap	412/tcp/udp	Trap convention port
smsp	413/tcp/udp	Storage management services protocol
infoseek	414/tcp/udp	InfoSeek®
bnet	415/tcp/udp	BNet
silverplatter	416/tcp/udp	Silverplatter
onmux	417/tcp/udp	Onmux
hyper-g	418/tcp/udp	Hyper-G (now Hyperwave)
ariel1	419/tcp/udp	Ariel™
smpte	420/tcp/udp	SMPTE
ariel2	421/tcp/udp	Ariel
ariel3	422/tcp/udp	Ariel
opc-job-start	423/tcp/udp	IBM operations planning and control start
opc-job-track	424/tcp/udp	IBM operations planning and control track
icad-el	425/tcp/udp	ICAD®
smartsdp	426/tcp/udp	Smartsdp
svrloc	427/tcp/udp	Server location
ocs_cmu	428/tcp/udp	OCS_CMU
ocs_amu	429/tcp/udp	OCS_AMU
utmpsd	430/tcp/udp	UTMPSD
utmpcd	431/tcp/udp	UTMPCD
iasd	432/tcp/udp	IASD
nnsp	433/tcp/udp	NNSP
mobileip-agent	434/tcp/udp	MobileIP-agent
mobilip-mn	435/tcp/udp	MobilIP-MN
dna-cml	436/tcp/udp	DNA-CML™
comscm	437/tcp/udp	Comscm

TABLE I-1   Well-Known Ports *(Continued)*

Service	Port/Protocol	Description
dsfgw	438/tcp/udp	Dsfgw
dasp	439/tcp/udp	Dasp
sgcp	440/tcp/udp	Sgcp
decvms-sysmgt	441/tcp/udp	Decvms-sysmgt
cvc_hostd	442/tcp/udp	Cvc_hostd
https	443/tcp/udp	Http protocol over TLS/SSL
snpp	444/tcp/udp	Simple network paging protocol
microsoft-ds	445/tcp/udp	Microsoft-DS
ddm-rdb	446/tcp/udp	DDM-RDB
ddm-dfm	447/tcp/udp	DDM-RFM
ddm-ssl	448/tcp/udp	DDM-SSL
as-servermap	449/tcp/udp	AS server mapper
tserver	450/tcp/udp	TServer
sfs-smp-net	451/tcp/udp	Cray® network semaphore server
sfs-config	452/tcp/udp	Cray SFS config server
creativeserver	453/tcp/udp	CreativeServer
contentserver	454/tcp/udp	ContentServer
creativepartnr	455/tcp/udp	CreativePartnr®
macon-tcp	456/tcp/udp	Macon-tcp
scohelp	457/tcp/udp	Scohelp
appleqtc	458/tcp/udp	Apple QuickTime®
ampr-rcmd	459/tcp/udp	Ampr-rcmd
skronk	460/tcp/udp	Skronk
datasurfsrv	461/tcp/udp	DataRampSrv
datasurfsrvsec	462/tcp/udp	DataRampSrvSec
alpes	463/tcp/udp	Alpes
kpasswd	464/tcp/udp	Kpasswd
urd	465/tcp/udp	URL rendesvous directory for SSM
digital-vrc	466/tcp/udp	Digital-vrc
mylex-mapd	467/tcp/udp	Mylex-mapd

TABLE I-1   Well-Known Ports *(Continued)*

Service	Port/Protocol	Description
photuris	468/tcp/udp	Proturis
rcp	469/tcp/udp	Radio control protocol
scx-proxy	470/tcp/udp	Scx-proxy
mondex	471/tcp/udp	Mondex®
ljk-login	472/tcp/udp	Ljk-login
hybrid-pop	473/tcp/udp	Hybrid-pop
tn-tl-w1	474/tcp/udp	Tn-tl-w1
tcpnethaspsrv	475/tcp/udp	Tcpnethaspsrv
tn-tl-fd1	476/tcp/udp	Tn-tl-fd1
ss7ns	477/tcp/udp	Ss7ns
spsc	478/tcp/udp	Spsc
iafserver	479/tcp/udp	Iafserver
iafdbase	480/tcp/udp	Iafdbase
ph	481/tcp/udp	Ph service
bgs-nsi	482/tcp/udp	Bgs-nsi
ulpnet	483/tcp/udp	Ulpnet
integra-sme	484/tcp/udp	Integra software management environment
powerburst	485/tcp/udp	Air Soft Power Burst
avian	486/tcp/udp	Avian™
saft	487/tcp/udp	Saft simple asynchronous file transfer
gss-http	488/tcp/udp	Gss-http
nest-protocol	489/tcp/udp	Nest-protocol
micom-pfs	490/tcp/udp	Micom® pfs
go-login	491/tcp/udp	Go-login
ticf-1	492/tcp/udp	Transport independent convergence for FNA
ticf-2	493/tcp/udp	Transport independent convergence for FNA
pov-ray	494/tcp/udp	POV-Ray
intecourier	495/tcp/udp	Intecourier
pim-rp-disc	496/tcp/udp	PIM-RP-DISC

TABLE I-1   Well-Known Ports *(Continued)*

Service	Port/Protocol	Description
dantz	497/tcp/udp	Dantz®
siam	498/tcp/udp	Siam®
iso-ill	499/tcp/udp	ISO ILL protocol
isakmp	500/tcp/udp	Isakmp
stmf	501/tcp/udp	STMF
asa-appl-proto	502/tcp/udp	Asa-appl-proto
intrinsa	503/tcp/udp	Intrinsa®
citadel	504/tcp/udp	Citadel
mailbox-lm	505/tcp/udp	Mailbox-lm
ohimsrv	506/tcp/udp	Ohimsrv
crs	507/tcp/udp	Crs
xvttp	508/tcp/udp	Xvttp
snare	509/tcp/udp	Snare®
fcp	510/tcp/udp	FirstClass protocol
passgo	511/tcp/udp	PassGo®
exec	512/tcp/udp	Remote process execution
login	513/tcp/udp	Remote login a la telnet
shell	514/tcp/udp	Cmd
printer	515/tcp/udp	Spooler
videotex	516/tcp/udp	Videotex
talk	517/tcp/udp	Like tenex link
ntalk	518/tcp/udp	Ntalk
utime	519/tcp/udp	Unixtime
efs	520/tcp/udp	Extended file name server
ripng	521/tcp/udp	Ripng
ulp	522/tcp/udp	ULP
ibm-db2	523/tcp/udp	IBM-DB2
ncp	524/tcp/udp	NCP®
timed	525/tcp/udp	Timed
tempo	526/tcp/udp	Newdate

TABLE I-1 Well-Known Ports *(Continued)*

Service	Port/Protocol	Description
stx	527/tcp/udp	Stock IXChange
custix	528/tcp/udp	Customer IXChange
irc-serv	529/tcp/udp	IRC-SERV
courier	530/tcp/udp	Rpc
conference	531/tcp/udp	Chat
netnews	532/tcp/udp	Readnews
netwall	533/tcp/udp	For emergency broadcasts
mm-admin	534/tcp/udp	MegaMedia® Admin
iiop	535/tcp/udp	Iiop
opalis-rdv	536/tcp/udp	Opalis-rdv
nmsp	537/tcp/udp	Networked media streaming protocol
gdomap	538/tcp/udp	Gdomap
apertus-ldp	539/tcp/udp	Apertus Technologies Load Determination
uucp	540/tcp/udp	Uucpd
uucp-rlogin	541/tcp/udp	Uucp-rlogin
commerce	542/tcp/udp	Commerce
klogin	543/tcp/udp	Klogin
kshell	544/tcp/udp	Krcmd
appleqtcsrvr	545/tcp/udp	Appleqtcsrvr
dhcpv6-client	546/tcp/udp	DHCPv6 Client
dhcpv6-server	547/tcp/udp	DHCPv6 Server
afpovertcp	548/tcp/udp	AFP over TCP
idfp	549/tcp/udp	IDFP
new-rwho	550/tcp/udp	New-who
cybercash	551/tcp/udp	Cybercash®
deviceshare	552/tcp/udp	Deviceshare
pirp	553/tcp/udp	Pirp
rtsp	554/tcp/udp	Real time stream control protocol
dsf	555/tcp/udp	Dsf
remotefs	556/tcp/udp	Rfs server

TABLE I-1   Well-Known Ports *(Continued)*

Service	Port/Protocol	Description
openvms-sysipc	557/tcp/udp	Openvms-sysipc
sdnskmp	558/tcp/udp	SDNSKMP
teedtap	559/tcp/udp	TEEDTAP
rmonitor	560/tcp/udp	Rmonitord
monitor	561/tcp/udp	Monitor
chshell	562/tcp/udp	Chcmd
nntps	563/tcp/udp	Nntp protocol over TLS/SSL (was snntp)
9pfs	564/tcp/udp	Plan 9® file service
whoami	565/tcp/udp	Whoami
streettalk	566/tcp/udp	StreetTalk®
banyan-rpc	567/tcp/udp	Banyan^SM rpc
ms-shuttle	568/tcp/udp	Microsoft shuttle
ms-rome	569/tcp/udp	Microsoft rome
meter	570/tcp/udp	Demon
meter	571/tcp/udp	Udemon
sonar	572/tcp/udp	Sonar
banyan-vip	573/tcp/udp	Banyan-vip
ftp-agent	574/tcp/udp	FTP software agent system
vemmi	575/tcp/udp	VEMMI
ipcd	576/tcp/udp	Ipcd
vnas	577/tcp/udp	Vnas
ipdd	578/tcp/udp	Ipdd
decbsrv	579/tcp/udp	Decbsrv
sntp-heartbeat	580/tcp/udp	SNTP HEARTBEAT
bdp	581/tcp/udp	Bundle discovery protocol
scc-security	582/tcp/udp	SCC Security
philips-vc	583/tcp/udp	Philips® video-conferencing
keyserver	584/tcp/udp	Key Server
imap4-ss	l585/tcp/udp	IMAP4+SSL
password-chg	586/tcp/udp	Password change

TABLE I-1 Well-Known Ports *(Continued)*

Service	Port/Protocol	Description
submission	587/tcp/udp	Submission
cal	588/tcp/udp	CAL
eyelink	589/tcp/udp	EyeLink™
tns-cm	1590/tcp/udp	TNS CML
http-alt	591/tcp/udp	FileMaker®, Inc
eudora-set	592/tcp/udp	Eudora set
http-rpc-epmap	593/tcp/udp	HTTP RPC Ep Map
tpip	594/tcp/udp	TPIP
cab-protocol	595/tcp/udp	CAB protocol
smsd	596/tcp/udp	SMSD
ptcnameservice	597/tcp/udp	PTC name service
sco-websrvrmg3	598/tcp/udp	SCO® Web Server Manager 3
acp	599/tcp/udp	Aeolon core protocol
ipcserver	600/tcp/udp	Sun IPC server
syslog-conn	601/tcp/udp	Reliable syslog service
	602-605	(Unassigned)
urm	606/tcp/udp	Cray unified resource manager
nqs	607/tcp/udp	Nqs
sift-uft	608/tcp/udp	Sender-initiated/unsolicited file transfer
npmp-trap	609/tcp/udp	Npmp-trap
npmp-local	610/tcp/udp	Npmp-local
npmp-gui	611/tcp/udp	Npmp-gui
hmmp-ind	612/tcp/udp	HMMP indication
hmmp-op	613/tcp/udp	HMMP operation
sshell	614/tcp/udp	SSLshell
sco-inetmgr	615/tcp/udp	Internet configuration manager
sco-sysmgr	616/tcp/udp	SCO System Administration Server
sco-dtmgr	617/tcp/udp	SCO Desktop Administration Server
dei-icda	618/tcp/udp	DEI-ICDA
digital-evm	619/tcp/udp	Digital EVM

TABLE I-1   Well-Known Ports *(Continued)*

Service	Port/Protocol	Description
sco-websrvrmgr	620/tcp/udp	SCO WebServer Manager
escp-ip	621/tcp/udp	ESCP
collaborator	622/tcp/udp	Collaborator
aux_bus_shunt	623/tcp/udp	Aux bus shunt
cryptoadmin	624/tcp/udp	Crypto admin
dec_dlm	625/tcp/udp	DEC DLM
asia	626/tcp/udp	ASIA
passgo-tivoli	627/tcp/udp	PassGo® Tivoli
qmqp	628/tcp/udp	QMQP
3com-amp3	629/tcp/udp	3Com AMP3
rda	630/tcp/udp	RDA
ipp	631/tcp/udp	IPP (internet printing protocol)
bmpp	632/tcp/udp	Bmpp
servstat	633/tcp/udp	Service status update (Sterling Software)
ginad	634/tcp/udp	Ginad
rlzdbase	635/tcp/udp	RLZ DBase
ldaps	636/tcp/udp	Ldap protocol over TLS/SSL
lanserver	637/tcp/udp	Lanserver
mcns-sec	638/tcp/udp	Mcns-sec
msdp	639/tcp/udp	MSDP
entrust-sps	640/tcp/udp	Entrust sps
repcmd	641/tcp/udp	Repcmd
esro-emsdp	642/tcp/udp	ESRO-EMSDP V1.3
sanity	643/tcp/udp	SANity®
dwr	644/tcp/udp	Dwr
pssc	645/tcp/udp	PSSC
ldp	646/tcp/udp	LDP
dhcp-failover	647/tcp/udp	DHCP Failover
rrp	648/tcp/udp	Registry registrar protocol (RRP)
aminet	649/tcp/udp	Aminet®

TABLE I-1   Well-Known Ports *(Continued)*

Service	Port/Protocol	Description
obex	650/tcp/udp	OBEX
ieee-mms	651/tcp/udp	IEEE MMS
hello-port	652/tcp/udp	HELLO_PORT
repscmd	653/tcp/udp	RepCmd
aodv	654/tcp/udp	AODV
tinc	655/tcp/udp	TINC
spmp	656/tcp/udp	SPMP
rmc	657/tcp/udp	RMC
tenfold	658/tcp/udp	TenFold®
	659/tcp/udp	(Unassigned)
mac-srvr-admin	660/tcp/udp	MacOS™ server admin
hap	661/tcp/udp	HAP
pftp	662/tcp/udp	PFTP
purenoise	663/tcp/udp	PureNoise™
secure-aux-bus	664/tcp/udp	Secure aux bus
sun-dr6	665/tcp/udp	Sun DR
mdqs	666/tcp/udp	Mdqs
doom	666/tcp/udp	Doom Id software
disclose	667/tcp/udp	Campaign contribution disclosures - SDR technologies
mecomm	668/tcp/udp	MeComm
meregister	669/tcp/udp	MeRegister
vacdsm-sws	670/tcp/udp	VACDSM-SWS
vacdsm-app	671/tcp/udp	VACDSM-APP
vpps-qua	672/tcp/udp	VPPS-QUA
cimplex	673/tcp/udp	CIMPLEX
acap	674/tcp/udp	ACAP
dctp	675/tcp/udp	DCTP
vpps-via	676/tcp/udp	VPPS Via
vpp	677/tcp/udp	Virtual presence protocol
ggf-ncp	678/tcp/udp	GNU Generation Foundation NCP

TABLE I-1   Well-Known Ports *(Continued)*

Service	Port/Protocol	Description
mrm	679/tcp/udp	MRM
entrust-aaas	680/tcp/udp	Entrust-aaas
entrust-aams	681/tcp/udp	Entrust-aams
xfr	682/tcp/udp	XFR
corba-iiop	683/tcp/udp	CORBA™ IIOP
corba-iiop-ssl	684/tcp/udp	CORBA IIOP SSL
mdc-portmapper	685/tcp/udp	MDC port mapper
hcp-wismar	686/tcp/udp	Hardware control protocol wismar
asipregistry	687/tcp/udp	Asipregistry
realm-rusd	688/tcp/udp	REALM-RUSD
nmap	689/tcp/udp	NMAP
vatp	690/tcp/udp	VATP
msexch-routing	691/tcp/udp	MS exchange routing
hyperwave-isp	692/tcp/udp	Hyperwave-ISP
connendp	693/tcp/udp	Connendp
ha-cluster	694/tcp/udp	HA-cluster
ieee-mms-ssl	695/tcp/udp	IEEE-MMS-SSL
rushd	696/tcp/udp	RUSHD
uuidgen	697/tcp/udp	UUIDGEN
olsr	698/tcp/udp	OLSR
accessnetwork	699/tcp/udp	Access network
	700-703	(Unassigned)
elcsd	704/tcp/udp	Errlog copy/server daemon
agentx	705/tcp/udp	AgentX
silc	706/tcp/udp	SILC
borland-dsj	707/tcp/udp	Borland® DSJ
	708	(Unassigned)
entrust-kmsh	709/tcp/udp	Entrust Key Management Service Handler
entrust-ash	710/tcp/udp	Entrust Administration Service Handler
cisco-tdp	711/tcp/udp	Cisco TDP

TABLE I-1   Well-Known Ports *(Continued)*

Service	Port/Protocol	Description
	712-728	(Unassigned)
netviewdm1	729/tcp/udp	IBM NetView DM/6000 server/client
netviewdm2	730/tcp/udp	IBM NetView DM/6000 send/tcp/udp
netviewdm3	731/tcp/udp	IBM NetView DM/6000 receive/tcp/udp
	732-740	(Unassigned)
netgw	741/tcp/udp	NetGW
netrcs	742/tcp/udp	Network based rev. cont. sys.
	743	(Unassigned)
flexlm	744/tcp/udp	Flexible license manager
	745-746	(Unassigned)
fujitsu-dev	747/tcp/udp	Fujitsu® Device Control
ris-cm	748/tcp/udp	Russell Info Sci Calendar Manager
kerberos-adm	749/tcp/udp	Kerberos administration
rfile	750/tcp/udp	Rfile
pump	751/tcp/udp	Pump
qrh	752/tcp/udp	Qrh
rrh	753/tcp/udp	Rrh
tell	754/tcp/udp	Send
	755-756	(Unassigned)
	757/tcp/udp	(Unassigned)
nlogin	758/tcp/udp	Nlogin
con	759/tcp/udp	Con
ns	760/tcp/udp	Ns
rxe	761/tcp/udp	Rxe
quotad	762/tcp/udp	Quotad
cycleserv	763/tcp/udp	Cycleserv
omserv	764/tcp/udp	Pmserv
webster	765/tcp/udp	Webster
	766	(Unassigned)
phonebook	767/tcp/udp	Phone

TABLE I-1   Well-Known Ports *(Continued)*

Service	Port/Protocol	Description
	768	(Unassigned)
vid	769/tcp/udp	Vid
cadlock	770/tcp/udp	Cadlock
rtip	771/tcp/udp	Rtip
cycleserv2	772/tcp/udp	Cycleserv2
submit	773/tcp/udp	Submit
rpasswd	774/tcp/udp	Rpasswd
entomb	775/tcp/udp	Entomb
wpages	776/tcp/udp	Wpages
multiling-http	777/tcp/udp	Multiling HTTP
	778-779	(Unassigned)
wpgs	780/tcp/udp	
	781-785	(Unassigned)
concert	786/tcp/udp	Concert
qsc	787/tcp/udp	QSC
	788-799	(Unassigned)
mdbs_daemon	800/tcp/udp	Mdbs_daemon
device	801/tcp/udp	Device
	802-809	(Unassigned)
fcp-udp	810/tcp/udp	FCP datagram
	811-827	(Unassigned)
itm-mcell-s	828/tcp/udp	Itm-mcell-s
pkix-3-ca-ra	829/tcp/udp	PKIX-3 CA/RA
	830-846	(Unassigned)
dhcp-failover2	847/tcp/udp	Dhcp-failover 2
	848-872	(Unassigned)
rsync	873/tcp/udp	Rsync
	874-885	(Unassigned)
iclcnet-locate	886/tcp/udp	ICL coNETion locate server
iclcnet_svinfo	887/tcp/udp	ICL coNETion server info

TABLE I-1   Well-Known Ports *(Continued)*

Service	Port/Protocol	Description
accessbuilder	888/tcp/udp	AccessBuilder™
	889-899	(Unassigned)
omginitialrefs	900/tcp/udp	OMG initial refs
smpnameres	901/tcp/udp	SMPNAMERES
ideafarm-chat	902/tcp/udp	IDEAFARM-CHAT
ideafarm-catch	903/tcp/udp	IDEAFARM-CATCH
	904-910	(Unassigned)
xact-backup	911/tcp/udp	Xact-backup
	912-988	(Unassigned)
ftps-data	989/tcp/udp	Ftp protocol, data, over TLS/SSL
ftps	990/tcp/udp	Ftp protocol, control, over TLS/SSL
nas	991/tcp/udp	Netnews Administration System
telnets	992/tcp/udp	Telnet protocol over TLS/SSL
imaps	993/tcp/udp	Imap4 protocol over TLS/SSL
ircs	994/tcp/udp	Irc protocol over TLS/SSL
pop3s	995/tcp/udp	Pop3 protocol over TLS/SSL
vsinet	996/tcp/udp	Vsinet
maitrd	997/tcp/udp	Maitrd
busboy	998/tcp/udp	Busboy
puprouter	999/tcp/udp	Pubrouter
cadlock2	1000/tcp/udp	Cadlock2
	1001-1009	(Unassigned)
surf	1010/tcp/udp	Surf
	1011-1022	(reserved)
	1023/tcp/udp	(reserved)

Bibliography

The following bibliography provides references to sources used in this book and references to sources we recommend, related to designing ISP architectures. The references are listed alphabetically by author within each subject area. This bibliography contains the following:

Architecture Design

Sun Professional Services. *Dot-Com & Beyond – Breakthrough Internet-Based Architectures and Methodologies*. Palo Alto, CA: Sun Microsystems, Inc., 2001.

Capacity Planning

Diggs, Brad, John Nguyen, and Ron Cotten. *Sun DNS/BIND Benchmarking and Sizing Guide*, Whitepaper, Sun Microsystems, Palo Alto, CA: March 2, 2001.

Menascé, Daniel and Virgilio Almeida. *Capacity Planning for Web Performance – Metrics, Models, & Methods*. Upper Saddle River, NJ: Prentice-Hall, 1998.

Wong, Brian. *Configuration and Capacity Planning for Solaris Servers*. Mountain View, CA: Sun Microsystems, Inc., 1997.

Database

Bobrowski, Steve. *Oracle8 Architecture*. Berkeley, CA: McGraw-Hill, 1998.

Directory Services

Bialaski, Tom and Michael Haines. *Solaris and LDAP Naming Services – Deploying LDAP in the Enterprise*. Palo Alto, CA: Sun Microsystems, Inc., 2001.

Howes, Tim, Gordon Good, and Mark Smith. *Understanding and Deploying LDAP Directory Services*. Macmillan Technical Publishing, 1998.

Howes, Tim and Mark Smith. *LDAP - Programming Directory-Enabled Applications with Lightweight Directory Access Protocol*. Macmillan Technical Publishing, 1997.

Lamothe, Robert. *Implementing and Troubleshooting LDAP*. New Riders Publishing, 1999.

Wilcox, Mark. *Implementing LDAP*. Wrox Press, Inc., 1999.

Messaging

Allman, Eric, Bryan Costales, and Neil Rickert. *Sendmail*. Sebastopol, CA: O'Reilly & Associates, Inc., 1993.

Mullet, Dianna and Kevin Mullet. *Managing IMAP*. Sebastopol, CA: O'Reilly & Associates, Inc., 2000.

Naming Services

Albitz, Paul and Cricket Liu. *DNS and BIND*. Third Edition. Sebastopol, CA: O'Reilly & Associates, Inc., 1998.

Diggs, Brad, John Nguyen, and Ron Cotten. *Sun DNS/BIND Benchmarking and Sizing Guide*, Palo Alto, CA: Sun Microsystems, Inc., March 2, 2001.

Droms, Ralph and Ted Lemon. *The DHCP Handbook – Understanding, Deploying, and Managing Automated Configuration Services*. New Riders Publishing, 1999.

Networking

Aelmans, Arjan, Floris Houniet, and M. M. Thomas. *BSCN – Building Scalable Cisco Networks*. McGraw-Hill, 2000.

Birkner, Matthew. *Cisco Internetwork Design*. Indianapolis, IN: Cisco Press, 2000.

Carolan, Jason and Mikael Lofstrand. *Service Delivery Network (SDN): Reference Architecture*, a Sun white paper (Part No. 816-2676-10), Palo Alto, CA: September 2001

Clark, Kennedy and Kevin Hamilton. *Cisco LAN Switching*. Indianapolis, IN: Cisco Press, 1999.

Comer, Douglas. *Internetworking with TCP/IP Volume I – Principles, Protocols, and Architecture*. Second Edition: Englewood Cliffs, NJ. Prentice-Hall, 1991.

Comer, Douglas and David Stevens. *Internetworking with TCP/IP Volume II – Design, Implementation, and Internals*. Englewood Cliffs, NJ: Prentice-Hall, 1991.

Comer, Douglas and David Stevens. *Internetworking with TCP/IP Volume III – Client-Server Programming and Applications*. Englewood Cliffs, NJ: Prentice-Hall, 1993.

Halabi, Sam and Danny McPherson. *Internet Routing Architectures*. Second Edition. Cisco Press, 2000.

Gast, Matthew and Mike Loukides. *T1: A Survival Guide*. Sebastopol, CA: O'Reilly & Associates, Inc., 2001.

Maufer, Thomas. *IP Fundamentals*. Upper Saddle River, NJ: Prentice-Hall, 1999.

McQuerry, Steve. *Interconnecting Cisco Network Devices*. Indianapolis, IN: Cisco Press, 2000.

Oppenheimer, Priscilla. *Top-Down Network Design*. Indianapolis, IN: Macmillan Technical Publishing, 1999.

Paquet, Catherine. *Building Cisco Remote Access Networks*. Indianapolis, IN: Cisco Press, 1999.

Paquet, Catherine and Diane Teare. *Building Scalable Cisco Networks*. Indianapolis, IN: Cisco Press, 2001.

Stevens, Richard. *TCP/IP Illustrated, Volume 1 – The Protocols*. Reading, MA: Addison Wesley®, 1994.

Stevens, Richard. *TCP/IP Illustrated, Volume 3 – TCP for Transactions, HTTP, NNTP, and the UNIX Domain Protocols*. Reading, MA: Addison Wesley, 1996.

Stevens, Richard and Gary Wright. *TCP/IP Illustrated, Volume 2 – The Implementation*. Reading, MA: Addison Wesley, 1995.

Raza, Khalid and Mark Turner. *Large-Scale IP Network Solutions*. Indianapolis, IN: Cisco Press, 2000.

Rossi, Louis and Thomas Rossi. *Cisco Catalyst LAN Switching*. McGraw-Hill, 1999.

Rossi, Louis and Thomas Rossi. *Cisco and IP Addressing*. McGraw-Hill, 1999.

Teare, Diane. *Designing Cisco Networks*. Indianapolis, IN: Cisco Press, 1999.

Webb, Karen. *Building Cisco Multilayer Switched Networks*. Indianapolis, IN: Cisco Press, 2000.

Operations and Management

SCN Education B.V. (Editor). *Application Service Providing – The Ultimate Guide to Hiring Rather Than Buying Applications*. Germany: Morgan Kaufmann Publishers, 2000.

Terplan, Kornel. *OSS Essentials – Support System Solutions for Service Providers*. John Wiley and Sons, Inc., 2001.

Verma, Dinesh. *Supporting Service Level Agreements on IP Networks*. Indianapolis, IN: Macmillan Technical Publishing, 1999.

Performance and Tuning

Cockcroft, Adrian and Richard Pettit. *Sun Performance and Tuning – Java and the Internet*. Second Edition. Palo Alto, CA: Sun Microsystems, Inc., 1998.

Security

Adams, Carlisle and Steve Lloyd. *Understanding Public-Key Infrastructure – Concepts, Standards, and Deployment Considerations*. Indianapolis, IN: Macmillan Technical Publishing, 1999

Amoroso, Edward. *Intrusion Detection – An Introduction to Internet Surveillance, Correlation, Trace Back, Traps, and Response*. Sparta, NJ: Intrusion.Net Books, 1999.

Bace, Rebecca. *Intrusion Detection*. Indianapolis, IN: Macmillan Technical Publishing, 2000.

Systems Architecture

Berg, Daniel and Bill Lewis. *Threads Primer – A Guide to Multithreaded Programming*. Prentice-Hall®, 1995.

Mauro, Jim and Richard McDougall. *Solaris Internals – Core Kernel Architecture*. Palo Alto, CA: Sun Microsystems, Inc., 2001.

Index

RADIUS services, FijiNet, 176
recommendations, selecting components, 132
root filesystems, 153
routers, 161
routers, FijiNet, 190
serial ports, 162
servers, 156
servers, FijiNet, 186
software, estimating, 133
software, estimating, FijiNet, 167
swap space, 153
switches, 162
switches, FijiNet, 191
uplink ports, 162
variables, during design phase, 123
web services, 136
web services, FijiNet, 171
capital, minimizing initial investment, 10
Central/Global Dispatch (software), 211
channelized T3, 74
Cisco Systems, 210
cluster environments, availability, 55
CoBox, 203
collision domains, 69
co-location solutions, 10
comments, providing about this book, xxviii
Committee of European Postal and Telephone
    hierarchy, network capacity, 304
Compaq enterprise servers, selecting, 207
comparison shopping, subscribers, 242
competitor offerings, subscriber expectations, 242
components
    console servers, selecting, 213
    console servers, selecting, FijiNet, 229
    data storage, selecting, 207
    data storage, selecting, FijiNet, 223
    failure, avoiding, 55
    firewalls, selecting, 211, 212
    firewalls, selecting, FijiNet, 228, 229
    functional decomposition, 58
    identifying, 45
    identifying, FijiNet, 60
    implementing, 237
    load balancers, selecting, 211
    load balancers, selecting, FijiNet, 228
    minimum services, 45
    NAS, selecting, 213

NAS, selecting, FijiNet, 230
network, capacity planning, 160
network, capacity planning, FijiNet, 190
network, selecting, 210
network, selecting, FijiNet, 225
operating environments, 50
operating platforms, 50
operating platforms, selecting, 205
product versions, 193
rack equipment, selecting, 214
rack equipment, selecting, FijiNet, 231
routers, selecting, 210
routers, selecting, FijiNet, 226
selecting, 193
servers, scaling, 52
servers, selecting, 206
servers, selecting, FijiNet, 221
services, 45
storage, selecting, 207
storage, selecting, FijiNet, 223
switches, selecting, 210
switches, selecting, FijiNet, 226
tape drives, selecting, 209
tape libraries, selecting, 209
tape libraries, selecting, FijiNet, 224
concurrency, estimating, 157, 158
concurrent active sessions
    assumptions, 17
    determining, FijiNet, 35
    industry average usage, 35
concurrent users
    bandwidth, determining average, 159
    modems, estimating capacity, 158
configurations
    cache servers, 74
    data storage, FijiNet, 223
    DHCP servers, 79
    DHCP, samples, 291
    directory servers, 78
    DNS servers, 77
    DNS, samples, 273
    implementing, 236
    implementing, tips, 238
    network, samples, 257
    NTP servers, 295
    services, 75
    services network, 75
    single-site, 67

design, 233
   prototypes, 234
implementations, FijiNet, prototype, xxiv
indexes, directory, 78
Informix Online, 199
infrastructure
   changing non-standard systems, 24
   network capacity, estimating, 157
   network, dividing, 70
   network, modeling, 70
   reliability, increasing, 57
infrastructure services, 48
   billing, 82
   capacity planning, 143
   capacity planning, FijiNet, 175
   DHCP, 48
   DNS, 48
   FijiNet, 60
   implementing, 238
   LDAP, 48
   NTP, 48
   RADIUS, 48
INN, 197
install scripts, 85
install servers, boot images, 85
interconnect, 75
interconnected (cascaded), 223
Intermail, 195
internal DNS, 77
internal DNS, FijiNet, 111
internal networks
   DNS not required, configuring, 77
internal servers, security, 71
Internet access, service, 46
Internet data center (IDC), 238
Internet mail access protocol (IMAP), 32
Internet news, service, 46
Internet relay chat (IRC), 47
Internet Software Consortium (ISC), 200
InterNetNews (INN), 197
Intrusion Detection Appliance (network-based), 212
intrusion detection system (IDS), *See* IDS
inverted list database models, 81
IOS DHCP, 202

IP address schema
   creating, 127
   creating, FijiNet, 165
   defining, 127
   implementing, 238
   sample, 127
IP addresses, 79
iPlanet Application Server (iAS), 199
iPlanet Directory Server (iDS), 201
iPlanet Messaging Server (iMS), 195
iPlanet Web Server (iWS), 196
IR Chat (IRC), services, 47
IRC (Internet relay chat), 47
ISC (Internet Software Consortium), 200
ISP architecture, defining, 2
ISP market
   data, obtaining, 6
   entering, 6
   fixed wireless technologies, 5
   high-speed access predictions, 5
   outsourcing, 8, 9
   requirements, outsourcing, 9
   revenues, increasing, 7
   satellite technologies, 5
ISP Planet, web site, 4
ISP services
   address book, 47
   basic services, 46
   calendar, 47
   designing, FijiNet, 60
   front-end access, 75
   infrastructure, 48
   installing, 75
   IRC, 47
   search engines, 47
   value-added, 47
   webmail, 47
ISPs
   interviewing, 13
   top companies, 4

J

Juniper Networks, 210

L

layers
  architectural models, 55
  network topology, 69
  network, system and data, 21
LDAP
  software, selecting, 201
  software, selecting, FijiNet, 217
LDAP data interchange format (LDIF), 177
LDAP servers
  configuring, 78
  implementing, 239
  masters, 82
  masters, CPU and RAM requirements, 78
  masters, updates, 89
  recommendations, 78
  replicas, 78
LDAP services
  capacity planning, 145
  capacity planning, FijiNet, 177
LDIF (LDAP data interchange format), 177
life cycle, 57
limitations, architectural, FijiNet, 41
limitations, hardware, selecting, 194
links, capacity planning, 159
Linux, 205
Linux distributors, web site, 205
load balancers
  ACEdiretor (switch), 211
  Big-IP/3-DNS, 211
  Central/Global Dispatch, 211
  implementing, 239
  Local/Distributed Director (appliance), 211
  RainSLB, 211
  selecting, 211
  selecting, FijiNet, 228
  ServerIron (switch), 211
local coverage area, 67
local hosts table, 77
Local/Distributed Director, 211
log archive, capacity planning, 153
log servers
  centralizing, 84
  defining, 84
  storage, 84
log services

capacity planning, 152
capacity planning, FijiNet, 183
logging, `syslogd(1m)`, 84
logical design, 65
logs, archiving, 84
loopback, 128
Lucent Technologies, 210

M

mail proxy
  partitioning, 70
  services networks, 76
mail relay
  defining, 72
  hardware, 72
  partitioning, 70
  purpose, 72
mail server, partitioning, 70
mail servers
  commercial or open source, 195
  Intermail, 195
  iPlanet Messaging Server (iMS), 195
  Qmail, 195
  Sendmail, 195
  software, selecting, 195
  software, selecting, FijiNet, 215
mail transfer agent (MTA), 215
MailStore, 81
manageability, 23
  architectural principles, 57
  content networks, 80
  FijiNet design, 63
  life cycle, 57
  monitoring services, 57
  products, 59
managed operation agreement, 10
management
  broadcast storms, preventing, 130
  disks, separating from system disk, 155
management networks
  access, restricting, 84
  boot/install servers, 85
  console server, 84
  defining, 84
  FijiNet, 112

applying, architectural, FijiNet, 63
private memory, 171
product versions, 193
ProFTPD, 198
protocol conversion, 75
protocols, listing, 309
prototypes, developing, 234
PSTN (public switched telephone network), 66
public switched telephone network (PSTN), 66

Q

Qmail, 195
Qpopper, 196
Qualstar tape libraries, 209
Quantum tape libraries, 209
questions
    ISP requirements interview, 13
    post implementation, 240
questions, ISP requirements interview, 243

R

rack equipment
    selecting, 214
    selecting, FijiNet, 231
RADIUS
    servers, AAA RADIUS Server, 202
    servers, freRADIUS, 202
    servers, implementing, 239
    servers, NAVISRADIUS, 202
    servers, Steel-Belted RADIUS, 202
    software, selecting, 202
    software, selecting, FijiNet, 218
RADIUS (remote access dial-in user service), 48
RADIUS local database entry, approximate
    size, 176
RADIUS services
    capacity planning, 144
    capacity planning, FijiNet, 176
RADIUS storage, Funk Software's
    recommendation, 176
RADIUS, network topology, 73
RAID (redundant array of independent disks), 41

RAID 0+1, 56, 186
RAID 5, 56
RAID controller, 207
RAID software, 207
RainSLB (software), 211
Randori News, 197
Raptor Firewall (software), 211
RealSecure (hybrid), 212
redundancy, architecture, 21
redundant array of independent disks (RAID), 41
regional ISP markets, 4
relational databases
    billing systems, 82
    defining, 81
    models, 81
    placing on networks, 81
relay agents, DHCP, 73, 79
reliability
    architectural principles, 57
    defining, 57
    defining, FijiNet, 42
    designing, 57
    designing, FijiNet, 40
    DNS servers, placing, 77
    FijiNet design, 63
    increasing, 57
    layers, 21
    MailStores, 81
    redundancy, 21
remote access dial-in user service (RADIUS), 48
remote access servers, Lucent Technologies, 213
remote coverage area, 67
replicas, LDAP, 78
requirements
    anticipating, challenges, 26
    billing, 25
    business, obtaining, 13
    design, 12
    design, capacity planning, 132
    evaluating, 16
    evaluating, challenges, 26
    evaluating, FijiNet, 31
    functional, 14
    news services, 37
    obtaining, 12
    obtaining, FijiNet, 28

W

WAP (wireless application protocol), 75
web content
    dynamic, 76
    performance, enhancing, 74
    static, 76, 81
    storing, 81
web farms, 76
web hosting
    requirements, 37
    services, 46
    storage, 38
web pages, server access, 76
web servers
    Apache, 196
    defining, 76
    fork/exec model, 196
    iPlanet Web Server (iWS), 196
    replacing or replicating, 24
    software, selecting, 196
    software, selecting, FijiNet, 216
    threaded model, 196
    WebSphere, 196
web services
    capacity planning, 136
    capacity planning, FijiNet, 171
web sites
    Alteon WebSystems (Nortel), 210
    Apache, 216
    Arrowpoint Communication (Cisco), 210
    Cisco Systems, 210
    docfeedback@sun.com, xxviii
    docs.sun.com, xxv
    Extreme Networks, 210
    fatbrain.com, xxv
    Foundry Networks, 210
    Internet Assigned Numbers Authority's
       (IANA), 309
    ISP Planet, 4
    Juniper Networks, 210
    LanStar, 214
    Linux distributors, 205
    Lucent Technologies, 210
    Nortel Networks, 210
    NTP solutions, 203
    Shark racks, 214
    SLAs, 242
    SouthWest Data Products, 214

storage estimates, 73
Sun BluePrints, xxii
Sun Microsystems, racks, 214
Sun OnLine, xxii
UW IMAP, University of Washington, 215
webmail, services, 47
WebSphere, 196
well-known ports, listing, 309
wireless application protocol (WAP), 75
wireless markup language (WML), 75
wireless, fixed, 5
WML (wireless markup language), 75
WU-FTP, 198

X

Xntpd, 203

Z

zone transfers, 82
zone updates, 82

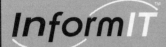